Microsoft® Office
Accounting Express 2007
Starter Kit

PAMELA PIERCE

800 East 96th Street, Indianapolis, Indiana 46240

This Book Is Safari Enabled

The Safari® Enabled icon on the cover of your favorite technology book means the book is available through Safari Bookshelf. When you buy this book, you get free access to the online edition for 45 days.

Safari Bookshelf is an electronic reference library that lets you easily search thousands of technical books, find code samples, download chapters, and access technical information whenever and wherever you need it.

To gain 45-day Safari Enabled access to this book:

- Go to http://www.quepublishing.com/safarienabled
- Complete the brief registration form
- Enter the coupon code BNBL-RHNB-8UUQ-PBBJ-1L6Z

If you have difficulty registering on Safari Bookshelf or accessing the online edition, please e-mail customer-service@safaribooksonline.com.

Microsoft® Office Accounting Express 2007 Starter Kit

ISBN-10: 0-7897-3685-3

ISBN-13: 978-0-7897-3685-7

Library of Congress Cataloging-in-Publication Data

Pierce, Pamela.

Microsoft Office Accounting Express 2007 starter kit / Pamela Pierce.

p. cm.

Includes index.

ISBN 0-7897-3685-3

1. Microsoft Office. 2. Accounting--Software. 3. Accounting--Computer programs. I. Title.

HF5679.P498 2007

657.0285'53--dc22

2007008953

Printed in the United States of America

First Printing: April 2007

10   09   08   07   4   3   2   1

Trademarks

Warning and Disclaimer

Bulk Sales

Que Publishing offers excellent discounts on this book when ordered in quantity for bulk purchases or special sales. For more information, please contact

U.S. Corporate and Government Sales
1-800-382-3419
corpsales@pearsontechgroup.com

For sales outside the United States, please contact

International Sales
international@pearsoned.com

Associate Publisher
Greg Wiegand

Acquisitions Editor
Loretta Yates

Development Editor
Kevin Howard

Managing Editor
Patrick Kanouse

Project Editor
Tonya Simpson

Copy Editor
Mike Henry

Indexer
Ken Johnson

Proofreader
Heather Wilkins

Technical Editor
Chris Schatte

Publishing Coordinator
Cindy Teeters

Book Designer
Anne Jones

Contents at a Glance

Table of Contents

About the Author

Pamela Pierce, author.

Pamela Pierce is certified through Microsoft Professional Accountants' Network (MPAN) in Microsoft Small Business Accounting. Pamela has been interviewed for articles on Microsoft Accounting 2007 in magazines such as *Accounting Technology* and *Accounting Today*.

Pamela has been working as a consultant, trainer, and coach for small businesses since the 1980s. She owned Applications Plus, Inc.—recommending, selling, and supporting accounting systems in the late 1980s. She is the author of *Wow! Look At Windows XP*, is a college instructor in PC repair and maintenance, and was one of the first Microsoft Partners and Microsoft Certified Solution Developers.

Owner of Empowering You!, Pamela has been transforming businesses through technology since 1993. Her company diagnoses and solves PC problems, improves PC security, and provides training and support for Microsoft Office Accounting 2007, Word, Access, Excel, Outlook, Publisher, and PowerPoint. Then Empowering You! works with the owners to take the business to the next level—creating company websites and modifying Office products to improve workflow and integrate them with Microsoft Office Accounting 2007.

You can contact the author through Empowering You!

http://www.empoweringyou.com
pam@empoweringyou.com
(440) 341-0955

The Empowering You! website also includes corrections to the book and other helpful resources. Please send any you wish to share.

Acknowledgments

I thought I knew Express inside and out until I started writing this book. Many people added to my knowledge and to the quality of the book.

In order of appearance, I'd like to thank

Microsoft Professional Accountants Network (MPAN) for providing great support and training for accountants.

Microsoft Support for its unfailing answers.

Ginny Musante, John Thuneby, Bob Lewis, Tracey Cummings, and Allen Goldberg—Microsoft angels I call on when all else fails.

Microsoft online newsgroup community.

> Microsoft—Jesper, Kollen Glynn, Jørn Lindhard Mortensen.

> And the many other contributors, including mT and Allan Martin, two of the most prolific.

Chris Schatte—Technical editor for this book, and the man with the most answers in the online newsgroup.

Ryan Staib—The person responsible for tearing my work apart with the aim of perfecting it.

The wonderful Que staff.

> Loretta Yates, acquisition editor and cheerleader.

> Kevin Howard, development editor.

The many people who have helped edit, proof, design, and market the book. It's a pleasure working with you.

Thanks also to my loving family and friends, especially Elaine Van Vliet, Shelley Boyle, and Al Burns. And, I can't forget my cat, Spooky.

I also want to thank Norma J. Rist for her dedication as a mentor to all small business owners, and my Boardroom Group members for their unfailing support.

We Want to Hear from You!

As the reader of this book, *you* are our most important critic and commentator. We value your opinion and want to know what we're doing right, what we could do better, what areas you'd like to see us publish in, and any other words of wisdom you're willing to pass our way.

As an associate publisher for Que Publishing, I welcome your comments. You can email or write me directly to let me know what you did or didn't like about this book—as well as what we can do to make our books better.

Please note that I cannot help you with technical problems related to the topic of this book. We do have a User Services group, however, where I will forward specific technical questions related to the book.

When you write, please be sure to include this book's title and author as well as your name, email address, and phone number. I will carefully review your comments and share them with the author and editors who worked on the book.

Email: feedback@quepublishing.com

Mail: Greg Wiegand
Associate Publisher
Que Publishing
800 East 96th Street
Indianapolis, IN 46240 USA

Reader Services

Visit our website and register this book at www.quepublishing.com/register for convenient access to any updates, downloads, or errata that might be available for this book.

Introduction

Welcome to the *Microsoft Office Accounting Express 2007 Starter Kit*! Inside you'll find lots of helpful tips and pictures showing how to set up and use this versatile accounting software.

The *Starter Kit* is a solid introduction to the software. It enables you to start quickly and set up properly. Read the book from beginning to end. You can refer to chapters after you've read them, but the best way to use the book is to follow the steps as they're laid out. That way, you'll set up everything correctly the first time.

The book starts with a comparison between the Express and Professional versions of Microsoft Office Accounting 2007. Learn which version is best for your company. If you need to upgrade, it's as easy as buying an upgrade key code. (See Chapter 1, "A Microsoft Accounting Products Comparison.") Then use the included CD or download the software from Microsoft, back up your computer, and install the software. The minimum system requirements and basic computer security are covered in Chapter 2, "Downloading and Installing."

In Chapter 3, "Registration and Setup Wizard," and Chapter 4, "Importing Data," you learn how to use the Setup Wizard to start a new company or import your data. Importing from Intuit QuickBooks, Microsoft Money, and Microsoft Excel are covered in depth. Follow the easy steps to prevent you from wasting time.

Company setup involves entering company, account, bank, customer, vendor, and employee information. You learn the techniques for this in Chapter 5, "Company Setup." Sales tax setup, a difficult subject, is made easier with this book.

In Chapter 6, "Basic Accounting Transactions," you learn how to enter your daily transactions, including invoices, payments, deposits, payroll, and general journal entries. This book explains the correct form to use for each type of transaction.

In Chapter 7, "Accounting Reports," you will see a complete list of reports and learn how to modify them. Each report is pictured and explained.

End-of-period processes are covered in detail in Chapter 8, "End of Period," including auditing data, editing and paying sales tax, and sending your books to your accountant. Express offers new choices for transferring data. This chapter explores the pros and cons and provides tips.

In Chapter 9, "Advanced Features," you walk through setting up and using the new features of Accounting Express, including PayPal, Equifax, eBay, ADP Payroll, and Outlook integration. In addition, you learn how to modify data entry and printed forms and create Word letters from your accounting information.

Appendix A, "Troubleshooting," contains commonly asked questions and their answers. You'll also learn how to restore, rebuild, or repair Express data files. For beginners, a guide to computers and Microsoft Windows is included, along with a list of additional help resources.

The glossary defines unfamiliar terms. The terms are italicized and defined in the chapter where they're first used.

Some users prefer to use the keyboard instead of the mouse. A list of Express shortcut keys are included on the inside cover of the book.

See the section "Author Information" in the front of the book to learn about the author and the additional support she can provide on her website.

Enjoy Express! It's extremely flexible, and is necessary for the growth of your business. This book provides the missing manual and essential guidance.

Book Conventions

What You'll Learn

Each chapter contains a "What You'll Learn" section that provides an overview of the topics covered in the chapter.

New Terms

Throughout the book, you will find new terms *italicized and defined* on first use to indicate that they appear in the glossary.

More Information

When a topic is covered in more detail in another section of the book, you will see this reference:

⇨   For more information about this topic, see page 2.

Notes, Tips, and Cautions

Notes, Tips, and Cautions appear in the margins. They provide valuable information.

NOTE
THIS IS A NOTE

A *note* contains useful information about options to consider.

TIP
THIS IS A TIP

A *tip* contains information that makes tasks easier.

CAUTION
THIS IS A CAUTION

A *caution* points out items that might cause trouble if not handled correctly. Pay close attention to cautions.

A Microsoft Accounting Products Comparison

Is Microsoft Office Accounting Express 2007 the best product for your needs? Here is a quick overview comparing the features of Microsoft small business accounting products.

Microsoft Office Accounting Advantages

Microsoft Office Accounting 2007 is solid, reliable accounting software for small business. It comes in two versions, the **free** Express version discussed in this book, and the Professional version, which includes additional features and is an easy upgrade from Express.

Both Express and Professional are **easy to use and full featured**. They include **customer invoicing and accounts receivable, vendor bill payment and accounts payable, banking and check writing, online sales integration, low-cost ADP Payroll integration**, and much more.

Your accountant will like using **Accountant View**, also included, to receive your accounting books, add end-of-period accountant's changes, and then send back and update your books without having to visit your business.

Microsoft Office Accounting's biggest advantage over its competition is **flexibility** and integration with other Microsoft and non-Microsoft products. It is built on Microsoft technology and **integrates with other Office products—Word, Excel, and Access**. This means that, for example, you can modify invoices using Word to include your logo, move and rename fields, or create multiple Word invoice templates for different types of customers.

Many companies have already written add-ins providing additional functionality in Microsoft Office Accounting 2007. Several come included in Microsoft Office Accounting—**eBay auctions, ADP Payroll, Equifax credit reports, and PayPal invoicing**. One of the many popular add-ins available from third-party vendors provides additional import capabilities to move data into Microsoft Office Accounting 2007, beyond the **many import options** already included.

If you want to integrate Microsoft Office Accounting with a different software program, add new screens full of information, or create completely new reports beyond the included customization capabilities, then use the Microsoft Office Accounting Software Development Kit (SDK). It is a free download from the Microsoft website.

Microsoft Office Accounting stores your information in Microsoft SQL Server 2005 Express. This powerful database works behind Microsoft Office Accounting 2007 to handle essentially **unlimited data**, limited only by your computer's hard drive storage capacity.

Underneath, Microsoft Office Accounting uses the Microsoft .NET technology. This means Microsoft Office Accounting is very flexible and **easy to customize** by someone experienced in programming.

Microsoft Office Accounting 2007 has the capability of growing with your business. You will never run out of account numbers, customers, or vendors, and you will be able to use your accounting data in new ways with other Microsoft and non-Microsoft programs.

Quick Feature Comparison Table

Table 1.1   Microsoft Accounting Products Feature Comparison

Features	Microsoft Small Business Accounting 2006 (SBA 2006)	Microsoft Office Accounting Express 2007 (MOA Express 2007)	Microsoft Office Accounting Professional 2007 (MOA Pro 2007)
Retail Price	$149	Free	$99.95 upgrade from 2006; $149.95 new
Customers, Vendors, and Accounts Limited Only by Hard Drive Space	Yes	Yes	Yes

Features	Microsoft Small Business Accounting 2006 (SBA 2006)	Microsoft Office Accounting Express 2007 (MOA Express 2007)	Microsoft Office Accounting Professional 2007 (MOA Pro 2007)
Professional-Looking Forms, Modifiable	Yes, limited	Yes	Yes
Integrates with Office 2003 or 2007: Word, Excel, and Outlook	Yes, limited	Yes. Not Outlook 2003, only 2007.	Yes. Not Outlook 2003, only 2007.
User-Defined Fields	Yes; however, the fields don't print	Yes, and they print on reports	Yes, and they print on reports
Custom Letters to Customers, Vendors, or Employees	Yes	Yes	Yes
Runs on SQL Server	MSDE version 2003	Installed on SQL 2005 Express, will run on all SQL Server 2005 versions	Installed on SQL 2005 Express, will run on all SQL Server 2005 versions
Audit Trail and Change Tracking	Yes	Yes	Yes
Back Up and Restore	Yes	Yes	Yes
Free Software Development Kit to Add Functionality	Downloadable	Downloadable	Downloadable
Microsoft Office Live Integration	No	Yes	Yes
Add-in Functionality Developed by Other Companies	Yes	Yes: Equifax credit reports, PayPal invoicing, eBay sales, receive credit card payments, and more	Yes: Equifax credit reports, PayPal invoicing, eBay sales, receive credit card payments, and more

Features	Microsoft Small Business Accounting 2006 (SBA 2006)	Microsoft Office Accounting Express 2007 (MOA Express 2007)	Microsoft Office Accounting Professional 2007 (MOA Pro 2007)
Company			
Set Up Multiple Companies	Yes	Yes	Yes
Setup Wizard	Yes	Yes, limited	Yes
Import Data From	SBA, comma-separated, Microsoft Access, Excel	SBA, comma-separated, Microsoft Access, Excel, Money, and most QuickBooks	SBA, comma-separated, Microsoft Access, Excel, Money, and most QuickBooks
Multilevel Chart of Accounts	Two levels	Five levels	Five levels
Company Home Page with Actions	Yes	No	Yes
Synchronize with Outlook Business Contacts Manager	Limited	Yes	Yes
Number of Reports	46 reports, plus many lists	23 reports, plus many lists	55 reports, plus many lists
Modifiable Reports	Yes	Yes	Yes
Auto-Graph Reports	Limited; export to Excel for more capabilities	Yes, or in Excel	Yes, or in Excel
Email Reports and Forms	Yes	Yes	Yes
Memorize Reports and Recurring Transactions	Yes	No	Yes

Features	Microsoft Small Business Accounting 2006 (SBA 2006)	Microsoft Office Accounting Express 2007 (MOA Express 2007)	Microsoft Office Accounting Professional 2007 (MOA Pro 2007)
Multiuser Functionality	Unlimited users on same computer; purchase to add additional computers	One user, one computer	Unlimited users on same computer; purchase to add additional computers
Multiple Currencies	No	No	Yes
Manages Fixed Assets, Depreciation Schedule	No	No	Yes
Accrual and Cash Basis Accounting	Yes, limited	Yes, limited	Yes
Class Tracking	Yes	No	Yes
Accountant Transfer Wizard	No	Yes	Yes
Multi-client Accountant Navigator	No	Yes	Yes
Cash Flow Reports and Forecasts	Yes	Cash flow report only	Yes
Accountant View	No	Yes	Yes
Customers			
Professional-Looking Quote, Sales Order, and Invoice, Modifiable	Yes, limited modifications	Quote and Invoice only, no Sales Order	Yes
Online Sales Integration	No	Yes	Yes
PayPal Payment Button on Invoices	No	Yes	Yes
Finance Charges	Yes	No	Yes

Features	Microsoft Small Business Accounting 2006 (SBA 2006)	Microsoft Office Accounting Express 2007 (MOA Express 2007)	Microsoft Office Accounting Professional 2007 (MOA Pro 2007)
Integration with eBay	No	Yes	Yes
Integrated Microsoft Retail Point of Sale	No	No	Yes
Multiple Price Levels	Yes	Yes	Yes
Sales Tax with Multiple Tax Agency, Item, or Location	Yes	Yes	Yes
Bank			
Online Banking	Yes, limited	Yes	Yes
Bank and Credit Card Statement Reconciliation	Yes	Yes	Yes
Vendors			
Professional-Looking Purchase Order, Modifiable	Yes, limited modification	No	Yes
Record, Pay, and Print Vendor and Expense Checks	Yes	Yes	Yes
Jobs			
Job Costing	Yes	Only job name	Yes
Inventory			
Inventory Creation and Tracking	Yes	No	Yes

Features	Microsoft Small Business Accounting 2006 (SBA 2006)	Microsoft Office Accounting Express 2007 (MOA Express 2007)	Microsoft Office Accounting Professional 2007 (MOA Pro 2007)
Employees and Payroll			
Timesheet	Yes	Yes	Yes
Accountant Payroll Center	No	Yes (with ADP)	Yes (with ADP)
1099 Reports	Yes	No	Yes
Integrates with ADP Payroll and Taxes	Yes	Yes	Yes
Excel-Based Manual Payroll	Yes	No, only ADP	Yes

Buy Express or Professional?

Express is great for businesses that are service oriented, home based, online, or selling products but that do not track inventory. Express has many features, but the Professional version has even more features. Express has

- **Customer invoicing and quoting, and customization to improve the professional image of your business, plus the ability to email invoices and receive customer payments via PayPal** but no sales orders.

- **Easy-to-create customer statements using a built-in wizard** but no finance charges.

- **Fully customizable reports**, but the customization cannot be saved as a memorized report available for viewing in the future.

- **Twenty-three reports and many lists**, but no home page with graphs summarizing cash flow, outstanding invoices, bills, and to-do lists.

- **A limit of one user on one computer**, not multiple users.

- **Subaccounts up to five levels deep within the Chart of Accounts**, but no classes; for example, divisions of a company.

- **Export to Excel, Access, or Word to analyze data**, but no job costing analysis.
- **Vendor bills**, but no vendor purchase orders.
- **Service and product items**, but no inventory tracking.
- **Easy-to-use low-cost ADP Payroll integration with checks printed on your printer and filled-in printable tax forms**, but no manual payroll or IRS 1099 forms.

If your company needs the extra features not included in Express, use the Professional version. If you are not sure, start with Express—it's included with the book! If you decide you need to upgrade, doing so is as easy as purchasing a Professional license and entering the product key in Express.

Should I Upgrade from 2006?

The first version of Office Accounting, Microsoft Small Business Accounting 2006, was a good introductory product by Microsoft. Most businesses will want to upgrade to take advantage of the new features and capabilities.

Microsoft Office Accounting 2007 offers improvements in customized fields, form and report customization, integration with Office products, improved cash basis accounting, and an accountant's view to work better with your accountant. New add-ins are also included for eBay auctions, PayPal payments, and ADP payroll.

Use this book to work with Express, and when you are ready, purchase the product key to turn on the extra Professional features and move your data from SBA 2006 to Professional 2007.

NOTE

YOU CAN'T SEE IT, BUT YOU ALREADY HAVE PROFESSIONAL

Microsoft Office Accounting Professional has more features than Express. However, Express and Professional are exactly the same program—the only difference is the product key. Express disables the additional features in Professional.

Moving from Express to Professional is very easy: Purchase a Professional product key and enter it in Express to view Professional.

NOTE

SBA 2006 ONLY UPGRADEABLE TO PROFESSIONAL

Previous users of Small Business Accounting 2006 (SBA 2006) should note that Microsoft Office Accounting Express 2007 is not an upgrade from 2006; only Professional has that capability.

Downloading and Installing

Before setting up and using Microsoft Office Accounting Express 2007, download the installation file or use the CD that comes with the book to install the program. This chapter provides tips and information to prepare you. Learn what kind of computer you need, and review some basic computer security and backup considerations before you begin. Then, download and install the software, guided by easy step-by-step instructions with pictures.

Minimum System Requirements

Install Microsoft Office Accounting Express 2007 on a computer with the following requirements:

- Processor: 1GHz (gigahertz) or better.

- Operating system (one of the following):

  - Windows XP with Service Pack 2

  - Windows Vista

  - Windows Server 2003 with Service Pack 1 or later

- Memory: 512MB (megabytes) or more.

- Display: 1024 × 768 or higher resolution (viewable dots in a 1" × 1" area of the display).

- Hard disk: 2GB or more.

- CD-ROM or DVD-ROM drive.
  - Single-sided CD, approximately 600MB of data
  - Single-sided DVD, approximately 4GB
  - Double-sided or dual-layer DVD, approximately 8GB
  - Dual-layer and double-sided DVD, approximately 16GB
- Internet connection and browser: For updates to Microsoft Office Accounting Express 2007 and for online sales, online credit reports, online banking, online credit card processing, and PayPal payments.
- (Optional) Microsoft Office Word, Outlook, Excel, and Access, versions 2003 or 2007, for additional data sharing and reporting. Express does not work with the 2003 version of Outlook's Business Contact Manager, but it does integrate with the 2007 version.

> NOTE
> **MORE MEMORY MEANS FASTER SPEED!**
>
> Your computer should have 1GB or more of memory. This is the easiest way to make your computer faster.
>
> If many applications are open at once, consider adding more memory. Read the computer manual to determine the maximum memory permitted in your computer (typically 2GB–4GB).

A Writable CD or DVD Drive Is Suggested

It is important to back up your data. This means that data copied from the computer is available later to restore important files to the same or a different computer if a problem occurs.

Make sure your CD or DVD drive is writable. A CD or DVD writer is the easiest and least expensive way to back up your data. A CD-ROM or DVD-ROM only reads. CD-R, DVD-R, DVD-DL, and DVD+R write once, and CD-RW, DVD-RW, DVD+RW, and DVD-RAM allow writing and erasing multiple times.

> TIP
> **HOW BIG IS IT?**
>
> From largest to smallest: 1GB is a thousand times bigger than 1MB, and 1MB is a thousand times bigger than 1KB (kilobyte). Each is a unit of storage describing the size of memory, hard drive, software, or documents in a computer.

How to Determine Display Resolution

To determine the display resolution of your computer:

1. Right-click an empty area of your computer desktop when the Windows Start button is visible and before applications open.
2. Click **Properties**, the last entry in the menu.
3. Click the **Settings** tab.
4. Under Screen Resolution, choose a size of **1024 × 768** or higher. Purchase a new graphics card and/or monitor if this size is not available or does not display well.
5. If the type is difficult to read, click the **Appearance** tab, and then change the **Font Size** setting.

Basic Computer Security

To protect your computer, first install the following:

- All Microsoft Windows and Office updates
- Firewall software
- Antivirus software
- Anti-spyware software
- Microsoft Baseline Security Analyzer

You Aren't Done Until Microsoft Says So!

Check to see whether your computer has all Windows and Office updates. Go online to the Microsoft Update website:

http://update.microsoft.com

After the initial updates install, be sure to return to the Microsoft Update website to check for more updates. There might be updates to the newly installed updates. Install the recommended updates and continue returning to the Microsoft Update website until it tells you there are no more updates to install. If Windows requests it, be sure to restart the computer between updates.

The Microsoft Way to Protect Your Computer

Search the Web and read reviews on security products to determine the best-rated products. Or use Microsoft's OneCare, which includes firewall, antivirus, anti-spyware, backup reminders, and periodic tune-ups—all bundled in one product. The OneCare website is

http://www.windowsonecare.com

Microsoft Baseline Security Analyzer is a separate download from Microsoft. It checks your computer and makes recommendations on any security risks found. For beginners, download and install the program, open it, and select the suggested settings by pressing the **Enter** key until the recommendations display.

Back Up Before Installing

Before installing any new software, it is always a wise choice to back up your computer in case of problems. Back up using one of the following options:

- The backup software included with some, but not all, Microsoft XP, Server, and Vista operating systems
- Software included with a DVD or CD burner
- Software purchased at a local computer store or downloaded from the Internet

Installing from CD

A free CD containing Express is included with the book. Insert the CD (with the writing side up) into your computer CD drive. It should automatically start. If it does not automatically start, click the **Start** menu, then **My Computer**. Double-click the Express CD to open the Express setup program. The next step is installing.

⇨ See "Installing," page 19.

Downloading

If you no longer have the CD that came with the book, download Express from the Internet to obtain the latest version. You will need an Internet connection, an Internet browser such as Internet Explorer, and sufficient hard drive space and time. Depending on your Internet connection, it could take from 15 minutes to 8 hours to download Express.

Open your Internet browser, as shown in Figure 2.1:

1. Click the **Start** button to open the menu.
2. Click **Internet Explorer** to open the Internet browser.

CAUTION

DO NOT CHOOSE SOFTWARE FROM EMAIL ADVERTISING

Never click a link in an email advertisement because malicious websites might give your computer a virus. Even when you know the product advertised, do not click an email link because the link might take you to a different website containing a virus.

Instead, type the correct website name into the browser address bar, or type the product name in a search engine and read reviews about the product.

Internet Explorer   My Documents

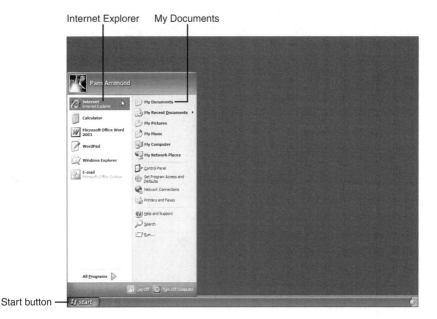

Start button

FIGURE 2.1   Open the Internet Explorer browser.

Enter the website address for Microsoft Office Accounting Express 2007, as shown in Figure 2.2:

1. Click the text in the address bar to highlight it.

2. Press the **Delete** key to remove the address text.

3. In the address bar, type the website address for Microsoft Office Accounting Express 2007:

   http://www.ideawins.com

   or

   http://office.microsoft.com/en-us/accountexpress

4. Press the **Enter** key.

Click the **Download Office Accounting Express** button, shown in Figure 2.3, to start using the product today. Or click the **Click Here to Order a CD** button to have a CD mailed to you.

Click the **Save** button to save Microsoft Office Accounting Express 2007 to a file on your computer, as shown in Figure 2.4. This prevents problems by saving the software to the computer and verifying that the download is correct before trying to install.

Address bar   Minimize button

Close
button

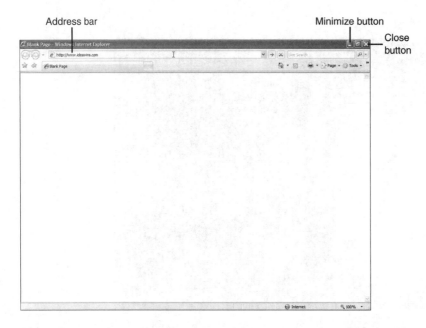

FIGURE 2.2   The Internet Explorer browser opens.

Download Office Accounting Express button

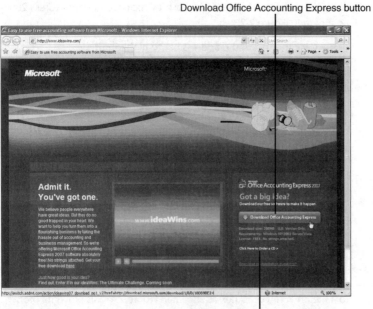

Click Here to Order a CD button

FIGURE 2.3   The Microsoft Office Accounting Express 2007 website opens.

Or, click the **Run** button to attempt to install the software without first saving it (not recommended).

Or, click **Cancel** to exit without downloading or installing the software.

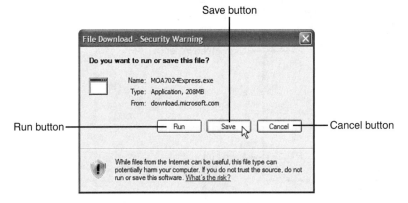

FIGURE 2.4   The File Download dialog box opens.

Suggested Save Location

It might be difficult to remember where files are stored. Save any new data, documents, and downloaded files to My Documents so you can easily locate them and back them up.

Create subfolders within My Documents for easy organization.

Save the downloaded files in the My Documents subfolder called My Received Files. If this folder does not exist, click the **My Documents** folder. This highlights My Documents, and its contents appear in the Folders and Files area. Then click the **Create New Folder** button and name the folder My Received Files.

Create a subfolder within My Received Files for each software company, in this case Microsoft. Create a subfolder within a company folder for each software program downloaded; in this case, Office Accounting Express 2007. Finally, before saving the downloaded software, double-check that the correct folder shows with the following steps:

1. Click the **Save In** drop-down list arrow, as shown in Figure 2.5, to open the file structure. This allows you to see the exact location where the file saves.

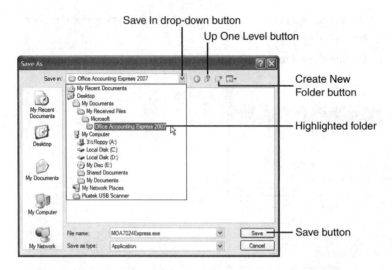

FIGURE 2.5   Choose the location to save the file.

2. Write down the file location by noting each folder and subfolder in the path (put a / between each folder and subfolder), and the filename. In this example:

   My Documents/My Received Files/Microsoft/Office Accounting Express 2007/MOA7024Express.exe

   Your folder and filenames might be different from the example.

3. Click the **Save** button to start the download.

Do not checkmark the **Close This Dialog Box When Download Completes** check box. If it is checkmarked, click the check box to remove the checkmark, so that it looks like the check box shown in Figure 2.6.

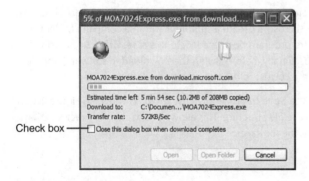

FIGURE 2.6   The Downloading Window shows the speed and length of time to download the file to your computer.

Installing

After downloading Express from the Internet or inserting the Express CD into the CD drive, the next step is to install the software.

When the download completes, click the **Open Folder** button, as shown in Figure 2.7, to open the folder containing the new downloaded file.

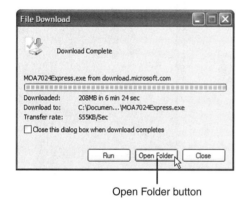

Open Folder button

FIGURE 2.7 Open the folder containing your downloaded file.

If the File Download window closed before you had a chance to click the Open Folder button, do the following:

1. On Windows Desktop, click the **Start** button to open the menu.

   ➪ See Figure 2.1, page 15.

2. Click **My Documents** to open the My Documents window.

3. Using the notes you wrote previously, locate the downloaded Microsoft Office Accounting Express file by double-clicking the correct subfolder(s).

   ➪ See "Suggested Save Location," page 17.

   Double-click the downloaded Express file, as shown in Figure 2.8, to open it.

Downloaded file

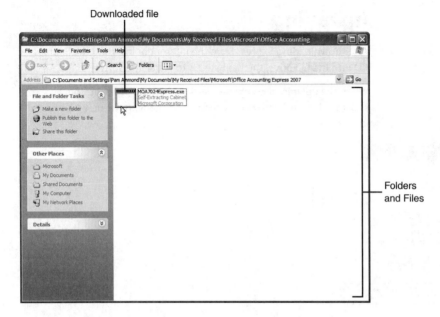

Folders
and Files

FIGURE 2.8 Open the downloaded file.

Click the **Run** button, as shown in Figure 2.9, to start the installation of Express.

Or, if you choose not to install Express at this time, click the **Cancel** button.

Wait while Windows puts the files on your hard drive.

Run button

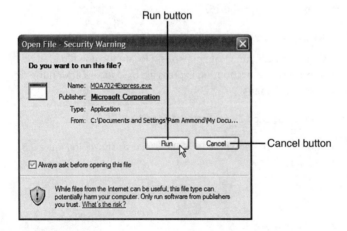

Cancel button

FIGURE 2.9 The Security Warning dialog box asks whether it is safe to install Express.

The Microsoft Office Accounting 2007 Setup Wizard opens.

Click the **Next** button, shown in Figure 2.10, in the Setup Wizard.

Or, click the **Advanced** button if you do not want to install SQL Express.

Or, click the **Cancel** button if you choose not to install Microsoft Office Accounting 2007 Express at this time.

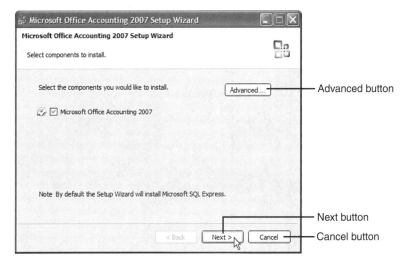

FIGURE 2.10   Select the **Next** button in Microsoft Office Accounting 2007 Setup Wizard.

SQL Server

Structured Query Language (SQL) is a programming language you can use to query the database where your company accounting information is stored. Microsoft Office Accounting 2007 comes with Microsoft SQL Express, which is a limited version of Microsoft SQL Server 2005. If you own a copy of Microsoft SQL Server 2005, you probably do not want to install SQL Express.

Microsoft Small Business Accounting 2006 (SBA 2006) came with MSDE, a limited version of Microsoft SQL Server 2003. Microsoft Office Accounting 2007 does not work with MSDE or Microsoft SQL Server 2003.

Microsoft Office Accounting 2007 Express cannot upgrade company accounting data from SBA 2006. Only the Professional version has this capability.

Click the **Next** button, as shown in Figure 2.11, to install Express in the recommended location (typically called the *default location* because it is already shown).

Or, click the **Browse** button to select a different location. (Not recommended—use the default location, if possible.) Then click the **Next** button.

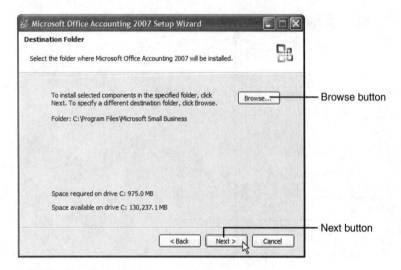

FIGURE 2.11 Choose where to install Express.

You have answered the installation questions. As shown in Figure 2.12, click the **Install** button to start the installation.

Or, click the **Back** button to change your answers.

Or, click the **Cancel** button if you choose not to install Microsoft Office Accounting 2007 Express at this time.

Wait while Express installs.

Click the **Finish** button shown in Figure 2.13 when Express completes the installation. The window will close.

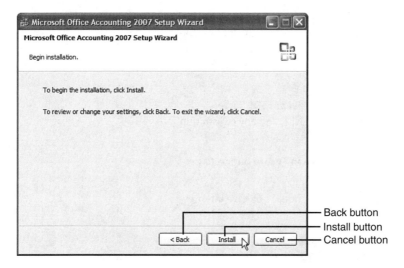

FIGURE 2.12 Ready to install.

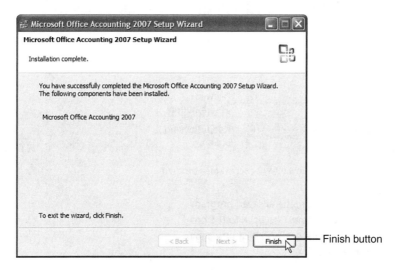

FIGURE 2.13 Microsoft Office Accounting Express 2007 is finished installing!

Firewall

A *firewall* stops malicious users and programs from entering or leaving your computer. It can also warn when an attempt is made to access your computer or the Internet.

If the software firewall is working properly, a pop-up window appears, asking permission to allow a specific program access to the Internet. Be careful! Make sure that the program to which you allow access is not a virus. If you are unsure, type the name of the program in a search engine and read the explanation.

Programs you should allow to access the Internet are SQL Server Express, Microsoft Office Accounting Express, .NET, and any registration for these products.

1. As shown in Figure 2.14, click the **Allow in Future** button to permit Internet access for the program.

   Or, click **Keep Blocking** if the program should not have Internet access.

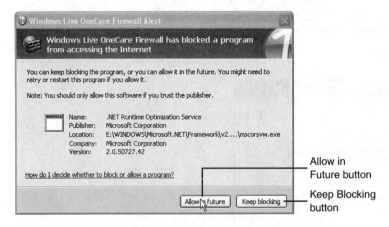

Allow in Future button

Keep Blocking button

FIGURE 2.14   **Carefully** decide whether to allow Internet access for a program.

2. After clicking the Allow in Future button, the allowed program has not yet accessed the Internet. You must go back to the program that was trying to access the Internet, and it can try again. This might mean restarting the program.

Registration and Setup Wizard

Now that you have downloaded and installed Express, you will learn to register and create your company. This chapter details the information you need before starting, and how to use the sample company. You also will learn how to use the New Company Wizard to complete the initial setup.

Registration

Registration sends your contact and company information to Microsoft. Activation verifies whether your software is legitimate. Express registers and activates the product online in one step. Express may be used up to 25 times before requiring activation and registration.

To start Microsoft Office Accounting Express 2007, follow these steps, as shown in Figure 3.1:

1. Click the **Start** button to open the Start menu.
2. Click **All Programs** to open the menu.
3. Click **Microsoft Office** to open the list of Microsoft Office programs installed on the computer.
4. Click **Microsoft Office Accounting 2007** to open Microsoft Office Accounting Express 2007.

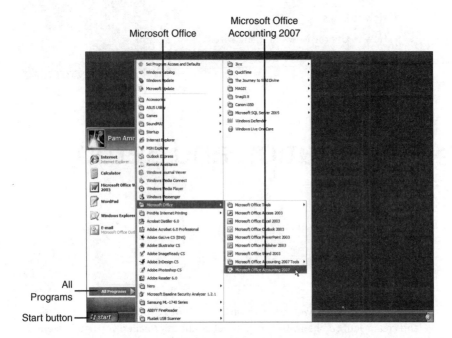

FIGURE 3.1   Start Microsoft Office Accounting Express 2007.

The Microsoft Office Accounting 2007 logo screen appears while the program starts.

Checkmark the **I Don't Want to Activate and Register Now** check box shown in Figure 3.2 if you do not want to provide your company and contact information to Microsoft. However, you may open the program only 25 times before it stops working; then you must register. Click the **Next** button to continue.

To accept the license agreement, follow these steps as shown in Figure 3.3:

1. Drag the slider bar downward on the scrollbar to read the text of the license agreement.

2. Click the **I Accept the Terms of This License Agreement** button if you agree to the license.

3. Click the **Next** button.

   Or, click the **Close** button if you do not want to use Express.

Product Key fields

I Don't Want to Activate and
Register Now check box

Next button

FIGURE 3.2   Because Express is free, the product key appears.

Slider bar on scrollbar

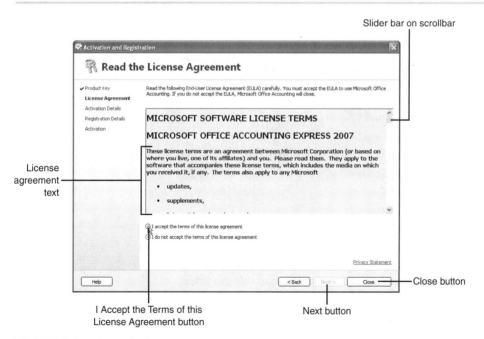

License
agreement
text

Close button

I Accept the Terms of this
License Agreement button

Next button

FIGURE 3.3   Accept the license agreement.

I Want to Activate the Software over the Internet is already selected. Microsoft does not provide telephone activation; Internet activation is the only choice for Express. Follow these steps and see Figure 3.4 to activate Express:

1. Verify that **I Want to Activate the Software over the Internet** is selected.

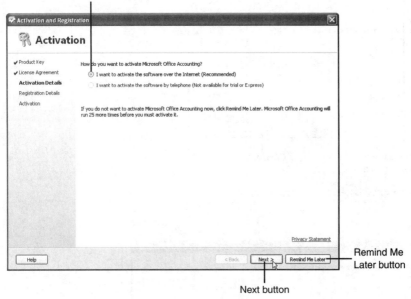

FIGURE 3.4   Activate Microsoft Office Accounting Express 2007 using the Internet.

2. Click the **Next** button to continue with activation.

   Or, click the **Remind Me Later** button to try Express up to 25 times before activating.

Enter information as shown in Figure 3.5.

1. Enter the registration information about you and your company. Microsoft receives the information. The only optional fields are a second address line and your company revenue. All other fields are required:

   - **Company Name**
   - **Street** (second address line optional)

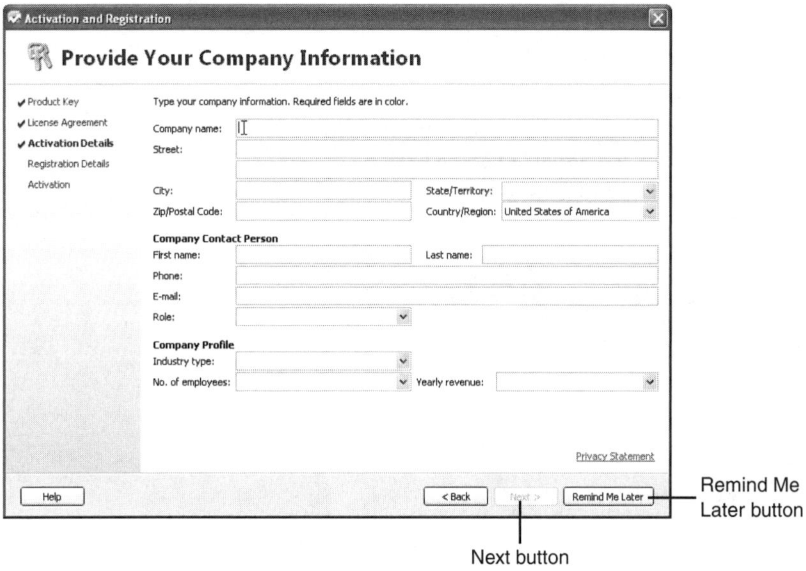

FIGURE 3.5 Enter your registration information.

- **City**
- **State/Territory**
- **Zip/Postal Code**
- **Country/Region**—Express is available only for United States of America businesses at this time; availability in other countries is expected soon
- **First Name**
- **Last Name**
- **Phone**
- **E-mail**
- **Role**—Accountant, Bookkeeper, General Manager, Manager, Office Manager, Owner, Partner
- **Industry Type**—Education, Financial Services, Government, Healthcare, Life Sciences, Manufacturing, Media & Entertainment, Nonprofit, Professional Services, Retail, Telecommunications, Transportation & Logistics, Utilities, Other
- **Number of Employees**—1–5, 6–10, 11–25, 25 or more
- **Yearly Revenue** (optional)—$0–250K, $250–500K, $500–1 Million, $1–2.5 Million, $2.5–5 Million, $5 Million or more

2. Click the **Next** button to continue with activation.

   Or, click the **Remind Me Later** button to try Express up to 25 times before activating.

If the firewall blocks the activation, click the **Allow in Future** button shown in Figure 3.6. The activation remains blocked this time, but Express saves your activation information.

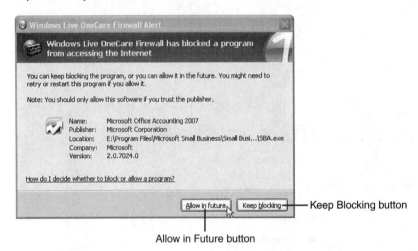

Allow in Future button

FIGURE 3.6 The software firewall might block Express activation.

Express will request activation each time it starts. If the computer has Internet access, the activation will continue. Otherwise, Express will open 25 times, and then not open until activated.

As shown in Figure 3.7, click the **OK** button to activate.

Or, click the **Cancel** button to continue using Express 25 times without activating the product.

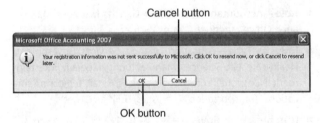

OK button

FIGURE 3.7 Express will continue to ask for activation each time it is started.

Initial Startup

Installation is done. You are ready to open Express for the first time!

To open Microsoft Office Accounting Express 2007, click the **Start** button, **All Programs**, **Microsoft Office**, **Microsoft Office Accounting 2007**.

Try, Play, Learn BEFORE Committing

Play with Express, look at what it does and does not do, look around the menus, and try out sample transactions. You can't hurt anything because it's just a sample company. After you know what to expect and see how easy Express is to use, you won't feel intimidated creating your own company. Go on; take it for a test drive! Figure 3.8 shows the options for opening or starting a company that are discussed next. To open a sample company

1. Click **Open a Sample Company** to see how Express works *before* setting up your own company.

   When you finish using the sample company:

2. Click the **File** menu to open the menu.

3. Click **Close Company**.

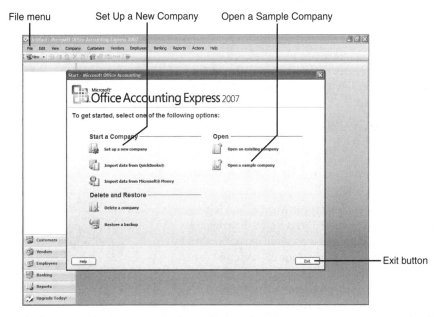

FIGURE 3.8   The Start screen displays multiple options. Set up a new company, import data from Money or QuickBooks, open a sample or existing company, or delete or restore a company.

You're ready to set up your own company! Follow these steps:

1. Click **Set Up a New Company**.

   Or, import data

   ⇨   See Chapter 4, "Importing Data."

   Or, open an existing company

   ⇨   See "Opening a Company," page 122.

   Or, open a sample company

   ⇨   See "Try, Play, Learn BEFORE Committing," page 31.

   Or, click the **Exit** button to close Express.

CAUTION

DON'T STOP UNTIL YOU ARE FINISHED

The wizard will not allow you to save partway through and continue later. If you cancel in the middle, you must start over.

New Company Wizard

Don't worry! The New Company Wizard helps you through a quick initial setup. If you make a mistake, it's okay. You can go backward in the wizard to a previous step. After the wizard completes, you can change your answers in Company Preferences.

Preparation

Here is a checklist of what to have ready before starting the wizard. It is best to enter all the information, but you can add any missing information after completing the wizard.

Locate the following information before starting the wizard:

- Company name, address, city, state, and ZIP code.
- Company phone and fax number, website address, and email address.
- Company *Federal Employer Identification Number*, also known as a *FEIN*, *EIN*, or *Federal tax ID number*. This is a nine-digit number containing two digits, a dash, and then seven digits. Obtain it by completing Internal Revenue Service form SS-4, via mail or on the Internet. Instead of the FEIN, the owner's Social Security number can be used for a sole proprietorship without employees.

NOTE

A VERY BASIC COMPANY SETUP

Express has a very basic company setup. Enter general ledger accounts, customers, vendors, and banking information later, after the wizard completes. Chapter 5, "Company Setup," is all you need to feel comfortable setting up accounts, vendors, and banking without the wizard's help. It also includes tips beyond what the Express Wizard provides.

- Sales tax rates and sales taxing authorities. If you have more than one sales tax rate or authority, the information is entered after the wizard completes.

Company and Preferences

The wizard asks for basic company information. You also choose which Express add-in features to use.

To start the New Company Wizard, click the **Next** button, as seen in Figure 3.9, to move from the Introduction screen to the Company Details screen.

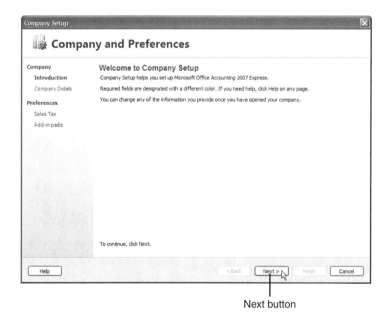

Next button

FIGURE 3.9   The New Company Wizard walks through the setup, starting with the Introduction screen.

Enter information as shown in Figure 3.10:

1. Enter the company details and press the **Tab** key after each entry: company name, legal name, street address, city, state, ZIP code, country, phone, fax, email, website, and federal tax ID.

   This basic company information is used throughout Express as the default on reports and invoices. Enter the information the way you would like your customers to see it.

   The company email address is used for the Accountant Transfer online feature to send your accounting records to your accountant.

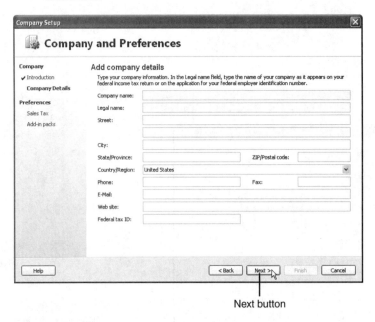

Next button

FIGURE 3.10 The Company Details screen allows you to enter basic company information used throughout Express.

2. Click the **Next** button to move from the Company Details screen to the Sales Tax screen.

The wizard enables you to enter only one sales tax for one taxing authority. If your company pays more than one rate or to more than one tax agency, do not enter your sales tax information in the wizard. Instead, complete the wizard, and then enter the sales tax setup information in Express preferences. Complete the Sales Tax screen, shown in Figure 3.11:

1. Click the **No** button if you do not pay sales tax or if you are not entering sales tax information in the wizard.

   Or, click the **Yes** button to set up one sales tax. The sales tax fields appear on the screen. Then do the following:

   - Enter the **Sales Tax Name**
   - Enter the **Sales Tax Rate**
   - Enter the **Sales Tax Agency**

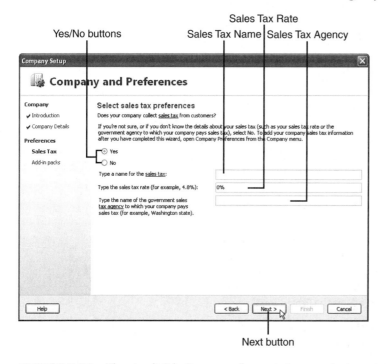

FIGURE 3.11 The wizard's Sales Tax screen allows entering one sales tax code for one taxing authority.

2. Click the **Next** button to move from the Sales Tax screen to the Add-In Packs screen, shown in Figure 3.12.

Enabled check boxes

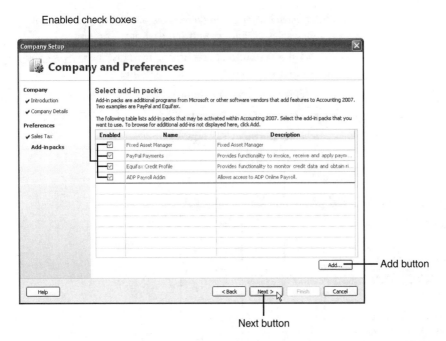

Add button

Next button

FIGURE 3.12   The Add-In Packs screen shows additional capabilities you can include in Express.

Add-ins are additional features that Microsoft or another company provides for Express. Microsoft includes the Fixed Asset Manager, PayPal
Payments, Equifax Credit Profile, and ADP Payroll add-ins in Express, as
shown in the following list. However, Express disables the Fixed Asset
Manager capability until you upgrade to the Professional version.

- **Fixed Asset Manager**—Tracks items that you own and their
  depreciation. Fixed Asset Manager is installed but disabled in
  Express.

- **PayPal Payments**—Receives, tracks, and reconciles payments
  from PayPal against invoices in Express. Emailed invoices include
  the capability of adding a PayPal payment button.

  ➪   See "PayPal," page 321 and "New Invoice," page 133.

- **Equifax Credit Profile**—Monitors credit information about your
  company, and its vendors and customers.

  ➪   See "Equifax," page 325.

- **ADP Payroll**—Provides three levels of service to calculate payroll, print checks, and prepare taxes.

➪ See "ADP Payroll," page 352.

Follow these steps to select add-ins:

1. All features are checkmarked for installation, as shown in Figure 3.12. Uncheck only those features that you don't want to use. Even though the features are installed, you can choose to disable an installed feature. Click the **File** menu, **Utilities**, **Add-in Manager**, and then checkmark or uncheck specific add-ins.
2. Click the **Next** button when you finish selecting add-ins.
3. Click the **Finish** button, shown in Figure 3.13, to finalize the setup.

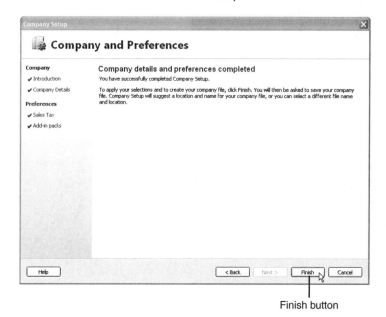

Finish button

FIGURE 3.13 Congratulations! You have completed the company setup.

As shown in Figure 3.14, follow these steps to save the new company file:

1. Use the company name provided, or type a different name in the **File Name** field.

Save In drop-down list arrow

Up One Level button

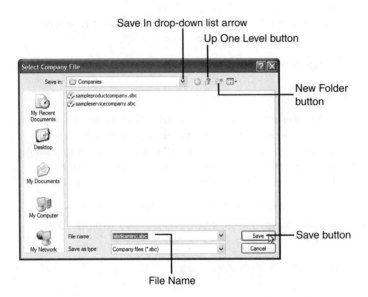

New Folder
button

Save button

File Name

FIGURE 3.14 Save the new company file.

2. Optionally, choose a different location for the file. However, using the default location provided is recommended.

3. Click the **Save** button.

A window appears and shows the software's progress. Express creates the company database and accounts, and then saves them. This might take several minutes. Do not interrupt the process.

You are now ready to use your new company!

WHAT YOU'LL LEARN

- How to Import Data From
- Intuit QuickBooks
- Microsoft Money
- Microsoft Excel
- Microsoft Access
- Comma-Separated Values File
- Other Sources

Importing Data

If your company had a previous accounting system, you might want to import the data from the old accounting system into Express.

Intuit QuickBooks Import

Move your company accounting data from QuickBooks to Express. Import only one company at a time.

To import data from QuickBooks, do the following:

1. Click the **File** menu, and then click **Close Company**. The company closes and the Welcome window opens.

2. As seen in Figure 4.1, click **Import Data from QuickBooks**. A warning window opens telling you that more data will be imported than you can see in Express—sales orders, purchase orders, inventory, and job costing features are missing.

   Import data in one of two ways, as shown in Figure 4.2:

   - **Master Records**—QuickBooks 2002 through 2006 Basic, Pro, Premier, and Accountant versions.

     Imports only the chart of accounts, customers, vendors, employees, items, and balance sheet account balances. Transactions and income statement balances are not imported.

- **All Data**—QuickBooks 2004 through 2006 Pro, Premier, and Accountant versions.

   Imports the chart of accounts, customers, vendors, employees, items, balance sheet account balances, and transactions for customer invoices and vendor bills.

⇨ See "Other Import Sources," page 49, to import from different versions.

3. If you choose All Data, click the **Microsoft Office Accounting Upgrade** link. Internet Explorer will open to the upgrade. Click the **Download** button and install the upgrade.

4. Click the **Next** button.

5. Click **All Data** or **Master Records Only**. Click the **Browse** button and locate the .qbw file to import. The file shows in Select File. Click the **Next** button. The Access and Migrate Your Data window opens.

6. Click the **Allow Access** button. QuickBooks opens, and warning windows appear in QuickBooks and Express. Allow access by clicking **Yes, Always** and following the directions. In QuickBooks, click the **Edit** menu, **Preferences**, **Integrated Applications**, **Company Preferences** tab. Allow Small Business Accounting or Office Accounting access to QuickBooks data and to log on automatically with Administrator rights. Close QuickBooks.

   In Express, checkmark **I Have Completed the Above Steps**. Click the **Next** button. The Company Details window opens.

7. Change the company data, if necessary, and then click the **Next** button. The Select Add-In Packs window opens.

8. Checkmark the required features. Click the **Next** button. The Define Fiscal Year window opens.

9. Enter the dates for the beginning and end of the fiscal year. Data outside this range will not be imported. Use the Import Wizard again, later, to import another fiscal year. Click the **Import** button.

10. The master records are imported. Review the logs, seen in Figure 4.3, for errors in My Documents/Small Business Accounting/Logs. Click the **Next** button. The Transaction Pending Import window opens.

CAUTION

BEFORE IMPORTING QUICKBOOKS DATA

To import data from QuickBooks successfully, first open QuickBooks and complete the following:

- Set credit card accounts to type Credit Card Account, not Liability.
- Archive and condense data for best performance.
- Set reports to accrual basis.
- Use account numbers for all accounts.
- Make inactive those accounts that are no longer used.
- If importing only Master Records, close the books so that only the Balance Sheet accounts have balances.
- All account and subaccount names must be unique.
- Change from multiple user to single user.
- The company file must be the same version as the QuickBooks software. Convert the file if necessary.

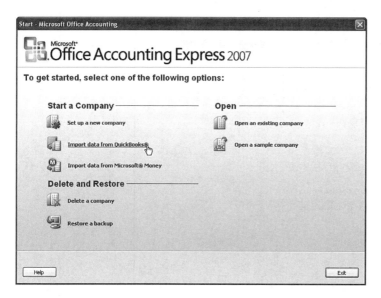

FIGURE 4.1 Import from QuickBooks.

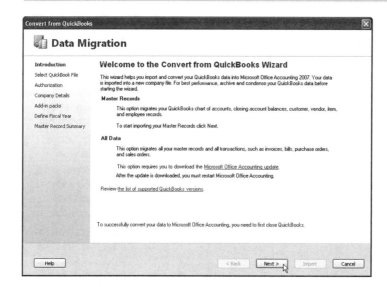

FIGURE 4.2 The QuickBooks Import Wizard opens.

Records Not Imported

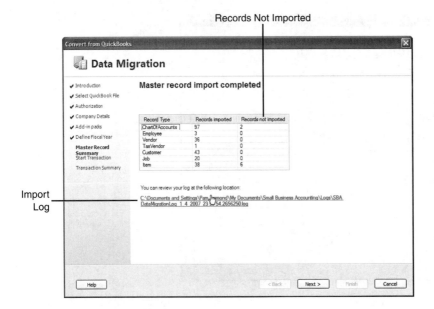

Import Log

FIGURE 4.3   Review the Master Record Summary.

11. Click the **Next** button. The transactions are imported.

12. The import status shows, as seen in Figure 4.4. Click the **Finish** button.

NOTE

QUICKBOOKS IMPORTED DIFFERENCES

The numbers might be different, but that might not be a problem:

- Look in the Job Resell income account for expenses or markups billed back to a customer.

- Customer Down Payments involves two entries in Accounts Receivable, not one as in QuickBooks.

- Purchase Cash Discounts might appear in Cash Discount Taken.

- Subaccounts with the same name are now in the parent account.

Import Status

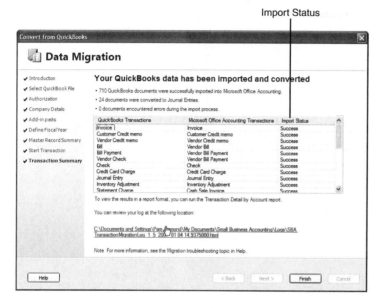

FIGURE 4.4 Success! The transactions were successfully imported from QuickBooks.

Microsoft Money Import

Move company accounting data from Microsoft Money to Express. Only one company or file may be imported at a time. Table 4.1 shows how the data will be imported.

Table 4.1 Imported Data Differences

Microsoft Money Data	Accounting 2007 Data
Account	Account
Payee—vendor	Vendor
Payee—customer	Customer
Bill	Bill
Deposit	Journal entry
Transfer	Journal entry
Paycheck	Check
Investment purchase	Other current asset
Invoice	Invoice

continues

43

Table 4.1   Imported Data Differences, continued

Microsoft Money Data	Accounting 2007 Data
Invoice (marked as estimate)	Quote
Service	Item
Reimbursable expense	Billable expense
Business category	Financial account
Sales tax	Sales tax group and tax code
Ship by	Shipping method
Payment terms	Payment terms
Non-inventory items	Non-inventory items
Fiscal years	Fiscal years
Company	Company

To import data from Money, do the following:

1. Click the **File** menu, and then **Close Company**. The company closes and the Welcome window opens.

2. Close Microsoft Money.

3. Click **Import Data from Microsoft Money**. A warning window opens telling you that more data will import than you can see in Express—sales orders, purchase orders, inventory, and job costing features are missing. Click the **No** button if you decide to use Express.

   Import data from Microsoft Money 2007 Home & Business, Premium, Deluxe and Essentials; Microsoft Money 2006 Small Business, Premium, Deluxe, and Standard; and Microsoft Money 2005 Small Business, Premium, Deluxe, and Standard.

4. Click the **Browse** button, shown in Figure 4.5, and locate the file to import. The file shows in Select File. The file might be located in the My Documents folder or in C:\Program Files\Microsoft Money. Click the **Next** button. The Migrate Accounts window opens.

5. Checkmark the accounts to migrate, as shown in Figure 4.6. Click the **Next** button. The Migrate Payees window opens.

6. Checkmark the payees as customers or vendors. Click the **Next** button. The Select Add-In Packs window opens.

7. Checkmark the add-in features to use. Click the **Next** Button. The Data Pending Migration window opens.

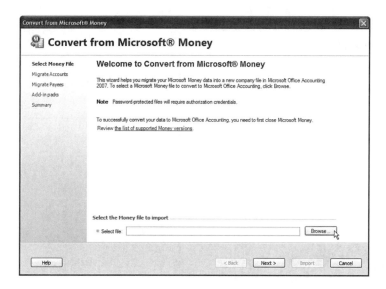

FIGURE 4.5 The Microsoft Money Import Wizard opens.

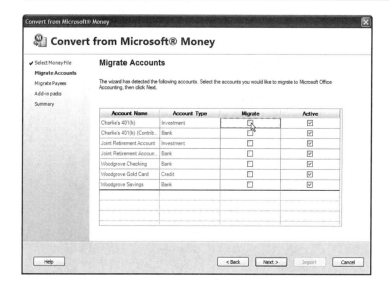

FIGURE 4.6 Select the accounts to migrate.

8. Click the **Import** button. The Data Migration Completed window opens.

9. The import status displays, as shown in Figure 4.7. Click the **Finish** button.

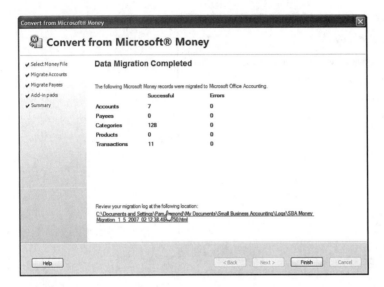

FIGURE 4.7   Review the data migration summary and the import log.

Import Utility

You can import from an Excel spreadsheet, an Access database, or a comma-delimited file.

As shown in Figure 4.8, to import, click the **File** menu, **Utilities**, **Import**.

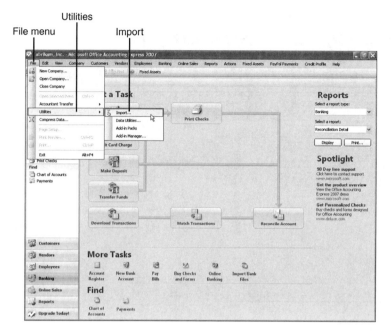

Utilities

File menu   Import

Excel Import

Express comes with an Excel spreadsheet to use as a template for importing data into Express. It might be located in the C:\Program Files\Microsoft Small Business\Small Business Accounting 2007\ Templates\Excel\ImportData.xls file.

The tabs on the bottom of the Excel spreadsheet, seen in Figure 4.9, indicate what can be imported into Express: Accounts, Customers, Vendors, Employees, Service Items, and Non-Inventory Items.

Use the Excel document as a template for importing your data. Before modifying the template, use Save As to give it a new name. Be sure not to modify the original template. Each Excel row is a record, and each cell imported must have the same formatting as the template. Right-click on an Excel cell and choose **Format Cell** to view the cell formatting.

If exporting to Excel from Peachtree, the signs on the liability, income, and equity accounts must be reversed. All negatives should be positives and all positives should be negatives.

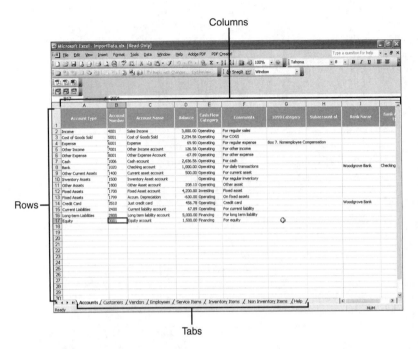

FIGURE 4.9   The Excel spreadsheet shows you how to format your information.

After the data is correct in Excel, save the modified spreadsheet and import the data. To import the data from Excel, do the following:

1. Click the **File** menu, **Utilities**, **Import**. The Import Data window opens.

2. Click **Microsoft Excel Worksheet (.xls, .xlsx)**, **OK**.

3. Browse to choose the Excel spreadsheet to import. Click the **Do Not Import Duplicate Records** button, or the **Import Duplicate Records** button. Then click the **Next** button.

4. Click the Excel worksheet, shown in Figure 4.10, and then click the Express data type. Click the **Map Fields** button.

5. The template automatically maps most fields, so you don't have to drag them. Drag any additional fields from the Excel worksheet to the Express fields. Any fields that do not match will not be imported. As shown in Figure 4.10, fields in Express marked with an asterisk (*) must be matched. Mapped Excel fields are shown with a checkmark. Click the **OK** button when you are finished mapping fields.

> **CAUTION**
>
> **THE DATA MUST BE IMPORTED IN A SPECIFIC ORDER**
>
> You must import the data in the following order:
>
> 1. Accounts
> 2. Vendors
> 3. Customers
> 4. Items
> 5. Employees
>
> Import only one data type at a time, and then restart the import process and import the next type.

Express Data Types

Excel Worksheets

Map Fields button

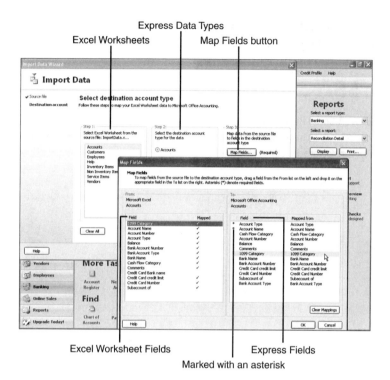

Excel Worksheet Fields

Express Fields

Marked with an asterisk

FIGURE 4.10   Choose the data type, and then map the data.

6. Click the **Next** button to begin importing data.

7. The link to the import log file appears. Click the link to view the file's details. Click the **Finish** button to exit the Import Wizard.

Finish importing each data type, one at a time.

Other Import Sources

Microsoft Access and comma-separated value files can be imported; however, these import methods are not recommended because they are more difficult than the other import methods. Click the **File** menu, **Utilities**, **Import**. The Import Data window opens. Select the appropriate type of import, and then select the source and destination files. Match the data. The process is similar to the Excel import discussed earlier.

Other companies have written import software for Express. Click the **Company** menu, **Business Services**, **Find Software Add-Ons**. Internet

Explorer opens to a list of vendors that write software that works with Express. Look for companies providing additional import capabilities.

Upgrading from SBA 2006

Express will not upgrade from Microsoft Small Business Accounting 2006 because it does not use purchase orders, sales orders, inventory, or job costing. Install Professional before upgrading from Small Business Accounting 2006.

WHAT YOU'LL LEARN

- Questions to Ask Your Accountant
- Basic Accounting Terms
- Company, Financial Accounts, and Sales Tax Settings
- Vendor, Customer, Employee, and Item Setup

Company Setup

The Company Wizard is complete and your new company files are set up. It's time to enter basic information about your company. This is the key to future happiness with Express or any other accounting system. **Complete this chapter before entering daily transactions.**

Setup is dependent on the type and form of company, taxes, and government regulations. Discuss the following with your accountant:

- **Company form**—Proprietorship, partnership, corporation: subchapter S, LLC, C
- **Company accounting basis**—Cash or accrual
- **Company year**—Fiscal year or calendar year
- **Start date**—Decide on the start date and request financial statements dated the day before the start date

Gather Before Setup

Instead of entering balances, try to find the records that make up each account balance for the bank, vendor, customer, and credit cards. For example, accounts payable is made up of individual vendor balances, and these contain unpaid or partially paid bills. You will be entering these bills.

Basic Accounting Terms Explained

Enter information about your business, using accounts and transactions, to obtain a better picture of where your business has been, as shown on reports.

Reports

Reports indicate the general health of the company. Three basic reports make up a financial statement:

- Balance sheet
- Income statement (also called Profit and Loss)
- Cash flow statement

The *balance sheet* shows what the company owns or is owed (*assets*), what it owes to others (*liabilities*), and what is left over for the owner(s) (*equity*). Equity includes the initial investment into the business by the owner(s), plus what the business made or lost. It is a snapshot of the business on a particular day.

The *income statement* shows whether the company is making money. It indicates what you sold (*income*, *revenue*, your services and products), less the direct costs of what you sold (*cost of goods sold*), less all the other indirect costs of staying in business (*expenses*). The end result is *net income*, or *net loss*.

The *cash flow statement* (also called a *statement of cash flow*) shows money moving into and out of your business. Because insufficient cash is one of the biggest reasons small businesses fail, keep a close watch on this report.

Accounts and Transactions

Transactions record an event within your business, such as buying stamps at the post office. *Accounts* contain the details of the transaction. There are always at least two accounts per transaction because the company trades one item to receive another. In this example, the company traded money (a bank check) for stamps. The transaction would show $30 coming out of the account called Bank and $30 going into an account called Postage.

Chart of Accounts

Express automatically sets up accounts and assigns them account numbers, as shown in Table 5.1. Ask your accountant whether you need to add, change, or delete accounts.

Table 5.1   Microsoft Express Chart of Accounts

Account Number	Account Name	Type of Account
1000	Undeposited Funds	Cash Account
1010	Checking	Bank
1100	Savings	Bank
1200	Accounts Receivable	Accounts Receivable
1250	Inventory	Inventory Asset
2000	Accounts Payable	Accounts Payable
2100	Credit Card	Credit Card
2110	Employee Payroll Liabilities	Payroll Liability
2200	Payroll Liabilities	Current Liability
2205	Payroll Liability: Federal Withholding, Social Security, Medicare	Current Liability
2210	Payroll Liability: Federal Unemployment Tax Act	Current Liability
2215	Payroll Liability: State and Local	Current Liability
2220	Payroll Liability: State Unemployment Tax Act	Current Liability
2225	Payroll Liability: 401K	Current Liability
2230	Payroll Liability: Profit Sharing	Current Liability
2235	Payroll Liability: Medical & Dental	Current Liability
2240	Payroll Liability: Section 125	Current Liability
2245	Payroll Liability: Union Dues	Current Liability
2250	Payroll Liability: Other	Current Liability
2300	Sales Tax Payable	Current Liability
2500	Pending Item Receipts	Current Liability
3050	Owner's Equity	Equity
3150	Opening Balance Equity	Equity
3200	Retained Earnings	Equity
4020	Sales	Income
4095	Write Off	Income
4100	Cash Discount Given	Income

continues

Table 5.1   Microsoft Express Chart of Accounts, continued

Account Number	Account Name	Type of Account
5000	Cash Discount Taken	Cost of Goods Sold
5015	Purchases	Expense
5500	Bank Charge	Expense
6010	Advertising and Promotion	Expense
6150	Insurance	Expense
6190	Meals and Entertainment	Expense
7110	Payroll Expenses - Employees	Expense
7125	Payroll Expense - Bonuses	Expense
7130	Payroll Expense - Benefits	Expense
7135	Employee - Meals 100%	Expense
7140	Medical	Expense
7145	Morale	Expense
7150	Retirement	Expense
7170	Payroll Tax Expense	Expense
7175	Payroll Tax Expense - Social Security; Medicare	Expense
7180	Payroll Tax Expense - FUTA - Federal Unemployment Tax Act	Expense
7185	Payroll Tax Expense - L&I - Company	Expense
7190	Payroll Tax Expense - SUTA - State Unemployment Tax Act	Expense
7310	Rent	Expense
7340	Supplies	Expense
7810	Utilities	Expense
7910	Vehicle Expense	Expense
8010	Interest Income	Other Income
8050	Miscellaneous Income	Other Income
8150	Interest Expense	Other Expense
8190	Miscellaneous Expense	Other Expense
8500	Federal Income Tax	Other Expense
10001	PayPal Expense Account	Expense

Adding an Account

Add the accounts for your company.

As seen in Figure 5.1, to add an account, click the **Company** menu, **Company Lists**, **Chart of Accounts** to open the Chart of Accounts list. Click **Add a New Account**, shown in Figure 5.2, to create a new account.

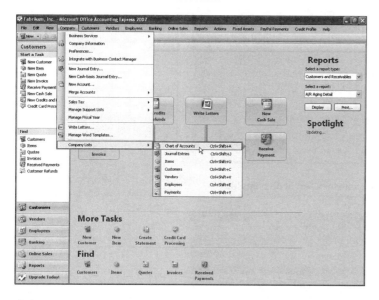

FIGURE 5.1   Check with your accountant to determine the best accounts and account numbers for your business.

Or, click the **Company** menu, **New Account** to create a new account, as seen in Figure 5.3.

Express opens a window asking which account type to use, seen in Figure 5.4.

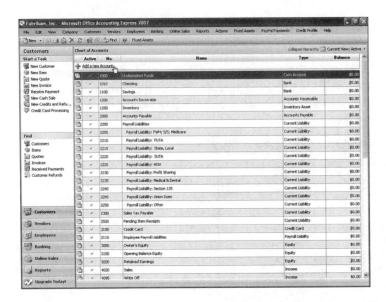

FIGURE 5.2 Add a new account from the Chart of Accounts list.

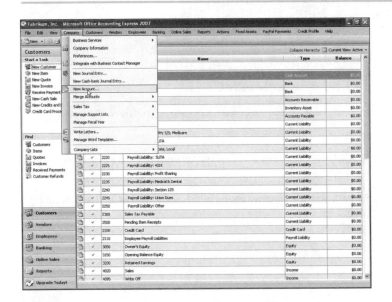

FIGURE 5.3 Add a new account using the Express menus.

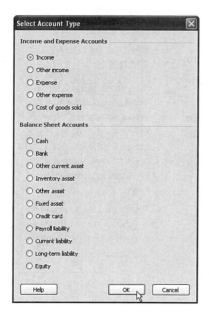

FIGURE 5.4 Choose the account type.

1. Select an account type:

   ■ **Income**—Earned by the company in the normal course of business

   ■ **Other Income**—Money received by the business that is not typically part of normal operations; for example, the sale of a noninventory asset

   ■ **Expense**—The indirect costs of staying in business

   ■ **Other Expense**—Indirect costs of the business that are not part of normal operations

   ■ **Cost of Goods Sold**—Direct costs of what was sold

   ■ **Cash**—Money on hand

   ■ **Bank**—Money in an account held by a third party

- **Other Current Asset**—Owned by the business for a year or less, but not Cash or Bank

- **Inventory Asset**—Product available for sale to a customer

- **Other Asset**—Owned by the business and not Cash, Bank, Other Current Asset, Inventory Asset, or Fixed Asset

- **Fixed Asset**—Owned by the business for more than one year; for example, furniture, fixtures, equipment, and cars

- **Credit Card**—Purchases made on a credit card

- **Payroll Liability**—Money owed for employee work

- **Current Liability**—Money owed for less than one year, but not for Credit Card, or Payroll

- **Long-term Liability**—Money owed for more than one year

- **Equity**—The earnings left over at the end of each year plus the amounts invested by the owner(s) into the business

⇨ See Table 5.1 on page 53 for more help in choosing the correct account type.

2. Click the **OK** button. Express closes the window and opens the account editing screen.

Editing an Account

Change the name, number, or status of any account. The account type may not be changed.

To open the account editing window, click the **Company** menu, **Company Lists**, **Chart of Accounts** to open the Chart of Accounts list. Right-click an account(s) to open a menu, seen in Figure 5.5. Click **Open Selected Items** to open the account.

The Account Type field may not be changed. If the account type is incorrect and the account does not yet have transactions, write down the information about the account, delete the account, and re-add it. All other information about the account may be changed.

> NOTE
>
> **SPECIAL ACCOUNT FEATURES**
>
> If an account has a statement to reconcile against, select an account type of Credit Card or Bank. These account types have an account register and allow reconciling with a statement.
>
> Payments can be made to or from accounts that are only of type Cash, Bank, or Credit Card.

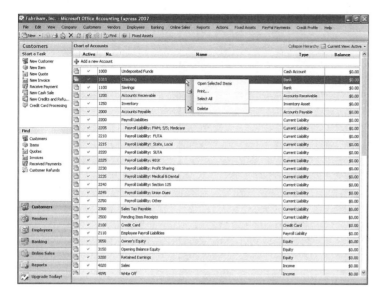

FIGURE 5.5 Right-clicking an account opens a menu with several options: Select Open Selected Items to edit an account, Print to print the chart of accounts, or Delete to permanently remove an account.

To edit an account, change one or more of the following fields, as shown in Figure 5.6:

- **Account No**—Shows only if Use Account Numbers is check-marked in Company Information. It's a good idea to use account numbers, to keep like accounts together, and to ask your accountant for advice on account numbers.

⮡ See "Company Preferences," page 80.

- **Account Name**—A required field. For clarity, do not use the same name for two different accounts. You could use one of the following methods to distinguish between accounts with dupli-cate names:
  - Add a category name after a duplicate name. For example, use the name Car for the asset you own, and the name Car Expense for the account under Repairs and Maintenance.
  - Use a dash or colon between parts of the account name. For example, use the name Car for the asset you own, and the name Repairs and Maintenance - Car for the account under Repairs and Maintenance.

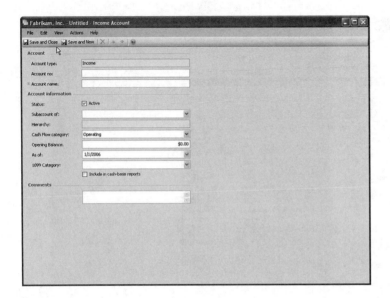

FIGURE 5.6   Add or edit the account.

- **Status**—Active is checkmarked by default. Unchecking the Active check box means the account does not show in dialog boxes, lists, forms, or wizards. The Chart of Accounts list enables you to show Active, Inactive, or All Accounts. Reports and previous transactions show the account. To use an inactive account, type the account name instead of choosing it from a list.

- **Subaccount Of**—Not shown for all accounts. Subaccount Of is optional, and if it is used, both the main and subaccount must be the same account type.

  Subaccounts break a large main account into multiple smaller accounts underneath the main account. Express allows up to five levels of subaccounts. For example, Payroll Expense may have Benefits as one of many subaccounts, and Benefits may have Medical as one of many subaccounts.

- **Hierarchy**—Does not show for all accounts and may not be changed. If Subaccount Of is filled in, the Hierarchy field will show the main account and the subaccounts underneath to reach this account. For example, Payroll Expense > Benefits > Medical.

- **Cash Flow Category**—The cash flow statement contains three categories: Operating, Financing, and Investing. Express uses the Cash Flow Category field to create the cash flow statement.

Select the correct cash flow category using the following list for guidance:

Operating—Cash receipts and payments from day-to-day operation of the business. Balance sheet accounts include

- Accounts payable
- Accounts receivable
- Cash
- Interest amortization
- Inventory
- Payroll payable
- Prepaid expenses
- Prepaid insurance
- Taxes payable

Income statement accounts include

- Cost of goods sold
- Dividends received
- Expenses
- Income
- Interest received

Non-cash items that are subtracted include

- Bad debt allowance
- Deferred income tax
- Depreciation
- Inventory allowance

Financing—Cash receipts and payments from financing when money is raised or dividends paid

- Bonds payable
- Dividends
- Loans received from others
- Long-term debt
- Mortgages
- Notes payable
- Owner's equity

- Paid-in capital in excess of par

- Retained earnings

- Stock the company issues or repurchases

Investing—Cash receipts and payments from investing in future growth

- Buildings

- Equipment

- Fixed assets

- Furniture and fixtures

- Investments

- Loans made to others

- Long-term assets

- Other businesses

- Property

- Property leases

- Vehicles

STOP! Do Not Enter Opening Account Balances

An account may not be deleted after an opening balance is entered, and the opening balance may not be changed. Make sure that the accounts are set up properly. Include all the accounts you need and remove any that are not used. Ask your accountant to review the Chart of Accounts. After finalizing the accounts, the opening balances will be entered using transactions.

 See "Opening Balance Overview," page 119, to enter opening transactions.

Do not be tempted to "save time" by entering opening balance amounts instead of taking the time to enter the transactions. You probably will *not* save time. Consider the frustration and time involved in paying vendor bills and receiving customer payments from invoices, when the original transactions are not in Express.

- **Opening Balance**—The amount the account shows just before the Company Preferences Start Date. **Do not enter an opening balance**; instead, use transactions. Press the **Enter** or **Tab** key to skip this field.

See "Opening Balance Overview," page 119, to enter opening transactions.

FIGURE 5.7 Entering an opening balance is not recommended. However, the year must be open if you enter an open balance.

- **As Of**—The date associated with the Opening Balance field. The As Of field defaults to the value of the Company Preferences Start Date field. Press the Enter or Tab key to skip this field.

- **1099 Category**—Not shown for all accounts. The 1099 report is available only in Professional. Press the Enter or Tab key to skip this field.

- **Include in Cash-Basis Reports**—Based on the account type, Express checkmarks or clears this check box for you. Make a change only after discussing it with your accountant. Otherwise, press the Enter or Tab key to skip this field.

- **Comments**—Optionally, enter comments about the account. They are used only by you; Express does not use them.

Click the **Save and New** button to save the account information, and then enter another account.

Or, click the **Save and Close** button to save the account information and close the window.

Deleting an Account

Deleting an account is not a difficult process, although certain accounts may not be deleted, as seen in Figure 5.8.

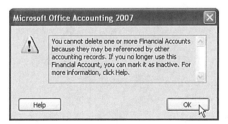

FIGURE 5.8 System accounts, accounts with a beginning balance, and accounts with transactions may not be deleted.

To delete an account, click the **Company** menu, **Company Lists**, **Chart of Accounts** to open the Chart of Accounts List. Right-click the account to delete it. As shown in Figure 5.9, a menu opens. Click **Delete**.

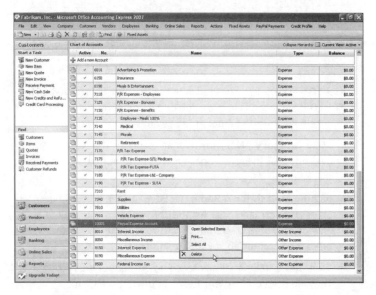

FIGURE 5.9   Deleting an account is easy!

Are you sure that you want to permanently delete the selected item(s)? Click the **Yes** button, seen in Figure 5.10, to delete the account, or click the **No** button to cancel.

FIGURE 5.10   Are you sure? Express gives you a chance to change your mind before deleting an account.

Sales Tax Setup

If your company does not report sales tax, skip this section. If the states in which you sell require sales tax reporting on the sale of your company's products and services, this is the next section to set up.

Express works with multiple taxing authorities and multiple sales tax rates for different products, services, types of customers, and locations—and any combination of the above.

Tax Agency

A *tax agency* is the government organization collecting a tax. Set up all tax agencies collecting sales tax on the company's products and services.

ADD A TAX AGENCY

To add a new tax agency, as shown in Figure 5.11, click the **Company** menu, **Sales Tax**, **New Tax Agency**. The Tax Agency window opens.

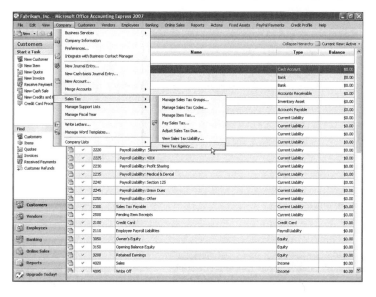

FIGURE 5.11   Add or edit a tax agency.

Enter the new tax agency information, seen in Figure 5.12, pressing the Enter or Tab key after each entry. An asterisk indicates a required field.

1. Enter the tax agency as you want it to appear on the check. For example, enter **Ohio Treasurer of State**.

2. **File As** automatically fills in the information entered for the Tax Agency field. Change it, if necessary, to indicate how you would like the tax authority displayed and sorted. For example, enter **Ohio Department of Taxation**.

3. Enter the business address. To format the address properly, click the **Business** button, shown in Figure 5.13, and enter the information.

65

Save and New button   Next Tax Agency button

Save and Close button   Previous Tax Agency button

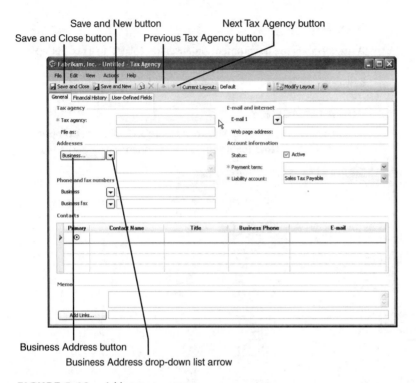

Business Address button

Business Address drop-down list arrow

FIGURE 5.12   Add a new tax agency.

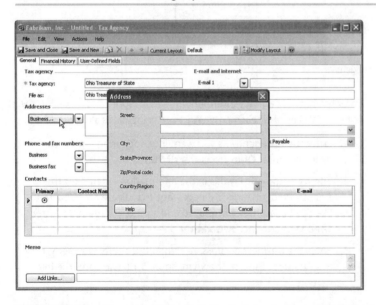

FIGURE 5.13   The address button indicates the type of address. Click the button to format the address correctly.

4. If this tax authority has multiple addresses, click the **Business address** drop-down list arrow, seen in Figure 5.14, and choose another address type:

   - Business
   - Bill To
   - Ship To
   - Warehouse
   - Home
   - Legal
   - Postal
   - Other

   A checkmark next to an address type indicates that it is used and may be changed. The bold address is the address currently being edited.

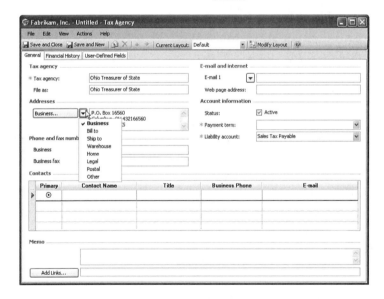

FIGURE 5.14   Click the Business address drop-down list arrow to choose another type of address.

5. Enter a value in the **Business Phone** field. A fast way to enter a number is to use the number pad on the right side of the keyboard, and enter only the 10 digits. Express automatically makes the number readable. For example, typing **8884054039** results in (888) 405-4039.

6. Click the **Business Phone** drop-down list arrow to enter additional phone numbers. The choices are

   - Business
   - Mobile
   - Home
   - Assistant
   - Other

   If the choices are not appropriate, you might want to enter additional phone information in the Contacts or Memo area.

7. Enter the business fax phone number.

8. Click the **Business Fax** drop-down list arrow to enter additional phone numbers. The choices are

   - Business fax
   - Home fax
   - Other fax

   If the choices are not appropriate, you might want to enter additional fax information in the Contacts or Memo area.

9. Enter an email address, if one is available.

10. Click the E-mail drop-down list arrow to enter additional email addresses.

11. Enter the company's web page address. This is useful if you pay taxes online.

12. The **Active Status** field is automatically checkmarked. Uncheck it if taxes are no longer paid to this tax agency.

13. Start typing in the **Payment Term** field. After the first few characters, Express completes the rest of the word for you. To see a list of choices, click the **Payment Terms** drop-down list arrow to make your selection. You must choose one of the payment terms in the list.

    To add a new payment term, click the **Payment Term** drop-down list arrow, and then click **Add a New Payment Term**. Payment terms such as "20 days after the end of the quarter" can easily be added.

    ⇨ See "Payment Terms List," page 88.

14. The **Liability Account** field automatically shows the sales tax liability account. You may change the account here. However, if you always use a different account, change it in Company Preferences.

   ⇨ See "Company Preferences," page 80.

15. For each contact, enter a **Contact Name**, **Title**, **Business Phone**, and **E-mail** in the appropriate field. Each item may contain any information you want. For example, Taxpayer Support Unit in Contact Name; 4485 Northland Ridge Blvd., Columbus, OH 43229-6596 in Title; (888) 405-4089 in Business Phone; and Fax: (614) 466-8892 in E-Mail.

16. If more than one contact is entered, choose the primary contact by clicking the **Primary** button for that contact.

17. Enter a **Memo**, if desired.

18. The **Add Links** button is used to attach one or more files. For example, scan in a universal sales tax form or the form instructions, save the file(s), and click the **Add Links** button. Then locate the file(s) on the computer and click the **OK** button. The filename shows in Add Links.

19. Click the **Save and Close** button to save the information and then close the window. Your completed form should look similar to Figure 5.15.

   Or, click the **Save and New** button to add another tax agency.

20. To edit a tax agency, click the **Previous Tax Agency** button or **Next Tax Agency** button to find the correct tax agency to edit.

Optionally, click the **User-Defined Fields** tab, seen in Figure 5.16, and then the **New Fields** button to include your own information—up to 21 alphanumeric text fields, 1 multiline text field, 6 date fields, 8 number fields, and 4 check box fields.

Customize forms to your needs. Click the **Modify Layout** button, shown in Figure 5.17, to change the fields and the layout of the form.

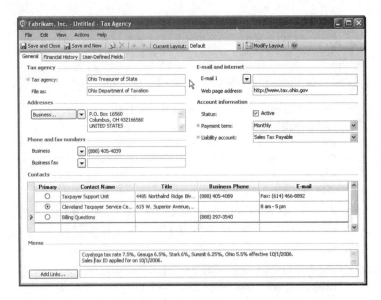

FIGURE 5.15 A completed tax agency form example.

User-Defined Fields tab

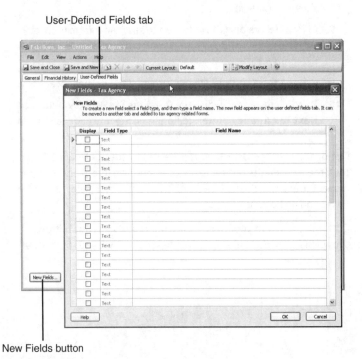

New Fields button

FIGURE 5.16 Click the New Fields button to add customized information to the form.

Modify Layout button

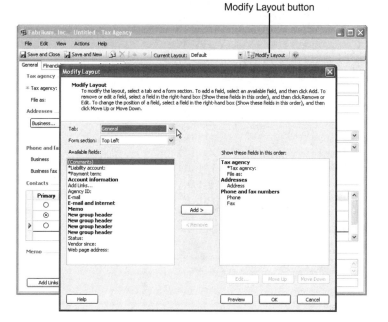

FIGURE 5.17   Click the Modify Layout button to customize forms.

Manage Sales Tax Codes

For each tax agency, define the tax code names and rates.

To manage tax codes, click the **Company** menu, **Sales Tax**, **Manage Sales Tax Codes**, as seen in Figure 5.18. The Manage Tax Codes window opens.

To add a new sales tax code, click the **Add** button, shown in Figure 5.19. The Add or Edit Tax Code window appears, as seen in Figure 5.20.

Tax code setup differs with each state's requirements. Ask your accountant.

- Typically, a tax code is set up for each county where a taxable product or service is delivered.

- Some states require a separate sales tax code for the state.

- Set up a tax code of Non-Taxable with a rate of 0% for items that are normally taxable but are delivered in a state or county that is nontaxable.

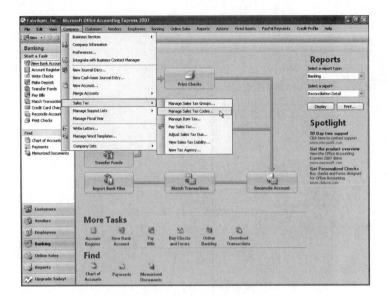

FIGURE 5.18   Manage sales tax codes.

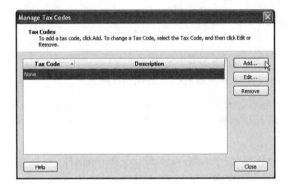

FIGURE 5.19   Add, edit, or remove a sales tax code.

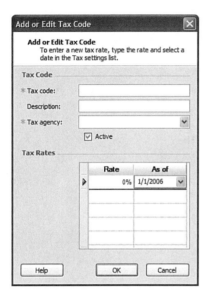

FIGURE 5.20 For each tax authority, enter all required tax codes and rates.

Enter the following information for each tax agency's tax code:

1. Enter a tax code. This is the short description of the tax, which shows on the invoice. For example, Cuyahoga Sales Tax.

2. Enter a description of the tax code. For example, Cuyahoga County Sales Tax.

3. Start typing in the **Tax Agency** field. After the first few characters, Express completes the rest of the word for you. To see a list of choices, click the **Tax Agency** drop-down list arrow to make your selection. You must choose one of the tax agencies in the list.

   To add a new tax agency click the **Tax Agency** drop-down list arrow, and then click **Add a New Tax Agency**.

   ⇨ See "Tax Agency," page 65.

4. **Active Status** is automatically checkmarked. Uncheck it if this tax code is no longer effective.

5. If the tax rates are changing, you can enter more than one tax rate per line, each with a different effective date. It does not matter which tax rate you enter first. Express looks at the As Of field date to determine which tax rate to use for each sale.

Enter a tax rate percentage. Express adds a % after the rate. For example, enter either **7.5** or **7.5%** and press the **Enter** or **Tab** key—Express will show 7.5%.

6. Enter the As Of effective date by typing it, or by clicking the **As Of** drop-down calendar arrow and clicking on a date in the calendar.

Click the **OK** button to save the information and close the window. The completed form should look similar to Figure 5.21. The Manage Tax Codes window reappears.

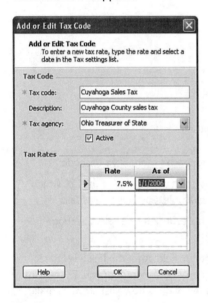

FIGURE 5.21   An example of a completed sales tax code.

To edit a tax code, highlight the **Tax Code** line and click the **Edit** button seen in Figure 5.22. Add, edit, or remove additional tax codes as needed. Then, click the **Close** button and the Manage Tax Codes window closes.

Manage Item Tax

An item tax is already set up named Non-Taxable. If no further breakdown of non-taxable or taxable sales is required on the sales tax reporting form sent to the government, set up one item tax named Taxable.

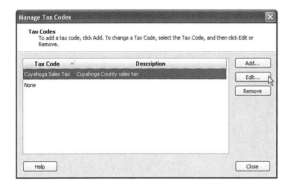

FIGURE 5.22   Click the Edit button to edit a tax code.

If the sales tax reporting form requires further breakdown of taxable or non-taxable sales, set up multiple item taxes. This will save time and improve accuracy when filling out the sales tax report. Express's Sales Tax Liability report includes a column and column total for each item tax that is set up.

To set up item taxes, click the **Company** menu, **Sales Tax**, **Manage Item Tax**, as seen in Figure 5.23.

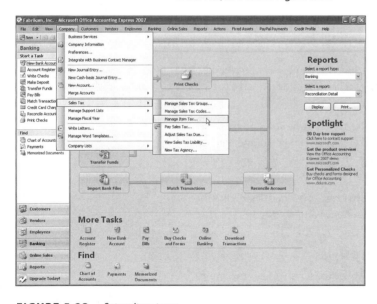

FIGURE 5.23   Set up item taxes.

To add a new item tax, click the **Add** button shown in Figure 5.24. The Item Tax window, seen in Figure 5.25, appears.

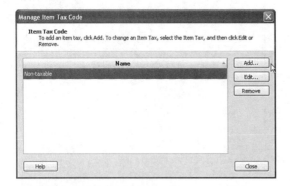

FIGURE 5.24   Add a new item tax.

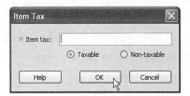

FIGURE 5.25   The Item Tax window adds new item taxes.

In the Item Tax window, enter the Item Tax name, indicate whether it is taxable or non-taxable, and then click the **OK** button to save the information.

To edit an item tax, highlight the **Item Tax Name** line, and then click the **Edit** button shown in Figure 5.26. Only the name of the item tax may be edited. To change whether an item is taxable or non-taxable, the item must be removed and then re-added.

Add, edit, or remove additional item taxes as needed. Then, click the **Close** button. The Manage Item Tax Code window closes.

Manage Sales Tax Groups

If the company charges sales tax, you must set up a sales tax group, even if only one sales tax code is in the group.

To manage sales tax groups, as seen in Figure 5.27, click the **Company** menu, **Sales Tax**, **Manage Sales Tax Groups**.

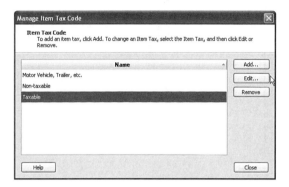

FIGURE 5.26   Add, edit, or remove an item tax.

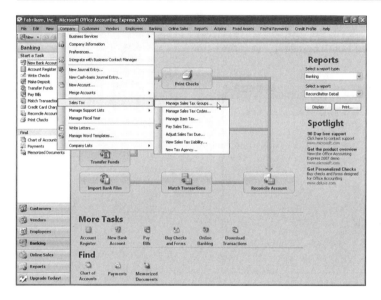

FIGURE 5.27   Manage sales tax groups.

To add a new sales tax group, click the **Add** button shown in Figure 5.28. The Tax Group window appears.

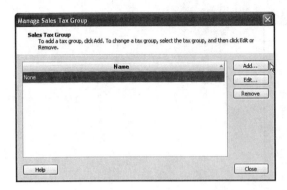

FIGURE 5.28   Add, edit, or remove a sales tax group.

Enter the new sales tax group information, as seen in Figure 5.29:

1. Enter a value in the **Selected Tax Group** field. This is the name for the tax group.

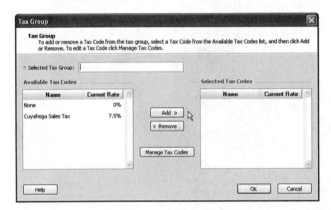

FIGURE 5.29   Add a new sales tax group.

2. As shown in Figure 5.30, on the left side, under Available Tax Codes, click the line containing the Available Tax Code Name and Available Tax Code Current Rate that you want to add to this group. The line highlights when selected.

3. Click the **Add** button. The line moves to Selected Tax Codes on the right side.

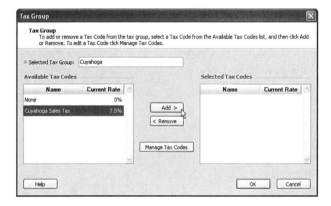

FIGURE 5.30 To create a group, move available tax codes from the left side into selected tax codes on the right side.

4. Continue moving codes from the left to the right side until the group is complete. For example, if your state requires you to collect both a state sales tax and a county sales tax, you would move both sales taxes from the left side to the right side to create a group.

To remove a tax code from the Selected Tax Codes box, highlight the code by clicking it, and then click the **Remove** button, shown in Figure 5.31. To add, edit, or delete a tax code created in a previous step, click the **Manage Tax Codes** button.

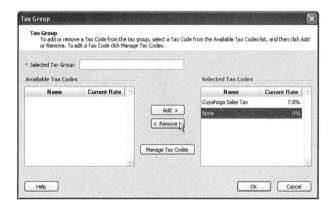

FIGURE 5.31 Remove a tax code.

5. Click the **OK** button to save the group and close the window. The Manage Sales Tax Group window reappears.

To edit a sales tax group, highlight the Item Tax Name line, and then click the **Edit** button shown in Figure 5.32.

Add, edit, or remove additional sales tax groups as needed. Then, click the **Close** button and the Manage Sales Tax Groups window closes.

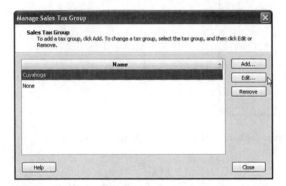

FIGURE 5.32   Add, edit, or remove a sales tax group.

Company Information and Preferences

Express uses the company information and company preferences extensively throughout the rest of the program. It's important to fill in the information before using Express for your daily transactions.

Company Information

The Company Information contains the company name and address used on customer invoices.

Click the **Company** menu, **Company Information**, as shown in Figure 5.33, to see basic information about the company.

Enter an optional Legal and Shipping address, as shown in Figure 5.34, if required.

Company Preferences

Company Preferences has tabs for Company, Online Sales, System Accounts, and General. Double-check that they are set up properly before using Express for daily transactions.

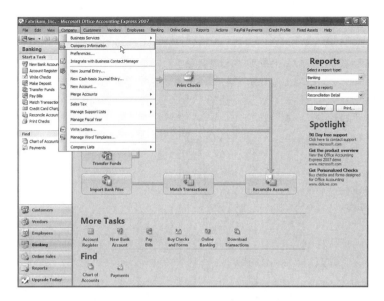

FIGURE 5.33   Company Information shows basic company information.

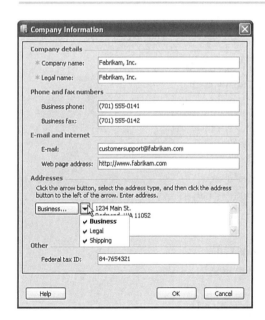

FIGURE 5.34   The Company Information window contains the information entered previously in the New Company Wizard.

Open the Company Preferences window by clicking the **Company** menu, **Preferences**, as seen in Figure 5.35.

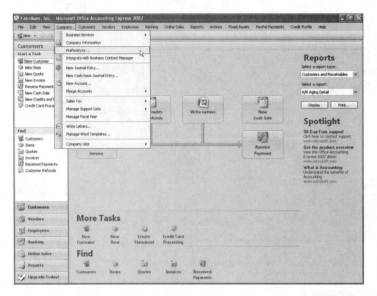

FIGURE 5.35   The Company Preferences window contains important configuration preferences.

It's important to set up company preferences properly for your specific company. Start with the **Company** tab, shown in Figure 5.36. Verify that the information on the Company tab is correct for your company:

- **Use Account Numbers**—This is checkmarked by default. An account number uniquely identifies the account. Use account numbers to prevent duplicate account names.

- **Use Customer ID**—A customer ID uniquely identifies the customer. Use customer IDs to prevent duplicate customer names.

- **Use Vendor ID**—A vendor ID uniquely identifies the vendor. Use vendor IDs to prevent duplicate vendors.

- **Use Employee ID**—An employee ID uniquely identifies the employee. Use employee IDs to prevent duplicate employee names.

- **Allow Duplicate Document Numbers**—This is checkmarked by default. Uncheck this to prevent entering duplicate documents.

FIGURE 5.36   The Company tab in Company Preferences contains company settings.

- **Prevent Posting Before**—You may not post transactions before this date. Choose a date before your oldest open items, yet recent enough to prevent entering erroneous data from previous years. Either type the date or click the drop-down calendar arrow to choose a date using the calendar.

- **First Day of the Week on Timesheet**—Sunday shows by default. Click the drop-down list arrow to choose a day.

- **Who Will Run Payroll When Using Accountant Transfer?**—The **I Would Like to Be Able to Run Payroll** option is selected by default. The other option is **My Accountant Will Run Payroll**.

⇨   See "Accountant Review," page 306.

- **Do You Pay Sales Tax?**—Checkmark this box, seen in Figure 5.37, if you pay sales tax.

- **Tax Groups** button—If **Do You Pay Sales Tax?** is checkmarked, this question is visible. You should already have set up sales taxes.

⇨   See "Sales Tax Setup," page 64.

FIGURE 5.37 Checkmarking Do You Pay Sales Tax? makes the remainder of the sales tax questions visible.

- **On What Basis Do You Pay Sales Tax?**—If **Do You Pay Sales Tax?** is checkmarked, this question is visible. Ask your accountant, and then choose **Accrual Basis** (when the customer is invoiced) or **Cash Basis** (when the customer pays the invoice).

If the company does not intend to sell online, uncheck the **Enable Online Sales** check box, shown in Figure 5.38.

⇨ See "Sell Online," page 328.

Click the **System Accounts** tab, shown in Figure 5.39. The accounts shown are probably the correct accounts to use for your business. Check with your accountant if you are not sure.

To change the account to a different account, click the **System Account** drop-down list arrow, and then choose a different account.

The Job Resell Account is intentionally left blank in Express. Job costing capabilities are available only by upgrading to Professional.

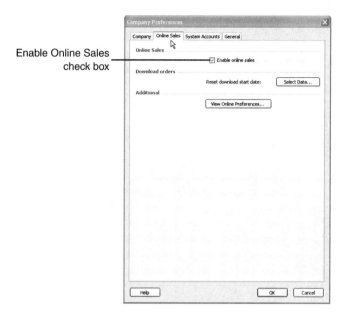

Enable Online Sales
check box

FIGURE 5.38 The information in the Online Sales tab is fine for now.

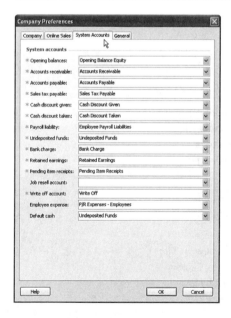

FIGURE 5.39 Verify with your accountant that the standard system accounts are correct for your company.

The **General** tab, seen in Figure 5.40, contains general settings for Express itself:

- **Provide Feedback with Sound to Screen Elements**—Express will make a sound as feedback for certain events.

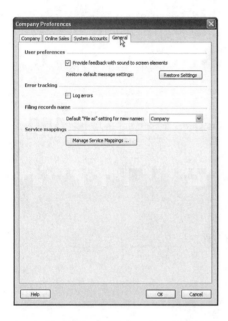

FIGURE 5.40   Click the General tab to check the settings.

- **Restore Default Message Settings**—You can turn off warning messages in Express by clicking **In the Future, Do Not Show This Message** when a message appears. Clicking the **Restore Default Message Settings** button turns the warning messages back on.

- **Log Errors check box**—Checkmark this option to save an informational error log at My Documents\Small Business Accounting 2007\Logs.

- **Default "File As" Setting for New Names**—Express files new customers, vendors, and employees by the company name. Click the drop-down list arrow to select either Last, First to sort by last name, or First, Last to sort by first name and then last name.

- **Manage Service Mappings button**—Double-click a service to edit it. The services are initially set up in Online Sales.

⟹ See "PayPal," page 321, and "Sell Online," page 328.

Click the **OK** button to save the Company Preferences settings.

Manage Support Lists

Add information to each support list now or when entering transactions. The information in the support lists is used for the drop-down lists in forms. New items may be added to a drop-down list anytime you are entering data on a form. To view and change a support list, click the **Company** menu, **Manage Support Lists**, as seen in Figure 5.41, and then click the appropriate list.

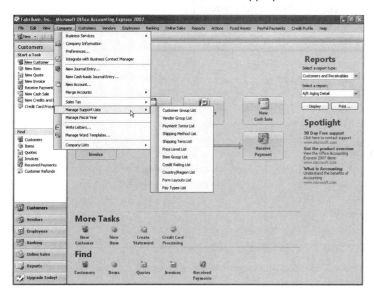

FIGURE 5.41   View the support lists.

Customer Group List

In the Manage Customer Group window, click the **Add** button shown in Figure 5.42 to add a new customer group. The Customer Group window opens. Type in a group name, and click the **OK** button. Customer groups may also be edited and deleted.

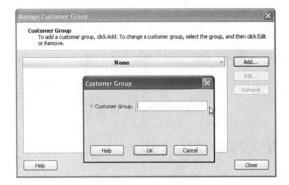

FIGURE 5.42 Customer groups enable you to group your customers together for reports. Compare groups of customers and see trends.

Vendor Group List

In the Manage Vendor Group window, click the **Add** button shown in Figure 5.43 to add a new vendor group. The Vendor Group window opens. Type in a group name, and click the **OK** button. Vendor groups may also be edited and deleted.

FIGURE 5.43 Vendor groups enable you to group your vendors together for reports. Compare groups of vendors and see trends.

Payment Terms List

Payment terms describe when the bill or invoice is due in full, and optionally, the discount percentage and date.

In the Manage Payment Term window, shown in Figure 5.44, click the **Add** button to add a new payment term.

Or, click a payment term to highlight it, and then click the **Edit** button to edit the term.

Or, click a payment term to highlight it, and then click the **Remove** button to delete the term.

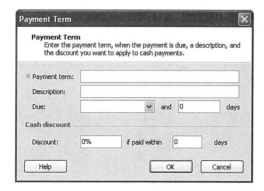

FIGURE 5.44 Based on company procedures, credit history, and volume of sales, the payment terms may vary for customers and vendors.

Enter Payment Term information, as seen in Figure 5.45:

- **Payment Term**—Enter the payment term as it will appear on invoices. For example, "2%/10, Net 30" means a discount of 2% of the invoice is given if paid within 10 days of the invoice date; otherwise, the invoice is due within 30 days of the invoice date.

FIGURE 5.45 Express is very flexible and can create practically any payment term.

- **Description**—Enter a description of the terms.
- **Due**—Leave this field blank or click the drop-down list arrow and choose from Current Month, Current Quarter, Current Half-Year, and Current Year.

- **Due Days**—Enter the number of days, after the invoice date, within which the invoice is due. For example, entering **20** would mean Net 20, indicating that the invoice is due within 20 days of the invoice date.

  If you leave the Due Days field blank and put Current Quarter in the previous field (Due), this would mean that the bill is due 0 days after the current quarter. In other words, the bill is due at the end of the current quarter.

- **Discount**—Enter the discount percentage taken off the invoice if paid early. If you enter a number, Express will automatically add a percentage sign after it. For example, a 2 becomes 2%.

- **If Paid Within XX Days**—Enter the number of days after the invoice date in which the invoice must be paid in order to obtain the discount.

- Click the **OK** button to save the payment term.

Shipping Method List

In the Manage Shipping Method window, shown in Figure 5.46, click the **Add** button to add a new shipping method. The Shipping Method window opens. Type in a shipping method and description, and then click the **OK** button. Shipping methods may also be edited and deleted.

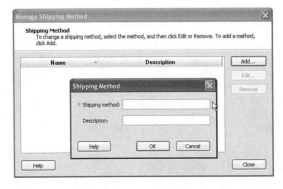

FIGURE 5.46   The shipping method describes how items ship. For example: UPS Ground, FedEx Overnight, U.S. Postal Service, Pick Up, Our Truck, and Hand Deliver are common methods.

Shipping Terms List

In the Manage Shipping Term window, seen in Figure 5.47, click the **Add** button to add a new shipping term. The Shipping Term window opens. Type in a shipping method and description, and then click the **OK** button. Shipping terms may also be edited and deleted.

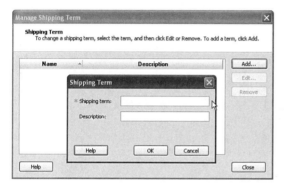

FIGURE 5.47   The shipping terms describe who pays for the shipment and who owns it while it is being shipped. For example, common terms are FOB Shipping Prepaid and FOB Destination Collect.

Price Level List

In the Manage Price Level window, shown in Figure 5.48, click the **Add** button to add a new price level. The Price Level window opens. Type in a price level name and the percentage to change the price, and click either the **Decrease Price Level by This Percentage** or the **Increase Price Level by This Percentage** button, and then click the **OK** button. Price levels may also be edited and deleted.

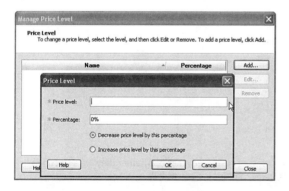

FIGURE 5.48   Price levels are the percentage increases or decreases in the price a customer pays. For example, Large Account Discount or Poor Payment Surcharge.

Item Group List

In the Manage Item Group window, seen in Figure 5.49, click the **Add** button to add a new item group. The Item Group Name window opens. Type in an item group, and then click the **OK** button. Item groups may also be edited and deleted.

FIGURE 5.49   Item groups enable you to group your items together for reports. Compare groups of items and see trends.

Credit Rating List

In the Manage Credit Rating window, shown in Figure 5.50, click the **Add** button to add a new credit rating. The Credit Rating window opens. Type in a credit rating, and then click the **OK** button. Credit ratings may also be edited and deleted.

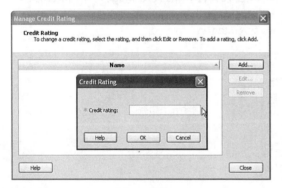

FIGURE 5.50   Credit ratings describe the creditworthiness of customers; that is, whether they are a good risk. For example, AAA is a top-quality company and D is a company that doesn't pay its bills.

Country/Region List

The Country/Region list contains the country or region abbreviation.

In the Manage Country/Region List window, shown in Figure 5.51, click the **Add** button to add a new country/region. The Country/Region window opens. Follow these steps to add country/region information:

1. Enter the full country/region name.

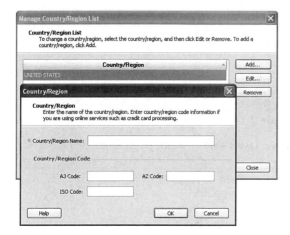

FIGURE 5.51 The Country/Region list is useful for worldwide online credit card sales.

2. Enter the A3 code, a three-character code for the country/region. For example, the A3 code for the United States is USA.

3. Enter the A2 code, a two-character code for the country/region. For example, the A2 code for the United States is US.

4. Enter the ISO code, a number used instead of characters for those countries/regions that do not use Latin-based letters, such as Japan. For example, the ISO code for the United States is 840.

Countries/regions may also be edited and deleted.

Forms Layout List

Forms Layout enables you to change the way the form looks when entering data on the screen. You can create and name multiple forms. You can create a different form for each printed form used in the business or each person entering data.

In the Remove Form Layout window, click the **Remove** button shown in Figure 5.52 to remove an unused customer layout form previously created in Invoices, Quotes, Bills, and so on. Deleting a custom form that was previously used to record a transaction is not recommended.

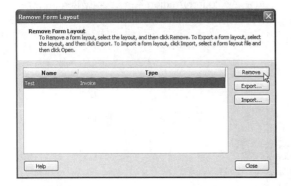

FIGURE 5.52   The Remove button on the Remove Form Layout window enables you to remove a custom form that is not used.

The Import and Export buttons are for advanced programming. Clicking the **Export** button saves the custom form as an XML document in My Documents/Small Business Accounting/Form Layouts or in another directory that you specify.

The Remove Form Layout window contains custom forms depending on where in Express you open the window. Opening the Remove Form Layout window from the Company menu shows all custom forms. Opening the Remove Form Layout window from a specific Express form will show only that form's customized versions. For example, opening the Remove Form Layout window from the Invoice form will show only customized Invoice forms.

Pay Types List

The Pay Types list contains a name and description for each type of payroll category; for example, Regular, Sick, Overtime, and Vacation. A payment type may be active or disabled if no longer used.

Express does not allow manual payroll (only Professional has this feature). As seen in Figure 5.53, click the **Disable Manual Payroll Pay Types** button if the company uses an outside payroll service. All the manual pay types are then disabled.

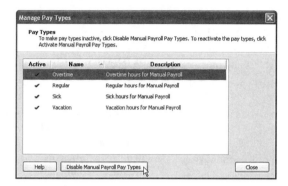

FIGURE 5.53   Manage or disable pay types.

Company Lists

To view the company Chart of Accounts, Journal Entries, Items, Customers, Vendors, Employees, or Payments, click the **Company** menu, **Company Lists**, as shown in Figure 5.54, and then click the appropriate list. Each list can be filtered to show All, Inactive, or Active list items.

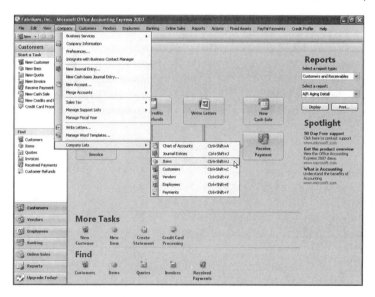

FIGURE 5.54   View the company lists.

Add information to each company list now, or add new customers, vendors, credit cards, and banks when you are entering transactions. The information in the company lists is used for the drop-down lists in forms. New information may be added to a drop-down list any time you enter data on a form.

Employees

Employees contains basic information about each employee for payroll, tax, and time-keeping purposes. You can add fields for additional information specific to your company.

As shown in Figure 5.55, click the **Employees** menu, **New Employee**. The Employee form opens.

Enter the employee information on the **General** tab, seen in Figure 5.56.

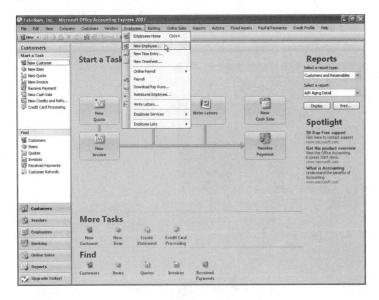

FIGURE 5.55   Add a new employee.

TIP

FULLY FILL OUT CUSTOMERS, VENDORS, AND BANKS!

The information from these lists is used throughout the program in many ways. If the information is not entered, when you enter data, you are continually returning to the customers, vendors, and banks to update information. Or, if you don't return to the customer, vendor, or bank and instead enter the information only on the specific form, you will have to enter the information again on the next form. In other words, it is best to complete the information on the customer, vendor, and bank forms completely and accurately the first time. This will save time and make your experience with Express more enjoyable.

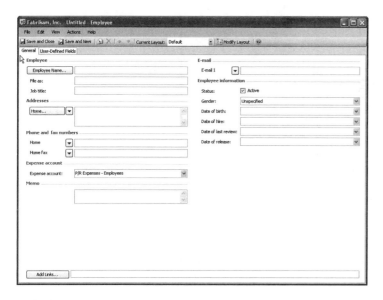

FIGURE 5.56   Enter employee information.

Click the **Employee Name** button to enter the details in the correct fields for reporting purposes:

1. Enter the employee's name by clicking the **Employee Name** button shown in Figure 5.57 and filling in the requested fields.

2. File As, seen in Figure 5.56, shows how the employee's name sorts in lists. It automatically sorts the way you entered it in the Check Full Name window, unless you change it by typing over the File As name.

3. Enter the employee's job title.

4. Click the **Addresses** drop-down arrow, as shown in Figure 5.58, to choose the correct address type. As seen in Figure 5.59, click the **Address** button and enter the information to format the address properly.

5. If this employee has multiple addresses, click the **Address** drop-down list arrow shown in Figure 5.58 and choose another address type:

   - Home
   - Business
   - Other

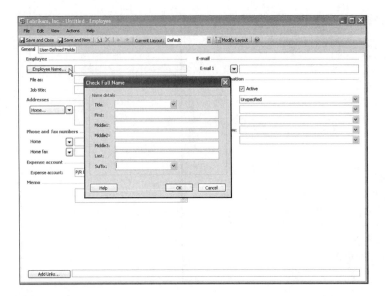

FIGURE 5.57   Enter the employee's name.

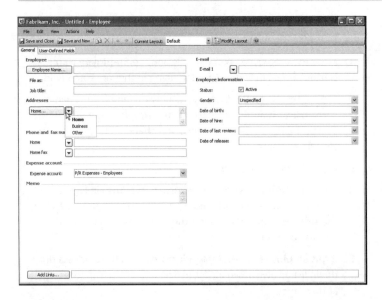

FIGURE 5.58   Click the Address drop-down list arrow to choose another type of address.

A checkmark next to an address type indicates that it is used and may be changed. The bold address is the current address being edited.

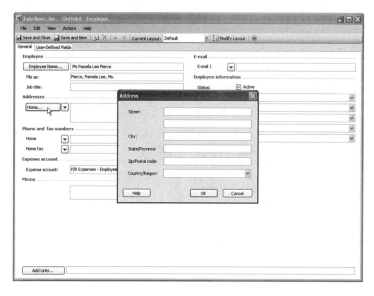

FIGURE 5.59 The Address button indicates the type of address selected. Click the button to format the address correctly.

6. Enter the phone number(s). The fastest way to enter a number is to use the number pad on the right side of the keyboard and to enter only the 10 digits. Express automatically makes the number readable. For example, typing **8884054039** results in (888) 405-4039.

7. Click the **Phone** drop-down list arrow to enter additional phone numbers. The choices are

   - Home

   - Business

   - Mobile

   - Assistant

   - Other

   If the choices are not appropriate, you might want to enter additional phone information in the Memo area.

8. Enter the fax phone number(s).

9. Click the **Business Fax** drop-down list arrow to enter additional phone numbers. The choices are

   - Home fax

   - Business fax

   - Other fax

If the choices are not appropriate, you might want to enter additional fax information in the Memo area.

10. Enter the expense account. The field defaults to the Company Preferences System Account for P/R Employee Expense (refer to the Company Preferences window), but may be changed.

11. Optionally, enter a memo comment.

12. Enter an email address, if one is available.

13. Click the email drop-down list arrow to enter additional email addresses.

14. Active Status is automatically checkmarked. Uncheck it if the employee is no longer with the company and no longer listed on company sales.

15. Enter the employee's gender as Unspecified, Male, or Female.

16. Enter the employee's date of birth, or click the drop-down calendar arrow and choose the date from the calendar.

17. Enter the employee's date of hire, or click the drop-down calendar arrow and choose the date from the calendar.

18. Enter the employee's date of last review, or click the drop-down calendar arrow and choose the date from the calendar.

19. If the employee is no longer with the company, enter the employee's date of release, or click the drop-down calendar arrow and choose the date from the calendar.

20. Click the **Save and Close** button to save the information and then close the window.

    Or, click the **Save and New** button to add another employee.

21. To edit an employee, click the **Previous Item** button or **Next Item** button to find the employee to edit.

Click the **User-Defined Fields** tab, seen in Figure 5.60, and then the **New Fields** button to include your own information—up to 21 alphanumeric text fields, 1 multiline text field, 6 date fields, 8 number fields, and 4 check box fields.

Customize forms to your needs. Click the **Modify Layout** button, shown in Figure 5.61, to change the fields and the layout of the form.

User-Defined Fields tab

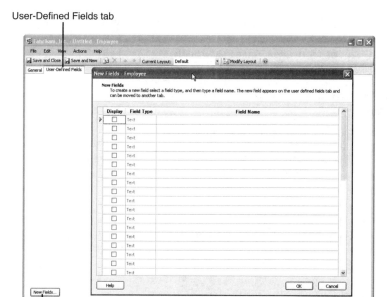

New Fields button

FIGURE 5.60   Click the New Fields button to add customized information to a form.

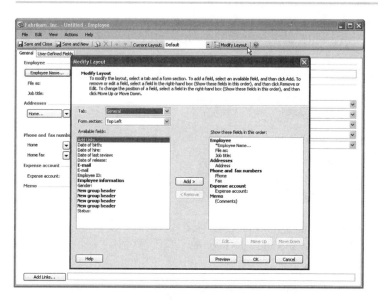

FIGURE 5.61   Click the Modify Layout button to customize forms.

Customers

Customers contains multiple screens of information. You can add fields for additional information specific to your company.

Click the **Customers** menu, **New**, **New Customer** as seen in Figure 5.62. The Customer form opens.

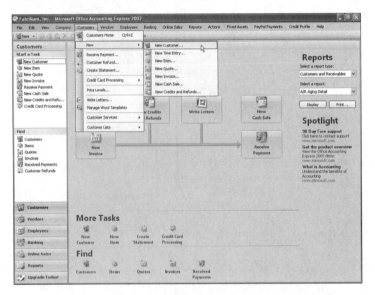

FIGURE 5.62 Open the customer form.

Start by entering customer information on the **General** tab, as shown in Figure 5.63. Enter the following information:

1. Enter the customer name as it will appear on invoices.

2. File As shows the sort order for filing. File As is automatically filled with the information entered in the Customer Name field. Change the order if desired. For example, The Company could be filed as Company, The.

3. Enter the business address. To format the address properly, click the **Business** button seen in Figure 5.64 and enter the information.

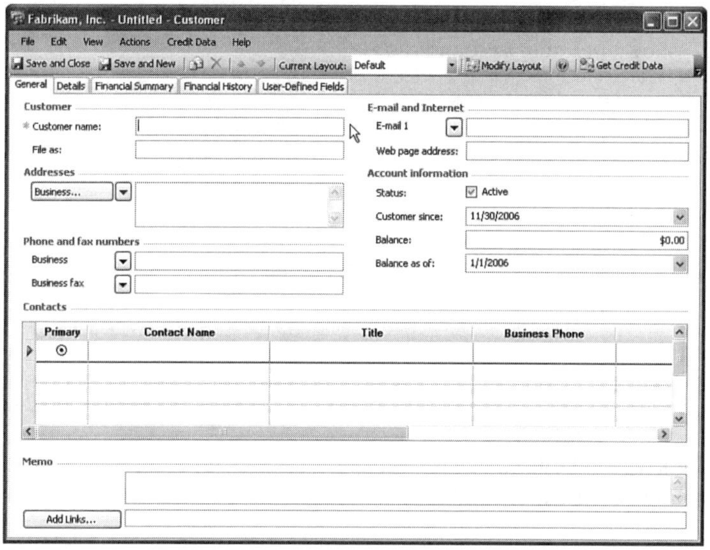

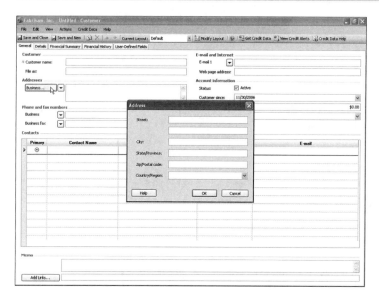

FIGURE 5.63   Enter customer information.

FIGURE 5.64   The Address button indicates the type of address. Click the button to format the address correctly.

4. If this customer has multiple addresses, click the **Business** address drop-down list arrow, shown in Figure 5.65, and choose another address type:

- Business
- Bill To
- Ship To
- Warehouse
- Home
- Legal
- Postal
- Other

A checkmark next to an address type indicates that it is used and may be changed. The bold address is the current address being edited.

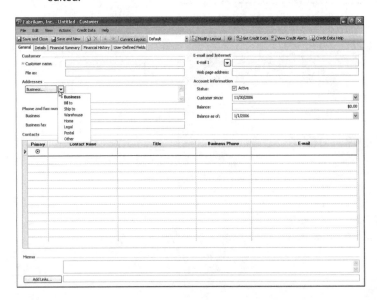

FIGURE 5.65   Click the Address drop-down list arrow to choose another type of address.

5. Enter the business phone. The fastest way to enter a number is to use the number pad on the right side of the keyboard and to enter only the 10 digits. Express automatically makes the number readable. For example, typing **8884054039** will result in (888) 405-4039.

6. Click the **Business Phone** drop-down list arrow to enter additional phone numbers. The choices are

    - Business
    - Mobile
    - Home
    - Assistant
    - Other

    If the choices are not appropriate, you might want to enter additional phone information in the Contacts or Memo area.

7. Enter the business fax phone number.

8. Click the **Business Fax** drop-down list arrow to enter additional phone numbers. The choices are

    - Business fax
    - Home fax
    - Other fax

    If the choices are not appropriate, you might want to enter additional fax information in the Contacts or Memo area.

9. Enter an email address, if one is available.

10. Click the **E-mail** drop-down arrow to enter additional email addresses.

11. Enter the company web page address.

12. Active Status is automatically checkmarked. Uncheck it if the customer no longer makes purchases.

13. The Customer Since field shows today's date. To change the Customer Since date, click the drop-down calendar arrow to open the calendar, and then choose a different date.

14. The Opening Balance shows only when you are creating a new customer. **Do not enter an opening balance**—instead, use transactions. Press the **Enter** key or **Tab** key to skip this field.

    ⇨ See "Opening Balance Overview," page 119.

15. Balance As Of shows only when you are creating a new customer. It is the date associated with the Opening Balance and defaults to the value of the Company Preferences Start Date field. Press the **Enter** or **Tab** key to skip this field.

CAUTION

STOP! DO NOT ENTER OPENING CUSTOMER BALANCES

A customer may not be deleted after an opening balance is entered, and the opening balance may not be changed. The opening balance is entered using transactions.

16. For each contact, enter a contact name, title, business phone, and email. Each item may contain any information you want.

17. If more than one contact is entered, click the **Primary** button for one contact.

18. Enter a **Memo**, if desired.

19. Add Links is used to attach one or more files. For example, scan in the customer's contract form or its tax-exempt certificate, save the file(s), and click the **Add Links** button. Then locate the file(s) on the computer and click the **OK** button. The filename shows in Add Links.

The following information, seen in Figure 5.66, is used for customer quotes and invoices. Enter the information accurately so that it automatically appears after you enter the customer name on the quote or invoice. Otherwise, if the customer information is not set up ahead of time, you must manually add or change the information on each quote or invoice.

1. Enter the salesperson or click the drop-down list arrow to see a list of employees. The salesperson must be an employee or be left blank.

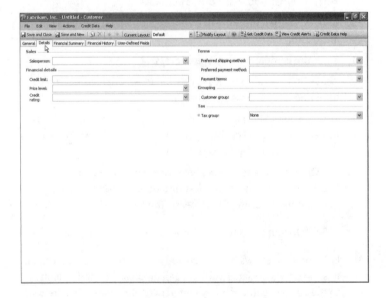

FIGURE 5.66 Enter the customer information on the Details tab.

2. Enter a value in the Credit Limit field for the customer, or leave it blank.

3. If the customer purchases at a non-standard rate, select the price level by clicking on the drop-down list arrow, or leave it blank.

4. Optionally, enter a credit rating by clicking on the drop-down list arrow.

5. Optionally, enter a preferred shipping method by clicking on the drop-down list arrow.

6. Optionally, enter a preferred payment method of cash, check, or credit card, or click the drop-down list arrow to make a selection.

7. Optionally, enter payment terms by clicking on the drop-down list arrow to make a selection.

8. Optionally, enter a customer group if this customer is part of a group for sorting and reporting purposes.

9. The Tax Group field is required. It indicates the taxable or non-taxable group for this customer. For example, a non-taxable group might be Out of State.

10. Click the **Save and Close** button to save the information and then close the window.

    Or, click the **Save and New** button to add another customer.

11. To edit a customer, click the **Previous Item** button or **Next Item** button to find the correct customer to edit.

Click the **User-Defined Fields** tab, shown in Figure 5.67, and then the **New Fields** button to include your own information—up to 21 alphanumeric text fields, 1 multiline text field, 6 date fields, 8 number fields, and 4 check box fields.

Customize forms to your needs. As seen in Figure 5.68, click the **Modify Layout** button to change the fields and the layout of the form.

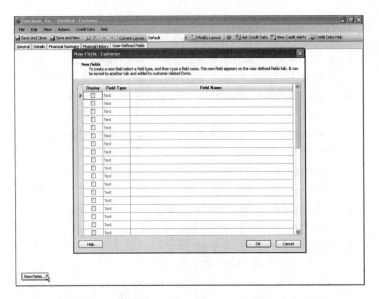

FIGURE 5.67 Click the New Fields button to add customized information to a form.

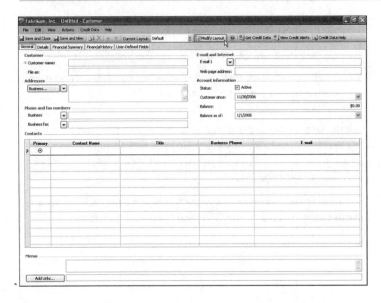

FIGURE 5.68 Click the Modify Layout button to customize forms.

Vendors

Enter information about the companies providing products and services. Create new vendor fields to customize the information to your needs.

Click the **Vendors** menu, **New**, **New Vendor**, as shown in Figure 5.69. The Vendor form opens.

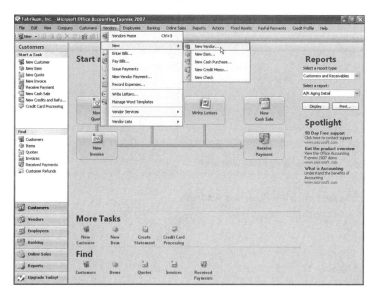

FIGURE 5.69 Add a new vendor.

Enter the following information, as seen in Figure 5.70:

1. The vendor name as it will appear on bills. (Express uses the term *bills* to describe vendor invoices. This prevents confusion between customer invoices and vendor bills.)

2. The File As field shows the sort order for filing. This field is automatically filled with the information entered in the Vendor Name field. Change the order if desired. For example, The Company could be filed as Company, The.

3. Enter the business address. To format the address properly, click the **Business** button and enter the information.

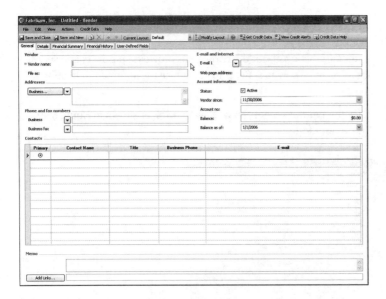

FIGURE 5.70   Start by entering vendor information on the General tab.

4. If this vendor has multiple addresses, click the **Business Address** drop-down list arrow and choose another address type:

   - Business
   - Bill To
   - Ship To
   - Warehouse
   - Home
   - Legal
   - Postal
   - Other

   A checkmark next to an address type indicates that it is used and may be changed. The bold address is the current address being edited.

5. Enter the business phone. The fastest way to enter a number is to use the number pad on the right side of the keyboard and to enter only the 10 digits. Express automatically makes the number readable. For example, typing **8884054039** will result in (888) 405-4039.

6. Click the **Business Phone** drop-down list arrow to enter additional phone numbers. The choices are

   - Business

   - Mobile

   - Home

   - Assistant

   - Other

   If the choices are not appropriate, you might want to enter additional phone information in the Contacts or Memo area.

7. Enter the business fax phone number.

8. Click the **Business Fax** drop-down list arrow to enter additional phone numbers. The choices are

   - Business fax

   - Home fax

   - Other fax

   If the choices are not appropriate, you might want to enter additional fax information in the Contacts or Memo area.

9. Enter an email address, if one is available.

10. Click the **E-mail** drop-down arrow to enter additional email addresses.

11. Enter the company's web page address.

12. Active Status is automatically checkmarked. Uncheck it if your company no longer purchases from this vendor.

13. The Vendor Since field shows today's date. To change the Vendor Since date, click the drop-down list arrow to open the calendar, and choose a different date.

14. The Opening Balance field shows only when creating a new vendor. **Do not enter an opening balance**—instead, use transactions.

   ➪ See "Opening Balance Overview," page 119.

   Press the **Enter** or **Tab** key to skip this field.

15. The Balance As Of field shows only when you are creating a new vendor. It is the date associated with the opening balance and defaults to the value of the Company Preferences Start Date field. Press the **Enter** or **Tab** key to skip this field.

CAUTION

STOP! DO NOT ENTER OPENING VENDOR BALANCES

A vendor may not be deleted after an opening balance is entered, and the opening balance may not be changed. The opening balance is entered using transactions.

16. For each contact enter a contact name, title, business phone, and email. Each item may contain any information you want.

17. If more than one contact is entered, click the **Primary** button for one contact.

18. Enter a memo, if desired.

19. Add Links is used to attach one or more files. For example, scan in the vendor contract form(s), save the file(s), and click the **Add Links** button. Then locate the file(s) on the computer and click the **OK** button. The filename shows in Add Links.

The following information, shown in Figure 5.71, is used for vendor bills. Enter the information accurately so that it automatically appears after you enter the vendor name on the bill. If the vendor information is not set up ahead of time, you must manually add or change the information on each bill.

1. Optionally, fill in the Expense Account field or click the drop-down list arrow to see a list of accounts.

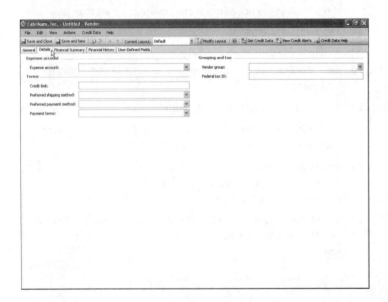

FIGURE 5.71 Enter the vendor information on the Details tab.

2. Enter a credit limit for the vendor, or leave it blank.

3. Optionally, enter a preferred shipping method by clicking on the drop-down list arrow.

4. Optionally, enter a preferred payment method of cash, check, or credit card, or click the drop-down list arrow to make a selection.

5. Optionally, enter payment terms by clicking on the drop-down list arrow to make a selection.

6. Optionally, enter a vendor group if this customer is part of a group for sorting and reporting purposes.

7. Optionally, enter the vendor's Federal Tax ID so that it is available to you when completing federal Form 1099 at the end of the year.

Click the **User-Defined Fields** tab, shown in Figure 5.72, and then the **New Fields** button to include your own information—up to 21 alphanumeric text fields, 1 multiline text field, 6 date fields, 8 number fields, and 4 check box fields.

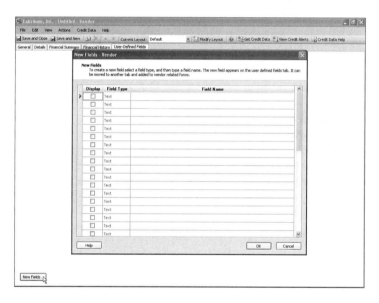

FIGURE 5.72   Click the New Fields button to add customized information to a form.

Customize forms to your needs. As seen in Figure 5.73, click the **Modify Layout** button to change the fields and the layout of the form.

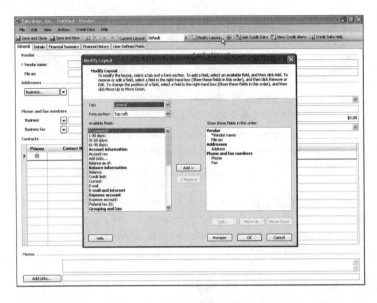

FIGURE 5.73   Click the Modify Layout button to customize forms.

Items

Items are products (non-inventory items), services, and additional quote and invoice line items; for example, a surcharge. Items in Express do not track inventory quantities or reorder points. Add items as line items on quotes and invoices from drop-down lists to eliminate additional typing and the potential for errors in data entry.

To open the items list, click the **Company** menu, **Company Lists**, **Items**, as shown in Figure 5.74.

You can locate the Items list under

- **Company** menu, and then **Company Lists**
- **Customer** menu, and then **Customer Lists**
- **Vendor** menu, and then **Vendor Lists**

All these locations contain the same items list.

To add an item, click **Add a New Item**, and then select a service or non-inventory item, as seen in Figure 5.75.

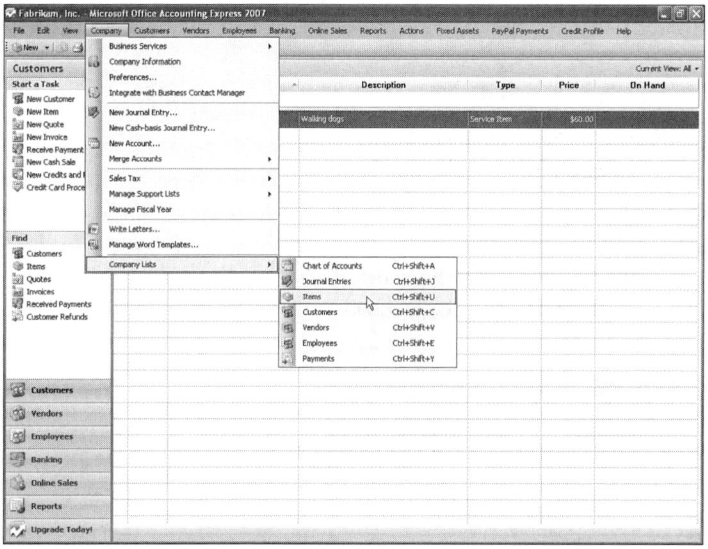

FIGURE 5.74 Open the items list.

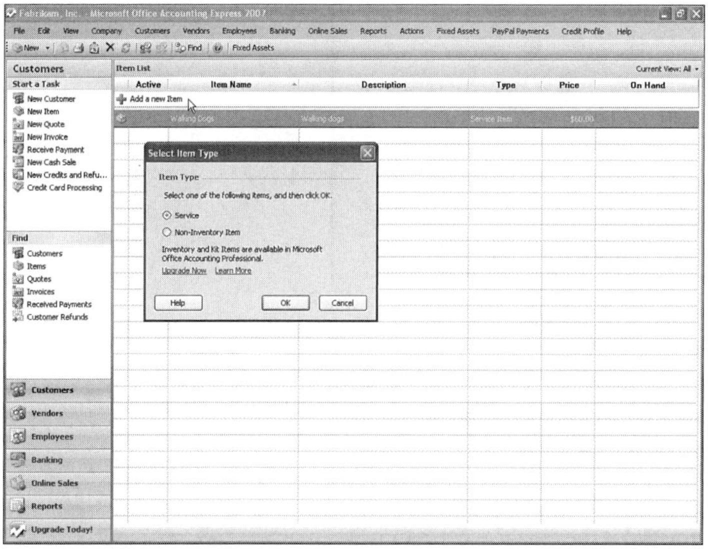

FIGURE 5.75 Add an item and select its type.

Enter the following information, shown in Figure 5.76 (the only required field is Item Name):

1. Enter the **Item Name**.

   Inside a form, typing the beginning of an item name will bring up the rest of that item's name. Therefore, enter a name that is easy to remember.

   Express does not use item numbers. You must upgrade to Professional, which has an item number field. Do not enter the item number in the Item Name field if you intend to eventually move to Professional. Instead, add a custom field.

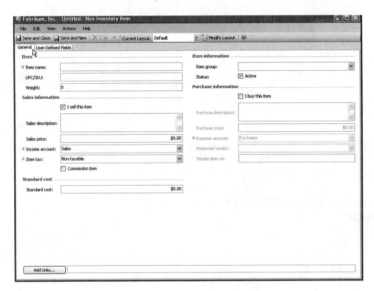

FIGURE 5.76 The only difference between the Service Item form and Non-Inventory Item form is that the Service Item does not contain Weight.

2. Enter the **UPC/SKU** (Universal Product Code/Stock-Keeping Unit) found on all products sold in the United States.

3. Enter the weight of the item only for products, not services.

4. Checkmarking **I Sell This Item** allows the next five fields to appear. Unchecking I Sell This Item means the item is not available for resale. This check box must be checkmarked if the item is sold online, or the listing process will fail.

5. Enter the sales description.

6. Enter the sales price in U.S. dollars.

7. The Item Account shows Sales, but click the drop-down list arrow to change the account. If you sell this item, an item account is required.

8. Click the drop-down list arrow to select an item tax, which is a required field if I Sell This Item is checkmarked.

9. Checkmark **Commission Item** if commission is paid for this item.

10. Enter the cost of the item in the **Standard Cost** field.

11. Click **Item Group** to choose an optional group to which this item belongs.

12. **Active Status** is checkmarked by default. Uncheck it if the item is inactive.

13. Checkmarking **I Buy This Item** allows the next five fields to appear. Unchecking I Buy This Item means the item is not purchased, but instead is manufactured.

14. Enter the purchase description.

15. Enter the purchase price.

16. The **Expense Account** is required if I Buy This Item is checkmarked. Click the drop-down list arrow to charge the purchase against an account.

17. Enter the name of the preferred vendor by clicking the drop-down list arrow and selecting a vendor.

18. Enter the vendor item number used by the preferred vendor for this item.

19. Click the **Save and Close** button to save the information and then close the window.

    Or, click the **Save and New** button to add or edit another customer.

20. To edit a customer, click the **Previous Item** button or **Next Item** button to find the correct customer to edit.

Click the **User-Defined Fields** tab, shown in Figure 5.77, and then the **New Fields** button to include your own information—up to 21 alphanumeric text fields, 1 multiline text field, 6 date fields, 8 number fields, and 4 check box fields.

Customize forms to your needs. As seen in Figure 5.78, click the **Modify Layout** button to change the fields and the layout of the form.

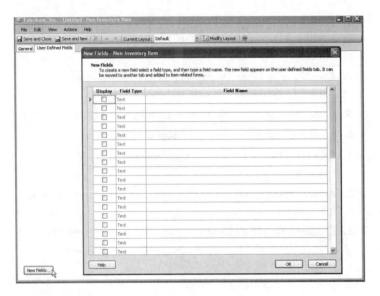

FIGURE 5.77   Click the New Fields button to add customized information to a form.

Modify Layout button

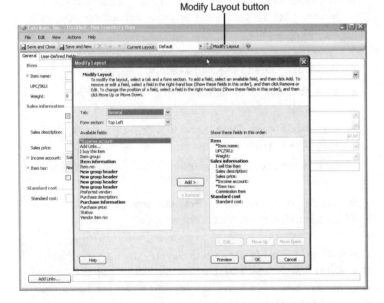

FIGURE 5.78   Click the Modify Layout button to customize forms.

Basic Accounting Transactions

Express opening balances for each account must match the opening balances in your Balance Sheet and Income Statement, then you are ready for your daily work. This chapter explains opening balance transactions for both new and existing businesses.

You will learn about each type of customer, vendor, employee, and banking transaction, plus general journal transactions. All the different types of daily transactions that you might have are explained in detail.

Opening Balance Overview

The basic setup of Office Accounting Express is complete except for one area: the opening balances. If you followed the directions, you have not yet entered opening balances and transactions in Express. This section explains the steps of creating opening balance transactions.

After you enter an opening balance or transaction, it cannot be deleted. To correct an incorrect entry, you must enter an opposite transaction, called a *reversing entry*, that cancels out the initial entry. Typically, you would enter a reversing entry yourself when you make a mistake. However, Express might do it for you when you change certain transactions.

Entering a transaction or a reversing transaction creates an *audit trail*, which shows all transactions and corrections. You and auditors use the audit trail to find problems in the accounting data and errors in entering the data. Starting properly, without reversing entries correcting mistakes, provides a clean, easy-to-understand audit trail.

There are multiple reasons why you might wait to enter beginning balances:

- The accounting system must be set up properly before use.

- All opening transactions, taken as a whole, must summarize to the numbers on the opening financial statement. The advantage of a journal entry is that Express will not let you complete a journal entry if it is not balanced. This means that both the debits and the credits must total the same amount. If you type a number incorrectly from your financial statement, Express won't save the journal entry until you find your mistake. If, instead, you enter an opening balance when setting up each new account, mistakes that require correction using reversing entries can occur.

The opening financial statement is dated the day immediately before your *start date*, the date you start using Express for normal transactions. Typically, a company has a start date of January 1, or the first date of its fiscal year. The beginning financial statement would be for December 31 of the previous year, or the last day of the previous fiscal year. This doesn't mean you can't start on a different date—ask your accountant for help.

It's important to back up at this point. If you create a backup and then make mistakes in your accounting system, you can always restore the backup and start over. Back up now!

⇨ See "Backup," page 371.

If the company is new, one large transaction is entered using the start date, showing how the company was capitalized—the money and assets brought into the new company, along with any startup loans and equity. This one large transaction, a journal entry, contains every non-zero account balance from the opening balance sheet of the financial statement.

⇨ See "New Journal Entry" on page 239 to learn how to create a journal entry.

If the company is not new, enter the detail of each account on the opening balance sheet. The detail of each account means, for example, that if the accounts payable balance is $1,234.56, the open amount of each individual vendor bill is entered using the Vendor's New Bills data entry form until the balance of all open vendor accounts totals exactly $1,234.56. Typically, enter each as an individual transaction on the date it actually occurred. When you are done entering the transactions for all accounts, the totals should match the balance sheet accounts on the financial statement.

Express permits transactions only in open years. Click the **Company** menu, **Manage Fiscal Year**, then the **New Fiscal Year** button to open a new fiscal year. The Create Fiscal Year window opens, as shown in Figure 6.1. Enter the beginning and ending dates of a fiscal year. Multiple years may be open. Repeat for each year containing open transactions.

FIGURE 6.1   The year must be open in Express before you can enter a transaction in that year.

Enter each opening transaction on the date it occurred, with all the usual detail that you would normally enter for that type of transaction. Then, later in the year, payments and receipts easily post against individual open bills and invoices, and statements easily reconcile against the detail in Express.

Enter the following transactions:

- Open accounts payable bills.

  ⇨   See "Enter Bills" on page 174.

- Open accounts receivable invoices.

  ⇨   See "New Invoice" on page 133.

- Unreconciled deposits, checks, and other amounts in each bank account, savings account, and other financial account.

  ⇨ See "Banking" on page 219.

- The ending balance of each credit card liability and any outstanding charges and credits.

  ⇨ See "Credit Card Charge" on page 229.

- Each asset and liability balance owed. For example, enter each car and each outstanding loan as a separate transaction using the correct form or a journal entry.

  ⇨ See "New Journal Entry" on page 239.

After entering all the opening balance detail, print a balance sheet summarizing the transactions, proving that all the transactions total to the opening balance sheet. Enter any accounts that do not have detail in one large entry. Find and correct errors. Print another balance sheet and compare it against the opening balance sheet. The opening balance sheet must match the printed balance sheet.

When the opening and printed balance sheets match, the previous period could be closed so that nothing more is entered by mistake with an incorrect date. However, I recommend keeping the period open until all invoices and bills for that period are no longer open.

Now you are ready to start posting transactions from your start date forward! Make a backup before starting. If necessary, you can later restore the backup as a different company to

- Prove that you started with good beginning balances
- Find problems if you mistakenly post future entries to dates before the start date

Opening a Company

After you set up a company, it must be opened for you to use it. You can choose to open one of the sample companies that come with Express or any company that you have already set up. Other than your hard disk space, there is no limit to the number of companies you can set up. However, only one company can be open at once.

Open a company by clicking the **File** menu, **Open Company**, and then choose the correct company.

Deleting or Changing Transactions

It's good accounting practice to not delete accounts or transactions because an unscrupulous person could cover fraud in this manner. For this reason, transactions cannot be deleted from Express after they are entered. Instead of deleting a transaction, Express either creates a reversing transaction for you, or you do it yourself.

You can change most transactions. Locate the transaction, open it, and then click the **Edit** button. After it's changed, save the transaction. If you attempt to close a transaction without saving your changes, Express will ask if you want to save your changes.

Daily Transactions

Daily transactions include entries for customers, vendors, employees, and banking. Any transaction that cannot be entered through forms on these screens is entered as a journal entry.

There are many ways to record any transaction. Various Express data entry forms can be used to record a transaction, depending on your preference.

You choose which form you prefer to use for data entry, and even the method you prefer to reach the form. Some Express users prefer to use menus. Users moving from other accounting products typically prefer the visual approach of clicking a button from a screen showing the workflow. Other users prefer to view similar transactions in a list and add or edit transactions from the list. Express accommodates your preferences.

Spend some time using the sample companies included with Express to explore and discover your preferences. An accounting system with many error-correcting transactions is difficult to use. This means that you should **understand basic accounting and the basics of Express before entering transactions so that there are few mistakes**.

Customers

Customers are the reason you are in business. They purchase your products and services, hopefully for a price high enough to make a profit. This section covers typical customer transactions.

- **Quote**—A *quote* explains what your company will provide the customer—the price and the terms. Some businesses record a quote even if the quote is verbal, without a written quote. In Express, a quote is optional because many customers make immediate purchases without requesting a quote. You can modify the quote several times as you negotiate terms and price with the customer. Eventually, the quote will be either rejected or accepted and turned into an invoice.

  ⇨ See "New Quote" on page 125.

- **Invoice**—An invoice describes the products and services sold and the terms of the sale. The invoice requests that the customer pay within a specific period of time, and may even offer a discount for early payment.

  ⇨ See "New Invoice" on page 133.

- **Cash Sale**—A cash sale records the sale and payment at the same time.

  ⇨ See "New Cash Sale" on page 144.

- **Credit Memo**—The credit memo records that money is owed to a customer. It can be used to refund money or be applied against previous or future sales, or any combination of the two.

  ⇨ See "Credit Memo" on page 152.

- **Receive Payment**—Receive Payment records the customer paying an invoice.

  ⇨ See "Receive Payment" on page 159.

- **Customer Refund**—Customer Refund records the intent to reimburse the customer. The check, credit card refund, or bank transfer can occur at the same time or later.

  ⇨ See "Customer Refund" on page 168.

- **New Credits and Refunds**—A *credit memo* is created to reverse all or part of a sale, signifying that the customer doesn't owe the full amount of the sale. The credit memo is used as payment for another invoice a customer owes or to create a customer refund. An immediate customer refund might also be created without a prior credit memo.

- **Receive Payment**—Payment is recorded at the time of a cash sale. Alternatively, all or partial payment is recorded later for one or more invoices.

NEW QUOTE

Quotes are usually the first step in the sales process. They can expire on the expiration date you set, be modified or deleted, be rejected by the customer, or be accepted and converted to an invoice if the customer decides to purchase. Rejected quotes can be edited to again become an open quote.

Add a quote using multiple methods:

On the Customers screen, click the **New Quote** button, as shown in Figure 6.2.

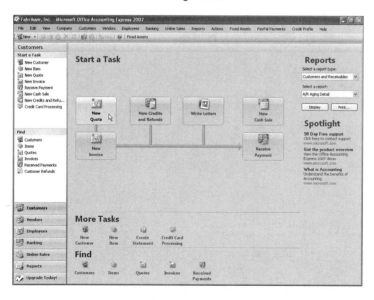

FIGURE 6.2 Create a new customer quote to propose how your company will meet the customer's needs.

Alternatively,

1. Click the **Customers** menu.

2. Click the **New** menu item.

3. Click the **New Quote** menu item.

Or, on the Customers screen, do the following:

1. Under either **Find** heading, click the **Quotes** link. The Quote List shows.

2. Click the **Add a New Quote** link. A new quote form shows.

Or, on the Customers screen, click the **New Quote** link under Start a Task.

To add a quote, as shown in Figure 6.3, enter the following information:

1. **Current Layout**—Use the default Express Quote data entry form, or click the **Current Layout** drop-down list arrow to select a custom form layout.

   ⇨ See "Modifying Entry Forms" on page 340 to create a custom data entry form.

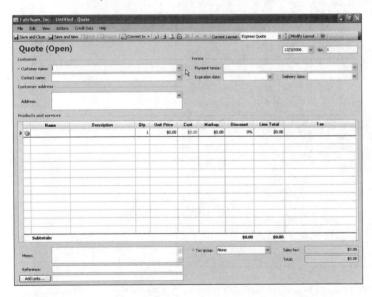

FIGURE 6.3   Enter the information about the customer quote. Customer Name and Tax Group are the only required fields.

2. **Date**—The date of the quote is automatically entered using today's date. If a different quote date is needed, type the date or click the drop-down arrow to select a date from the calendar.

3. **Quote Number**—The Quote Number is automatically incremented and the next available number appears. You can type in a different number. If the company preferences do not allow duplicate document numbers, the quote number must be a unique number.

➪ See "Company Preferences" on page 80.

4. **Customer Name**—A Customer Name is required. Do one of the following:

   ■ Click the drop-down list arrow and choose the correct customer from the list. If the customer is new, click the first line in the list, **Add a New Customer**.

   ■ Start typing the customer name and the full name will appear if it has already been added as a customer. When you are finished, press the **Enter** or **Tab** key. If the customer is new, a window will appear asking whether you would like to add the customer.

   If the new customer warning window appears, as shown in Figure 6.4, do one of the following:

   ■ Click the **Set Up** button to add the customer. Enter as much information as you can about the customer, filling in the information on both the General and Details tabs. From that point on, Express enters the customer's information on new quotes and invoices. This saves time.

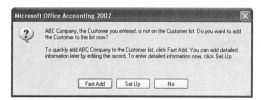

FIGURE 6.4   Choose Set Up, which takes you to the new customer form. Add the customer information on each tab, and then save the information. From then on, Express fills in the customer information on new quotes and invoices.

   ■ Click the **Fast Add** button to add only the name of the customer. Later, when you save the quote, Express tells you that the information about the customer has changed (for example, the address and payment terms) and asks whether you would like to save the new information permanently in the customer file.

- Click the **No** button if you made a spelling error. Then either correct the spelling of the customer's name or choose the customer using the drop-down list arrow.

5. **Contact Name**—Filled in from the primary contact entered when the customer was added. If a different customer contact is needed, choose it using the drop-down list arrow. Express will not permit a contact that is not in the customer's Contacts list.

6. **Address**—Filled in from the business address entered when the customer was added. If a different address is needed, choose it using the drop-down list arrow, or type in the address.

7. **Payment Terms**—Filled in from the payment terms entered when the customer was added. If a different payment term is needed, do one of the following:

   - Click the drop-down list arrow and choose the correct payment term from the list of all payment terms. If the payment term is new, click the first line in the list, **Add a New Payment Term**.

   - Start typing the payment term and the full name appears. When you are finished, press the **Enter** or **Tab** key. If the payment term is new, a window appears asking whether you would like to add the term to the Payment Terms list.

8. **Expiration Date**—The last date on which you agree to sell the product or service to the customer with these terms. Type the date, or click the drop-down arrow to select a date from the calendar.

9. **Delivery Date**—The expected date to deliver the product or service to the customer. Type the date, or click the drop-down arrow to select a date from the calendar.

Each line in the Products and Services section shows on the printed quote sent to the customer.

In the Products and Services section, as shown in Figure 6.5, enter the following:

10. **Name**—Click the drop-down list arrow, and then click one of the following:

  - **Item**—A product or service. Also, enter the quantity, price, type of tax, and optionally the cost, markup, and discount.

  ⇨ See "Items" on page 114 to add a new item.

  - **Comment**—A multiline descriptive comment in the Description column. A comment can also be a blank line.

  - **Sales Tax**—A tax on the sale other than the typical sales tax; for example, a hospitality tax. Also, enter a description of the tax.

  ⇨ See "Sales Tax Setup" on page 64 to add a new sales tax.

  - **Account**—A financial account to post to; for example, the Freight expense account. Also, enter the quantity, price, type of tax, and, optionally, the description.

  ⇨ See "Adding an Account" on page 55 to add a new account.

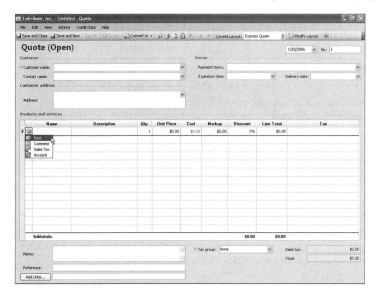

FIGURE 6.5 The middle of the quote form contains multiple lines—product and service items, comments, sales tax, and miscellaneous accounts (for example, a surcharge).

11. **Description**—Multiple lines of text on Item, Comment, Sales Tax, and Account line items. A description can also be blank.

12. **Qty**—Quantity, a required field for Item and Account line items. Quantity can be a positive number, a negative number, or 0.

13. **Unit Price**—Used for Item and Account line items. Unit price can be only a positive number or 0. Unit price minus cost determines the markup. Changing the unit price also changes the markup.

14. **Cost**—Used for Item line items only, and is not editable. Cost is edited in the **Item, Standard Cost**.

    ⇨ See "Items" on page 114 to change the cost.

15. **Markup**—Used for Item line items only. Cost plus markup determines the unit price. The unit price changes to reflect a change in markup. Markup can be 0 or a positive dollar amount.

16. **Discount**—Used for Item line items only. The discount is a percentage of the unit price. For example, enter either **5%** or **5** and Express displays 5%. A discount must be a positive number between .01% and 100%. Changing the Discount field automatically changes the line total; changing the line total automatically changes the Discount field.

17. **Line Total**—A calculated total, line total equals quantity multiplied by price, then the discount is subtracted. The line total can be edited. If you change the line total to a higher amount, the markup and unit price change. Markup equals unit price minus cost, and unit price equals line total divided by quantity. If you change the line total to a lower amount, the discount percentage changes.

18. **Tax**—If previously set up in the Item, the Tax category will display, as shown in Figure 6.6.

    ⇨ See "Items" on page 114 to add the correct tax category to this item.

    Alternatively, click the Tax drop-down list arrow, and then click a previously set up sales tax category.

    ⇨ See "Sales Tax Setup" on page 64 to add a new sales tax category.

    The Discount Subtotal and Line Total Subtotal calculate automatically.

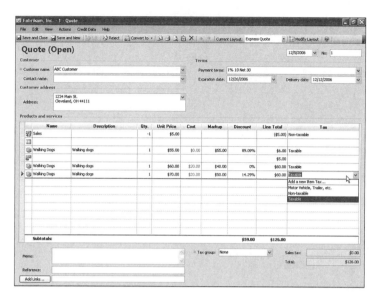

FIGURE 6.6   Decide whether the item is taxable.

19. **Memo**—Not typically printed. You might want to use the Memo field to detail any changes made to the quote and why.

20. **Reference**—Prints on the quote, but does not automatically print on Word templates. You might want to enter the customer's purchase order number when they accept the quote.

21. **Add Links button**—Used to attach one or more files. For example, scan in the customer's Request for Quote, save the file(s), and click the **Add Links** button. Then locate the file(s) on the computer and click the **OK** button. The filename shows in Add Links.

22. **Tax Group**—If previously set up for the customer, the correct Tax Group will display, and the tax will be calculated and displayed. Otherwise, click the **Tax Group** drop-down list arrow and choose a previously set up tax group, as shown in Figure 6.7.

> See "Manage Sales Tax Groups" on page 76 to set up a new tax group.

The Sales Tax and Total fields display and are not editable.

When a quote is complete, click the **Save and Close** button. The information is saved and the window closes. Alternatively, click the **Save and New** button. The information saves and the form clears, ready for a new quote.

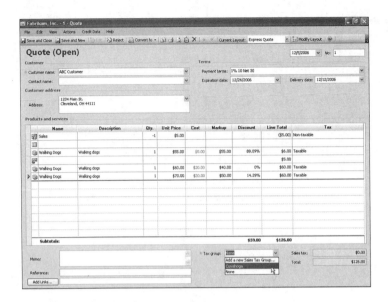

FIGURE 6.7 Choose the correct tax group.

After a quote is saved, you can do the following:

- Click the **Edit** button to edit the quote.

- Click the **Reject** button to mark the quote as rejected by the customer. A rejected quote cannot be converted into an invoice, but it can be edited to turn it back into an open quote.

- Click the **Convert To** button, as shown in Figure 6.8, and then click **Convert to Invoice**. An invoice window opens with the quote information already shown. The quote is marked as Accepted.

- Click the **E-mail** button to email the quote to your client, as shown in Figure 6.9. The primary contact email address appears. If the primary contact does not have an email address, the first available email address appears. Enter an email address if the email address is not already set up for the customer.

- Click the **Print** button to send the quote to the printer.

  ⇨ See "Modifying Printed Forms" on page 345 to customize the printed form.

- Click the **Print Preview** button to open a window to see how the quote will look printed.

- Click the **Send to Word** button to edit the quote in Microsoft Word.
- Click the **Delete** button to permanently delete the quote.
- Click the **Previous** button to see the previous quote.
- Click the **Next** button to see the next quote.
- Click the **Current Layout** drop-down list arrow to choose the data entry form layout.
- Click the **Modify Layout** button to edit the form. Add or delete fields on the form, or move fields to a different position on the form.

⇨ See "Modifying Entry Forms" on page 340 to customize the data entry form.

NEW INVOICE

An invoice is created for a customer sale. You can convert a quote to an invoice or create an invoice without a previous quote. An invoice records only a sale, not a payment. Use the Cash Sale form instead of New Invoice to record payment in full at the time of sale.

⇨ See "New Cash Sale" on page 144.

Add a new customer invoice using multiple methods:

On the Customers screen, click the **New Invoice** button, as shown in Figure 6.10.

Alternatively,

1. Click the **Customers** menu.
2. Click the **New** menu item.
3. Click the **New Invoice** menu item.

Or, on the **Customers** screen, under **Start a Task**, click the **New Invoice** link.

Or,

1. On the Customers screen under the **Find** heading, click the **Invoices** link. The Invoice list shows.
2. Click the **Add a New Invoice** link. A new invoice form shows.

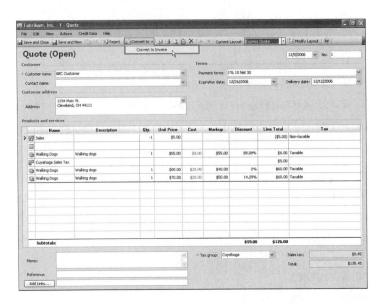

FIGURE 6.8   After completing a quote, it can be edited, rejected, converted into an invoice, emailed, printed, sent to Microsoft Word, or deleted.

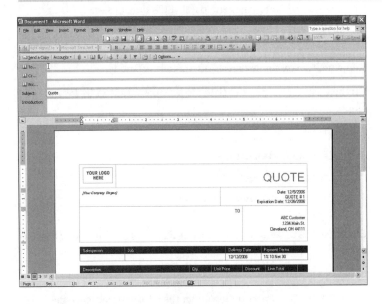

FIGURE 6.9   Email a quote to a client.

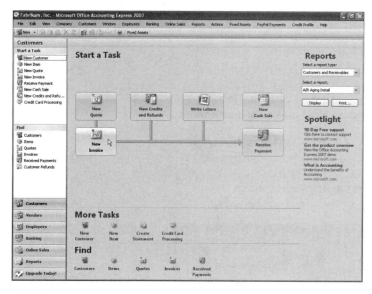

FIGURE 6.10 Create a new customer invoice to request payment for a product or service.

Convert an existing quote to an invoice using multiple methods:

From a new invoice, click the **Create From** button, as shown in Figure 6.11. Click a quote, and then click **OK**. The invoice fills in using the information from the quote.

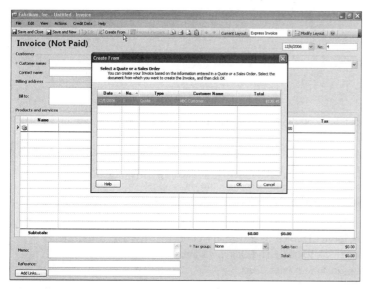

FIGURE 6.11 Create an invoice from a quote.

Alternatively, from a quote, click the **Convert To** button. Click **Convert to Invoice**. The quote is marked as Accepted. The invoice window opens containing the information from the quote.

Enter the following information to add an invoice:

1. **Current Layout**—You can use an invoice data entry form that you created, as shown in Figure 6.12, or use one of the following:

   ⇨ See "Modifying Entry Forms" on page 340 to create a custom data entry form.

   ■ **Express Invoice**—The simplest invoice, shown in Figure 6.12.

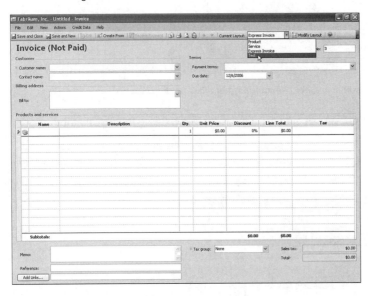

FIGURE 6.12   Choose the invoice form layout: an Express invoice, product invoice, service invoice, or one of the invoice forms that you design yourself.

   ■ **Product Invoice**—Includes Ship To, Phone, Salesperson, Shipping Terms, Shipping Method, and Delivery Date fields, as shown in Figure 6.13. The invoice totals include a price level.

   ■ **Service Invoice**—The Service Invoice, as shown in Figure 6.14, includes the Phone, Salesperson, and Delivery Date fields. The invoice totals include a Price Level.

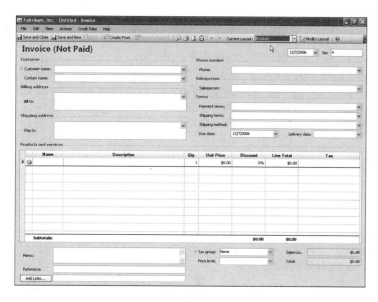

FIGURE 6.13 The product invoice.

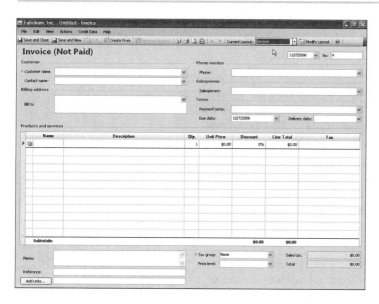

FIGURE 6.14 The service invoice.

2. **Date**—The date of the invoice is automatically entered using today's date. If a different invoice date is needed, type the date or click the drop-down arrow to select a date from the calendar.

3. **Invoice Number**—The invoice number is automatically incremented and the next available number appears. You can enter a different number. If the company preferences do not allow duplicate document numbers, the invoice number must be a unique number.

⇨   See "Company Preferences" on page 80.

4. **Customer Name**—The Customer Name is required. Do one of the following:

    ■ Click the drop-down list arrow and choose the correct customer from the list. If the customer is new, click the first line in the list, **Add a New Customer**.

    ■ Start typing the customer name and the full name will appear if the name has already been added as a customer. When you're finished, press the **Enter** or **Tab** key. If the customer is new, a window will appear asking whether you would like to add the customer.

    If the new customer warning window appears, do one of the following:

    ■ Click the **Set Up** button to add the customer and as much information as you can about them. From that point on, Express will enter the customer's information on new quotes and invoices. This saves time.

    ■ Click the **Fast Add** button to add only the name of the customer. Later, when you save the invoice, Express tells you that the information about the customer has changed (for example, the address and payment terms) and asks whether you would like to save the new information permanently in the customer file.

    ■ Click the **No** button if you made a spelling error. Then either correct the spelling of the customer's name or choose the customer using the drop-down list arrow.

5. **Contact Name**—Filled in from the primary contact entered when the customer was added. If a different customer contact is needed, choose it using the drop-down list arrow. Express will not permit a contact that is not in the customer's Contacts list.

6. **Billing Address**—Filled in from the bill-to address entered when the customer was added. If the bill-to address is not in the customer record, the business address is used. If a different address is needed, choose it using the drop-down list arrow or type in the address.

7. **Payment Terms**—Filled in from the payment terms entered when the customer was added. If different payment terms are needed:

   - Click the drop-down list arrow and choose the correct payment term from the list of all payment terms. If the payment term is new, click the first line in the list, **Add a New Payment Term**.

   - Alternatively, start typing the payment term and the full name will appear. When you are finished, press the **Enter** or **Tab** key. If the payment term is new, a window will appear asking whether you would like to add the term to the payment terms list.

8. **Due Date**—The last date for the customer to pay the invoice without being late. Express fills in the due date based on the invoice date and the payment terms entered when the customer was added. To change the due date, type the date or click the drop-down arrow to select a date from the calendar.

Each line in the Products and Services section shows on the invoice sent to the customer.

In the Products and Services section, enter the following:

9. **Name**—Click the drop-down list arrow, as shown in Figure 6.15, and then click one of the following:

   - **Item**—A product or service. Also, enter the quantity, unit price, type of tax, and optionally the discount.

   - **Comment**—A multiline comment in the Description column. A comment can also be a blank line.

   - **Sales Tax**—A tax on the sale other than the typical sales tax; for example, a hospitality tax. Also, enter a description of the tax.

   - **Account**—A financial account to which to post; for example, the Freight expense account. Also, enter the quantity, unit price, type of tax, and optionally the description.

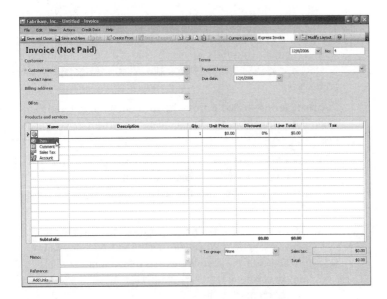

FIGURE 6.15 The middle of the invoice contains line items—product and service items, comments, sales tax, and miscellaneous accounts (for example, a surcharge).

10. **Description**—Multiple lines of text on Item, Comment, Sales Tax, and Account line items.

11. **Qty**—Quantity, a required field for Item and Account line items. Quantity can also be a positive number, a negative number, or 0.

12. **Unit Price**—Used for Item and Account line items. Unit Price can be only a positive number or 0.

13. **Discount**—Used for Item line items only. The discount is a percentage of the unit price. For example, enter either **5%** or **5** and Express displays 5%. A discount must be a positive number between .01% and 100%. Changing the Discount field automatically changes the line total; changing the line total automatically changes the Discount field.

14. **Line Total**—A calculated total. Line total = (quantity multiplied by price) less discount. The line total can be edited.

15. **Tax**—If previously set up in the Item, the Tax category will display.

⇨ See "Items" on page 114.

Alternatively, click the **Tax** drop-down list arrow, and then click a previously set up sales tax category.

↪ See "Sales Tax Setup" on page 64.

The Discount Subtotal and Line Total Subtotal calculate automatically.

16. **Memo**—A comment. You might want to use the Memo field to detail any changes made to the invoice and why.

17. **Reference**—A comment. You might want to enter the customer's purchase order number.

18. **Add Links button**—Used to attach one or more files. For example, scan in the customer's purchase order, save the file(s), and click the **Add Links** button. Then locate the file(s) on the computer and click the **OK** button. The filename appears in Add Links.

19. **Tax Group is required**—If previously set up for the customer, the correct tax group will display, and the tax will be calculated and displayed. Otherwise, click the **Tax Group** drop-down list arrow and choose a previously set up tax group.

↪ See "Manage Sales Tax Groups" on page 76.

The Sales Tax and Total fields display and are not editable.

When an invoice is complete, click the **Save and Close** button. The information is saved and the window closes. Alternatively, click the **Save and New** button. The information saves and the form clears, ready for a new invoice.

After an invoice is saved, do the following:

- Click the **Edit** button to edit the invoice, as shown in Figure 6.16.
- Click the **Receive Payment** button to receive all or a portion of the money from the customer to pay the invoice.
- Click the **E-mail** button to email the invoice to your client. The first time an invoice is sent via email, Express asks which template to use, as shown in Figure 6.17. You have the option of adding a PayPal button to the invoice, as shown in Figure 6.18, to receive payment via PayPal.

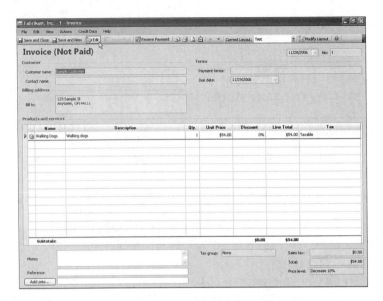

FIGURE 6.16 After completing an invoice, it can be edited, emailed, printed, sent to Microsoft Word, or voided (but not deleted).

The primary contact email address appears. If the primary contact does not have an email address, the first available email address appears. Enter an email address if no email address is set up for the customer.

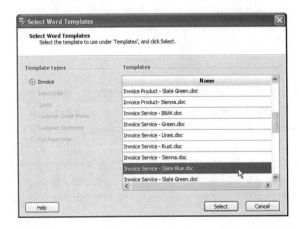

FIGURE 6.17 Choose a template to format the invoice for email.

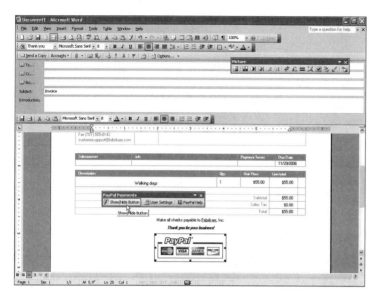

FIGURE 6.18   If you choose, add a button on the email invoice to allow customer payment via PayPal.

- Click the **Print** button to send the invoice to the printer.

  ⇨ See "Modifying Printed Forms" on page 345 to customize the printed form.

- Click the **Print Preview** button to open a window to see how the invoice will look printed.

- Click the **Send to Word** button to edit the invoice in Microsoft Word.

- Click the **Previous** button to see the previous invoice.

- Click the **Next** button to see the next invoice.

- Click the **Current Layout** drop-down list arrow to choose the form layout.

- Click the **Modify Layout** button to edit the form. Add or delete fields on the form, or move fields to a different position on the form.

  ⇨ See "Modifying Entry Forms" on page 340 to create a custom data entry form.

Click the **Actions** menu, **Print Packaging Slip** to print a packing slip for the invoice, as shown in Figure 6.19.

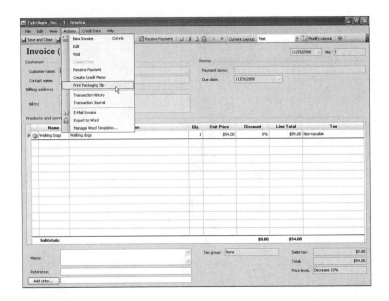

FIGURE 6.19   A packing slip can also be printed for an invoice.

NEW CASH SALE

A new cash sale automatically records both the sale and the receipt of payment when the cash sale invoice is saved. (An invoice records only the sale.)

Add a new cash sale using multiple methods:

On the Customers screen, click the **New Cash Sale** button, as shown in Figure 6.20, to open the Cash Sale form.

Alternatively,

1. Click the **Customers** menu.

2. Click the **New** menu item.

3. Click the **New Cash Sale** menu item.

Or, on the **Customers** screen, under **Start a Task**, click the **New Cash Sale** link.

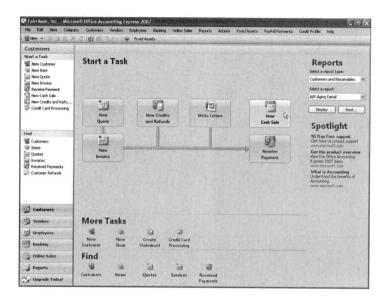

FIGURE 6.20   Create a new cash sale.

Enter the following information to add a cash sale:

1. **Current Layout**—You can use a cash sale data entry form that you created, or use one of the following:

   ⇨   See "Modifying Entry Forms" on page 340 to create a custom data entry form.

   - **Service form**—The simplest cash sale form, as shown in Figure 6.21.
   - **Product form**—Includes all the fields on the Service cash sale form plus Ship To, Shipping Terms, and Shipping Method, as shown in Figure 6.22.

2. **Date**—The date of the cash sale is automatically entered using today's date. If a different cash sale date is needed, type the date, or click the drop-down arrow to select a date from the calendar.

3. **Cash Sale No.**—The cash sale number is automatically incremented and the next available number appears. You can type in a different number. If the company preferences do not allow duplicate document numbers, the cash sale number must be a unique number.

   ⇨   See "Company Preferences" on page 80.

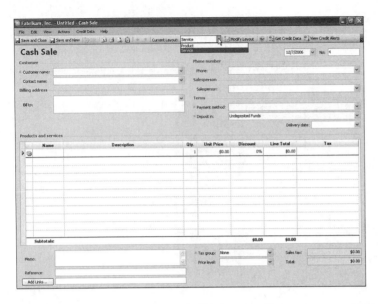

FIGURE 6.21 Choose the cash sale form layout: service, product, or one of the cash sale forms that you design yourself.

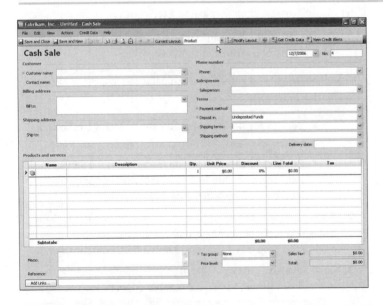

FIGURE 6.22 The Product Cash Sale form also includes Ship To, Shipping Terms, and Shipping Method fields.

4. **Customer Name**—The Customer Name is required. Do one of the following:

   - Click the drop-down list arrow and choose the correct customer from the list. If the customer is new, click the first line in the list, **Add a New Customer**.

   - Start typing the customer name, and the full name will appear if the name has already been added as a customer. When you're finished, press the **Enter** or **Tab** key. If the customer is new, a window will appear asking whether you would like to add the customer.

   If the new customer warning window appears, do one of the following:

   - Click the **Set Up** button to add the customer and as much information as you can about them. From that point on, Express will enter the customer's information on new quotes and invoices. This saves time.

   - Click the **Fast Add** button to add only the name of the customer. Later, when you save the invoice, Express tells you that the information about the customer has changed (for example, the address and payment terms) and asks whether you would like to permanently save the new information in the customer file.

   - Click the **No** button if you made a spelling error. Then either correct the spelling of the customer's name or choose the customer using the drop-down list arrow.

5. **Contact Name**—The Contact Name field is filled in from the primary contact entered when the customer was added. If a different customer contact is needed, choose it using the drop-down list arrow. Express will not permit a contact that is not in the customer's Contacts list.

6. **Billing Address**—The Billing Address field is filled in from the bill-to address entered when the customer was added. If the bill-to address is not in the customer record, the business address is used. If a different address is needed, choose it using the drop-down list arrow, or type in the address.

7. **Shipping Address**—The Shipping Address field, which is used on the Product form and not on the Service form, is filled in from the ship-to address entered when the customer was added. If the ship-to address is not in the customer record, the business

address is used. If a different address is needed, choose it using the drop-down list arrow, or type in the address.

8. **Phone**—The Phone field is filled in from the phone number entered when the customer was added. If a different phone number is needed, choose it using the drop-down list arrow or type it in yourself.

9. **Salesperson**—The Salesperson field is filled in from the salesperson entered when the customer was added. If a different salesperson is needed, choose one using the drop-down list arrow showing all employees, or add a new employee.

10. **Payment Method**—The Payment Method field is required. Click the drop-down list arrow and choose Cash, Check, or Credit Card.

11. **Deposit In**—The Deposit In field is required. Express displays the Undeposited Funds account automatically. To change the financial account, click the drop-down list arrow, and then choose a different account.

12. **Shipping Terms**—The Shipping Terms field is used on the Product form and not on the Service form. It is filled in from the shipping terms entered when the customer was added. If the shipping terms are not in the customer record, or if different shipping terms are needed, choose it using the drop-down list arrow or click **Add a New Shipping Term**.

13. **Shipping Method**—The Shipping Method field is used on the Product form and not on the Service form. It is filled in from the shipping method entered when the customer was added. If the shipping method is not in the customer record, or if a different shipping method is needed, choose it using the drop-down list arrow or click **Add a New Shipping Method**.

14. **Delivery Date**—The Delivery Date field can be typed in, or you can click the drop-down list arrow to select a date from the calendar.

Each line in the Products and Services section shows on the printed cash sale form given to the customer.

In the Products and Services section, as shown in Figure 6.23, enter the following:

15. **Name**—Click the drop-down list arrow, and then click one of the following:

    ■ **Item**—A product or service. Also, enter the quantity, unit price, type of tax, and, optionally, the discount.

    ■ **Comment**—A multiline comment in the description column. A comment can also be a blank line.

    ■ **Sales Tax**—A tax on the sale other than the typical sales tax; for example, a hospitality tax. Also, enter a description of the tax.

    ■ **Account**—A financial account to which to post; for example, the Freight expense account. Also, enter the quantity, unit price, type of tax, and, optionally, the description.

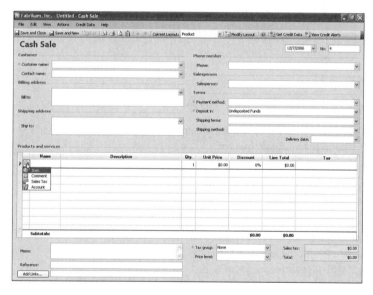

FIGURE 6.23 The middle of the cash sale form contains line items—product and service items, comments, sales tax, and miscellaneous accounts (for example, a surcharge).

16. **Description**—Multiple lines of text on Item, Comment, Sales Tax, and Account line items.

17. **Qty**—Quantity, a required field for Item and Account line items. Quantity can also be a positive number, a negative number, or 0.

18. **Unit Price**—Used for Item and Account line items. Unit price can be only a positive number or 0.

19. **Discount**—Used for Item line items only. The discount is a percentage of the unit price. For example, enter either **5%** or 5 and Express displays 5%. A discount must be a positive number between .01% and 100%. Changing the Discount field automatically changes the line total; changing the line total automatically changes the Discount field.

20. **Line Total**—A calculated total. Line total equals quantity multiplied by price, then the discount is subtracted. The line total can be edited.

21. **Tax**—If previously set up in the item, the Tax category will display.

    ⇨ See "Items" on page 114 to change the tax on an item.

    Alternatively, click the **Tax** drop-down list arrow, and then click a previously set up sales tax category or add a new sales tax category.

    ⇨ See "Manage Item Tax" on page 74.

The Discount Subtotal and Line Total Subtotal calculate automatically.

22. **Memo**—Not typically printed. You might want to use the Memo field to detail any changes made to the cash sale invoice and why.

23. **Reference**—Prints on the cash sale invoice. You might want to enter the customer's purchase order number.

24. **Add Links button**—Used to attach one or more files. For example, scan in the customer's purchase order, save the file(s), and click the **Add Links** button. Then locate the file(s) on the computer and click the **OK** button. The filename appears in Add Links.

25. **Tax Group is required**—If previously set up for the customer, the correct tax group will display, and then tax will be calculated and displayed. Otherwise, click the **Tax Group** drop-down list arrow and choose a previously set up tax group.

    ⇨ See "Manage Sales Tax Groups" on page 76.

26. **Price Level**—If previously set up for the customer, the correct price level will display and the total of the cash sale invoice will be increased or decreased. Alternatively, click the **Price Level** drop-down list arrow, and then click a previously set up price level or add a new one.

The Sales Tax and Total fields display and are not editable.

When a cash sale invoice is complete click the **Save and Close** button. The information is saved and the window closes. Alternatively, click the **Save and New** button. The information saves and the form clears, ready for a new cash sale invoice.

After a cash sale is saved, do the following:

- Click the **Edit** button to make changes to the saved information.
- Click the **E-mail** button to email the cash sale invoice to your client. The first time a cash sale invoice is sent via email, Express asks which template to use.

  The primary contact email address appears. If the primary contact does not have an email address, the first available email address appears. Enter an email address if no email address is set up for the customer.

- Click the **Print** button to send the invoice to the printer.

  ⇨ See "Modifying Printed Forms" on page 345 to customize the printed form.

- Click the **Print Preview** button to open a window to see how the printed invoice will look, as shown in Figure 6.24.
- Click the **Send to Word** button to edit the invoice in Microsoft Word.
- Click the **Previous** button to see the previous invoice.
- Click the **Next** button to see the next invoice.
- Click the **Current Layout** drop-down list arrow to choose the form layout.
- Click the **Modify Layout** button to edit the form. Add or delete fields on the form, or move fields to a different position on the form.

  ⇨ See "Modifying Entry Forms" on page 340 to create a custom data entry form.

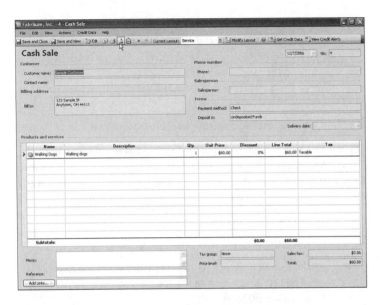

FIGURE 6.24 After completing a cash sale invoice, it can be edited, emailed, printed, sent to Microsoft Word, or voided (but not deleted).

CREDIT MEMO

A credit memo reverses a previous customer transaction, indicating that the company owes the customer. After a credit memo is issued, a customer refund form can be used to refund money, or the credit memo can be applied against outstanding invoices.

On the Customers screen, as shown in Figure 6.25, click the **New Credits and Refunds** button.

Alternatively, on the Customers screen, under Start a Task, click the **New Credits and Refunds** link.

Or click the **Customers** menu, **New**, **New Credits and Refunds**.

Or, on the Customers screen, under either **Find** heading, click **Invoices**. The Invoice list appears. Right-click an invoice, and then choose **Create Credit Memo**, as shown in Figure 6.26. The credit memo form opens.

Or, convert an existing invoice or cash sale to a credit memo. Click the **Actions** menu, **Create Credit Memo**. The credit memo form opens, filled in with the invoice information.

Or, open a credit memo, click the **Create From** button, select an invoice, as shown in Figure 6.27, and then click the **OK** button. The Credit Memo form fills with the invoice information.

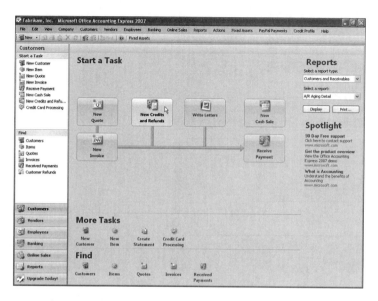

FIGURE 6.25   Refund money to a customer or create a credit memo.

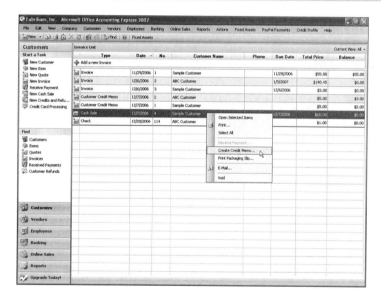

FIGURE 6.26   Create a credit memo from an invoice in the invoice list.

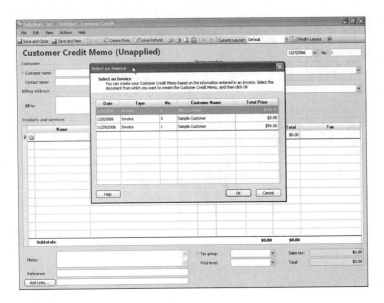

FIGURE 6.27 Open a new credit memo form, and then create a credit memo from an invoice or cash sale.

To add a credit memo, as shown in Figure 6.28, enter the following information:

1. **Current Layout**—Create your own credit memo form or use the default form.

   ⇨ See "Modifying Entry Forms" on page 340 to create a custom data entry form.

2. **Date**—The date of the credit memo is automatically entered using today's date. If a different credit memo date is needed, type the date or click the drop-down list arrow to select a date from the calendar.

3. **Credit Memo No.**—The credit memo number is automatically incremented and the next available number appears. You may type in a different number. If the company preferences do not allow duplicate document numbers, the credit number must be a unique number.

   ⇨ See "Company Preferences" on page 80.

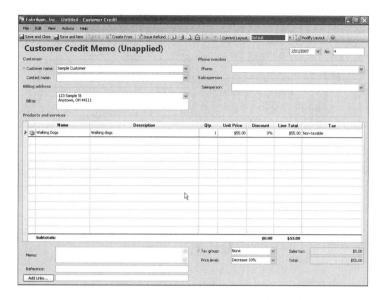

FIGURE 6.28   Complete the Credit Memo form.

4. **Customer Name**—The customer name is required. Do one of the
   following:

   - Click the drop-down list arrow and choose the correct cus-
     tomer from the list.

   - Start typing the customer name and the full name will
     appear. When you are finished, press the **Enter** or **Tab** key.

5. **Contact Name**—The Contact Name field is filled in from the primary contact entered when the customer was added. If a different customer contact is needed, choose it using the drop-down
   list arrow. Express will not permit a contact that is not in the customer's Contacts list.

6. **Billing Address**—The Billing Address field is filled in from the
   bill-to address entered when the customer was added. If the bill-
   to address is not in the customer record, the business address is
   used. If a different address is needed, choose it using the drop-
   down list arrow or type in the address.

7. **Phone**—The Phone field is filled in from the phone number
   entered when the customer was added. If a different phone number is needed, choose it using the drop-down list arrow or type it
   in.

8. **Salesperson**—The Salesperson field is filled in from the salesperson entered when the customer was added. If a different salesperson is needed, choose one using the drop-down list arrow showing all employees, or add a new employee.

Each line in the Products and Services section shows on the printed credit memo form.

In the Products and Services section, enter the following:

9. **Name**—Click the drop-down list arrow, and then click one of the following:

   - **Item**—A product or service. Also, enter the quantity, unit price, type of tax, and, optionally, the discount.

   - **Comment**—A multiline comment in the Description column. A comment can also be a blank line.

   - **Sales Tax**—A tax on the sale other than the typical sales tax; for example, a hospitality tax. Also, enter a description of the tax.

   - **Account**—A financial account to which to post; for example, the Freight expense account. Also, enter the quantity, unit price, type of tax, and, optionally, the description.

10. **Description**—Multiple lines of text.

11. **Qty**—Quantity, a required field for Item and Account line items. Quantity can also be a positive number, a negative number, or 0.

12. **Unit Price**—Used for Item and Account line items. Unit Price can be only a positive number or 0.

13. **Discount**—Used for Item line items only. The discount is a percentage of the unit price. For example, enter either **5%** or 5 and Express displays 5%. A discount must be a positive number between .01% and 100%. Changing the Discount field automatically changes the line total; changing the line total automatically changes the Discount field.

14. **Line Total**—A calculated total. Line total = (quantity multiplied by price) less discount. The line total can be edited.

15. **Tax**—If previously set up in the Item, the Tax category will display.

    Alternatively, click the **Tax** drop-down list arrow, and then click a previously set up sales tax category or add a new sales tax category.

The Discount Subtotal and Line Total Subtotal calculate automatically.

16. **Memo**—A comment. You might want to use the Memo field to detail any changes made to the credit memo and why.

17. **Reference**—A comment. You might want to enter the original document number the credit memo references.

18. **Add Links button**—Used to attach one or more files. For example, scan in the documentation to defend the decision to issue a credit memo, save the file(s), and click the **Add Links** button. Then locate the file(s) on the computer and click the **OK** button. The filename shows in Add Links.

19. **Tax Group is required**—If previously set up for the customer, the correct tax group displays and the tax will be calculated and displayed. Otherwise, click the **Tax Group** drop-down list arrow and choose a previously set up tax group.

20. **Price Level**—If previously set up for the customer, the correct price level will display and the total of the credit memo will be increased or decreased. Alternatively, click the **Price Level** drop-down list arrow, and then click a previously set up price level or add a new one.

The Sales Tax and Total fields display and cannot be edited.

When a credit memo is complete, click the **Save and Close** button. The information is saved and then the window closes. Alternatively, click the **Save and New** button. The information saves and then the form clears, ready for a new credit memo.

After a credit memo is saved, you can do the following:

- Click the **Edit** button to make changes to the saved information.

- Click the **Issue a Refund** button to open a Customer Refund form.

  ➪ See "Customer Refund" on page 168.

- Click the **E-mail** button to email the credit memo to your client. The first time a credit memo is sent via email, Express asks which template to use.

  The primary contact email address appears. If the primary contact does not have an email address, the first available email address appears. Enter an email address if no email address is set up for the customer.

- Click the **Print** button to send the credit memo to the printer.

- Click the **Print Preview** button to open a window to see how the printed credit memo will look.

- Click the **Send to Word** button to edit the credit memo in Microsoft Word.

- Click the **Previous** button, as shown in Figure 6.29, to see the previous credit memo.

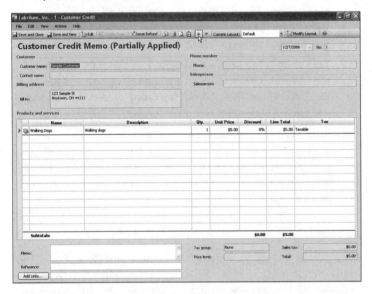

FIGURE 6.29   After completing a credit memo, you can use it to issue a refund, or it can be edited, emailed, printed, sent to Microsoft Word, or voided (but not deleted).

- Click the **Next** button to see the next credit memo.

- Click the **Current Layout** drop-down list arrow to choose a form you created or the default form layout.

- Click the **Modify Layout** button to edit the form. Add or delete fields on the form, or move fields to a different position on the form.

⇨   See "Modifying Entry Forms" on page 340 to create a custom data entry form.

For example, create a credit memo for $5 from an open invoice for $3, and then save the credit memo. On the Invoice list, the invoice will be reduced by the amount of the credit memo, showing an invoice balance of $0. The credit memo ($5) will be reduced by the amount of the invoice ($3), showing a credit memo balance of $2 and indicating that it is partially applied, as shown in Figure 6.30.

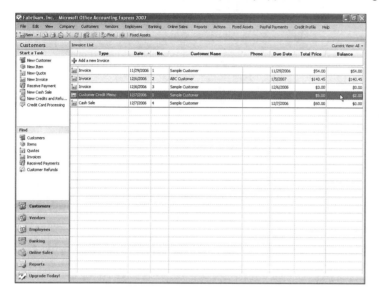

FIGURE 6.30   The result of a $5 credit memo applied to a $3 invoice.

RECEIVE PAYMENT

Receive Payment records money from a customer to pay outstanding invoices.

On the Customers screen, click the **Receive Payment** button, as shown in Figure 6.31.

Alternatively, on the Customers screen, under **Start a Task**, click the **Receive Payment** link.

Or, click the **Customers** menu, **Receive Payment**.

Or, on the Customers screen, under either **Find** heading, click the **Received Payments** link. The Received Payments list shows. Click the **Add a New Payment** link, as shown in Figure 6.32. The Received Payment form opens.

To receive payment on an existing invoice, open the invoice and click the **Receive Payment** button, as shown in Figure 6.33.

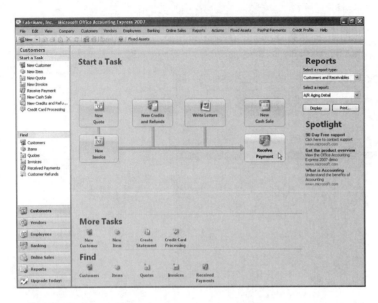

FIGURE 6.31   Receive payment from a customer.

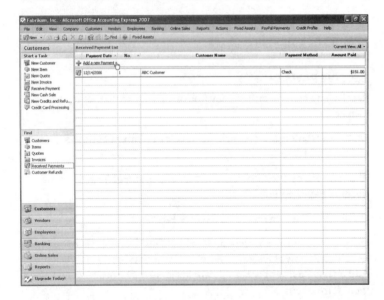

FIGURE 6.32   Add a new receipt of payment from the Received Payments list.

Alternatively, open an invoice, and then click the **Actions** menu. Click **Receive Payment**. The customer payment form opens, filled with the invoice information.

FIGURE 6.33 Receive payment on an existing invoice.

Or, from the Customers window, under either **Find** heading, click the **Invoices** link. The Invoice list opens. Right-click on an invoice. A menu opens. Click **Receive Payment**, as shown in Figure 6.34. The customer payment form opens, filled with the invoice information.

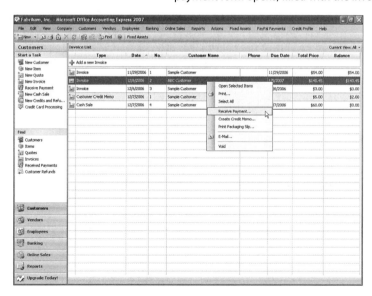

FIGURE 6.34 Receive payment on an existing invoice.

When clicking the **Receive Payment** button from an existing invoice, the customer payment form opens, filled with the customer's open invoices, as shown in Figure 6.35. The selected invoice is already check-marked for payment.

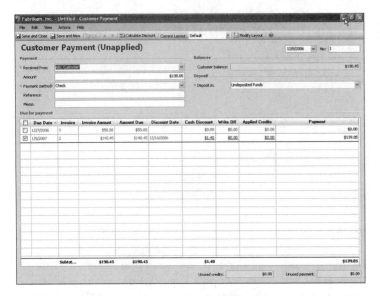

FIGURE 6.35   The default Customer Payment form, with an invoice automatically selected.

To add a customer payment, enter the following information:

1. **Current Layout**—You can create your own customer payment form or use the default form.

2. **Date**—The date of the customer payment is automatically entered with today's date. If a different customer payment date is needed, type the date or click the drop-down list arrow to select a date from the calendar.

3. **Customer Payment No.**—The customer payment number is automatically incremented and the next available number appears. You can type in a different number. If the company preferences do not allow duplicate document numbers, the customer payment number must be a unique number.

⟹   See "Company Preferences" on page 80.

4. **Received From**—The Received From *customer name* field is required. Do one of the following:

- Click the drop-down list arrow and choose the correct customer from the list. If the customer is new, click the first line in the list, **Add a New Customer**.

- Start typing the customer name and the full name will appear if the name has already been added as a customer. When you are done, press the **Enter** or **Tab** key.

When the customer is found, the Due for Payment section fills with the customer's open invoices. Unused credits also show at the bottom.

5. **Amount**—This is the amount of payment received from the customer. Express calculates payment discounts on each invoice based on the payment date, and then automatically pays invoices, until all the money is used. You can then modify the payment allocation, as shown in Figure 6.36.

If you change the amount of payment received from the customer, a window opens asking whether you want Express to automatically decide which invoices to pay, as shown in Figure 6.37. If you want to manually distribute the money according to the check detail, click the **No** button, and then enter the payment allocated to each invoice.

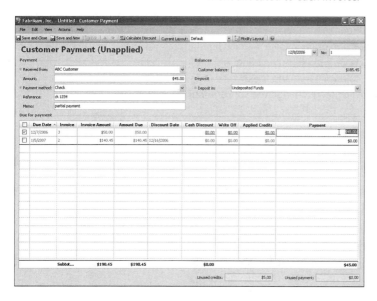

FIGURE 6.36   The default Customer Payment form, with an invoice automatically selected.

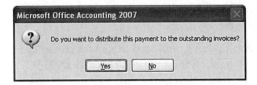

FIGURE 6.37   Click Yes to have Express automatically distribute the payment, or click No to distribute it manually.

6. **Payment Method**—Type **Cash**, **Check**, or **Credit Card**, or use the drop-down list arrow and click the correct method.

7. **Reference**—If the customer is paying by check, enter the customer's check number.

8. **Memo**—Enter comments.

The customer balance is not editable.

9. **Deposit In**—Express displays the Undeposited Funds financial account. This is typically the correct account because a bank deposit that also includes other checks is made later.

⇨   See "Make Deposits" on page 233.

To change the financial account, click the drop-down list arrow to select a different account.

The Due for Payment section shows one open invoice on each line. Change how the invoices sort by clicking a column heading. A small sort by arrow appears next to the column name and the invoice rows sort by that column. Click the arrow again to change the sort order of the column from A–Z to Z–A.

Click the **Select All** check box to select all invoices for payment. The invoices to be paid have a checkmark. Uncheck a specific invoice to stop paying it. Checkmark an invoice to pay it.

In the Due for Payment section, you can change the following for each invoice:

10. **Cash Discount**—The amount the invoice is reduced because of an early payment made by a specific date. For example, 1%/10 Net 30 allows a 1% cash discount if payment is made within 10 days of the invoice date. For a $500 invoice, the cash discount would be $5.

The Cash Discount field shows an incorrect amount when the calculated cash discount amount is rounded differently from the customer's check, the customer takes a discount after the discount date, or the customer forgets to take the cash discount. Decide how you want to resolve the difference. Click the **Cash Discount** button to calculate the discount automatically. Or, click the **Cash Discount** amount field to open the Cash Discount window, as shown in Figure 6.38, and change the cash discount account and amount.

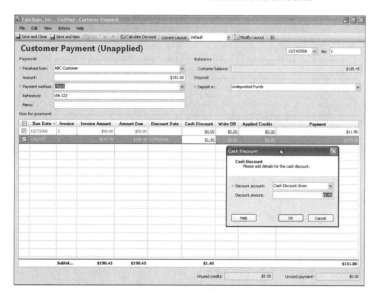

FIGURE 6.38 If you want to distribute the payment differently, change the Cash Discount, Write Off, Applied Credits, or Payment amounts for each invoice. Click the Cash Discount button to automatically calculate the discount.

You also can change the Write Off, Applied Credits, and Payment amounts.

11. **Write Off**—The dollar amount owed as a bad debt when the customer does not pay the invoice. Click the **Write Off** amount field to open the Write Off window, as shown in Figure 6.39.

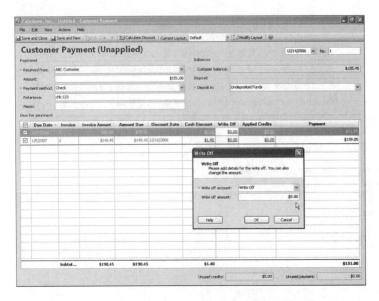

FIGURE 6.39 Click the Write Off amount field to open the Write Off window, and then change the write off account or amount.

12. **Applied Credits**—Shows applied credit memo amounts. Unused Credits shows credit memo amounts unapplied to invoices. To use some of or all the unused credits:

   - Click the **Applied Credits** amount. The Applied Credits and Payments window opens, as shown in Figure 6.40.

   - Uncheck the **Applied Credits** check box if a specific credit memo is not applied against this invoice, or checkmark the **Applied Credits** check box if the credit memo is applied against this invoice.

   - Change the **Amount to Use** field if the full amount of the credit memo is not applied against this invoice.

   - Click the **Adjust** button to save the changes and close the Applied Credits and Payments window.

13. **Payment**—Enter the portion of the check that will be used to pay this invoice.

The subtotal calculates automatically and is not editable. The Unused Credits and Unused Payment, in most cases, are both $0.00.

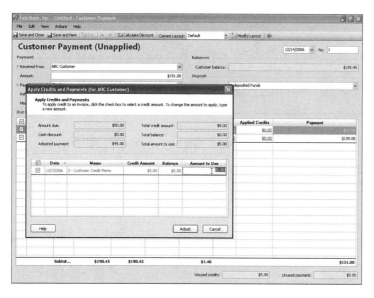

FIGURE 6.40 Click the Applied Credits amount to open the Applied Credits and Payments window, and then change the Applied Credits amount.

Follow these steps when a customer payment is complete:

14. Click the **Save and Close** button. The information is saved and the window closes. Alternatively, click the **Save and New** button. The information saves and the form clears, ready for a new credit memo.

- Click the **Previous** button to see the previous invoice.

- Click the **Next** button to see the next invoice.

- Click the **Current Layout** drop-down list arrow to choose the form layout.

- Click **Modify Layout** to edit the form. Add or delete fields on the form, or move fields to a different position on the form.

When you click the **Save and Close** or **Save and New** button, a warning window appears, as shown in Figure 6.41, if one of the following is true:

- **Unused Payment is less than $0**—Express does not allow the Unused Payment amount to be less than zero. In other words, the check amount must be more than or equal to the payments applied against the invoices.

- **Unused Payment is more than $0**—The check amount is more than the amount applied against invoices. Click **No** and correct the mistake, or click **Yes** and the unapplied amount of the check will be available as a credit to pay invoices in the future.

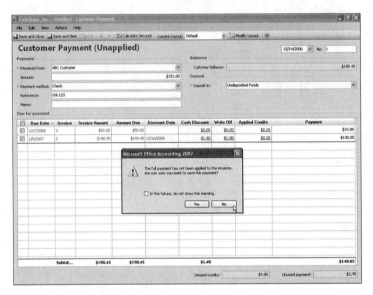

FIGURE 6.41 Usually, the check payment amount will equal the payment subtotal (the amounts applied against invoices) and the unused payment is $0.

CUSTOMER REFUND

Issue customer refunds directly from the **Customers** menu or from a credit memo. Refund the money to the customer from the Customer Refund form using cash, check, credit card, or an electronic payment through online banking.

Issue a customer refund using multiple methods:

Click the **Customers** menu, and then click the **Customer Refund** menu item, as shown in Figure 6.42. The Customer Refund form opens.

Alternatively, on the Customers screen:

1. Under the left **Find** heading, click the **Customer Refunds** link. The Customer Refunds list appears.

2. Click the **Add a New Customer Refund** link. The Customer Refund form opens.

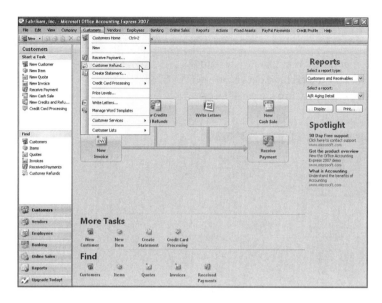

FIGURE 6.42   Refund a payment to a customer.

Or, to issue a refund on an existing credit memo, open the credit memo and click the **Issue Refund** button, as shown in Figure 6.43. The Customer Refund form opens, filled with the credit memo information.

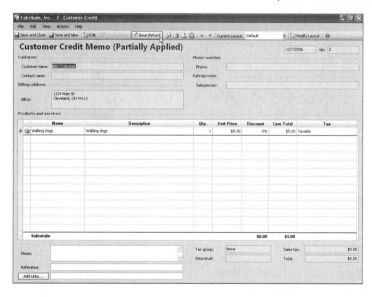

FIGURE 6.43   Issue a refund from an existing credit memo.

To add a customer refund, as shown in Figure 6.44, enter the following information:

1. **Date**—The date of the customer refund is automatically entered with today's date. If a different customer refund date is needed, type the date, or click the drop-down list arrow to select a date from the calendar.

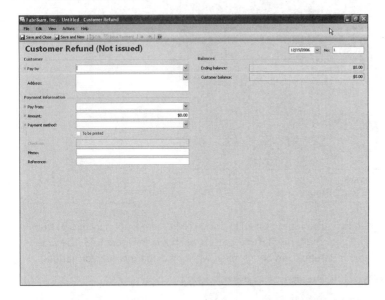

FIGURE 6.44 Complete the Customer Refund form when returning money to a customer.

2. **Customer Refund No.**—The customer refund number field is automatically incremented and the next available number appears. You may type in a different number. If the company preferences do not allow duplicate document numbers, the customer refund number must be a unique number.

⇨ See "Company Preferences" on page 80.

3. **Pay To**—The customer Pay To *name* field is required. Do one of the following:

   - Click the drop-down list arrow and choose the correct customer from the list.
   - Start typing the customer name and the full name appears. When you are done, press the **Enter** or **Tab** key.

     When the customer is found, the remainder of the window fills with the customer's information.

4. **Address**—The Address field is filled in from the bill-to address information entered when the customer was added. If a different address is needed, choose it using the drop-down list arrow or type in the address.

5. **Pay From**—The Pay From field is required. The payment type is a cash, bank, or credit card financial account. Do one of the following:

   - Click the drop-down list arrow and choose the correct financial account from the list.

   - Start typing the financial account. Type the name, or type the account number and the name will appear. When you are finished, press the **Enter** or **Tab** key.

6. **Amount**—The Amount field is required. Enter the dollar amount to refund to the customer.

7. **Payment Method**—The Payment Method field is required. Choose the payment method by typing **Cash**, **Check**, or **Credit Card**; or use the drop-down list arrow and click the correct payment method. If online banking is enabled, Electronic Payment is also available.

8. **To Be Printed**—The To Be Printed check box is checked if you choose Check as the payment method. If a handwritten check is used, uncheck the check box and enter the check number in the Check No. field.

9. **Check No.**—Check No. appears only if the payment method is a check. If a handwritten check is used, enter the check number.

10. **Memo**—Enter comments.

11. **Reference**—Optionally, enter a reference number. For example, the original invoice number of the sale.

The ending balance of the financial account used to pay the refund cannot be edited.

The customer's current balance cannot be edited.

When a customer refund form is complete, click the **Save and Close** button. The information is saved and the window closes. Alternatively, click the **Save and New** button. The information saves and the form clears, ready for a new customer refund.

After the customer refund is saved, you can do the following:

- Click the **Edit** button to change the customer refund.

- Click the **Issue Payment** (or **Reissue Payment** if the customer refund has been edited) button to enter the cash or credit card payment, or to print the check. The Cash Refunds list changes to show the cash refund status as Issued, as shown in Figure 6.45.

  ⇨ See "Print Checks" on page 225 in this chapter.

  If online banking is enabled, Electronic Payment is also available.

- Click the **Previous** button to see the previous invoice.

- Click the **Next** button to see the next invoice.

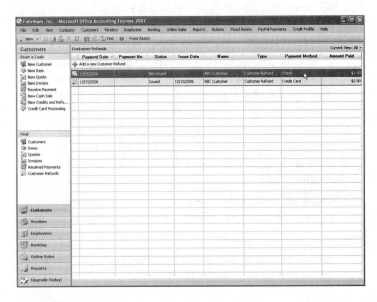

FIGURE 6.45   A customer refund via check will not show as issued unless the check is either handwritten or the check is actually printed.

Vendors

You probably purchase products and services from vendors to use in your business, either as part of products or services to resell or for direct sale to customers. This section covers typical vendor transactions:

- **Vendor Bill**—Vendor Bill records the purchase of products and services with no payment or partial payment.

  ⇨ See "Enter Bills" on page 174.

- **Cash Purchase**—Cash Purchase records both the purchase and immediate payment. Payment forms include cash, check, credit card, and online forms of payment.

  ➪ See "New Cash Purchase" on page 178.

- **Credit Memo**—Credit Memo records a full or partial amount owed to your company by a vendor. It can be used to offset current or future bills or a vendor refund. A credit memo is also important as a reminder if the vendor forgets to send a check or credit card refund, or sends the wrong amount. Refunds to the company credit card do not use a credit memo; use the Credit Card account instead.

  ➪ See "New Vendor Credit Memo" on page 183.

- **Pay Bills**—Pay Bills selects vendor bills to pay and records the intent to pay. The actual payment may be made at the same time or remain unissued and paid later using Issue Payment, Write Checks, or Credit Card Charge.

  ➪ See "Pay Bills" on page 189.

- **Issue Payment**—Issue Payment issues payment for an unissued payment. For example, when a vendor payment check is waiting to be printed until funds are available, use Issue Payment to finally print the check.

  ➪ See "Issue Payment" on page 197.

- **Vendor Payment**—Use vendor payments to record an advance deposit or prepayment of any type (check, cash, or credit card).

  ➪ See "Vendor Payment" on page 201.

- **Record Expenses**—Record Expenses first asks for the type of payment. It uses Cash Purchase for cash payments, Write Checks for check purchases, and Credit Card Charge for credit card purchases.

  ➪ See "Record Expenses" on page 205.

Notice that some transactions could be recorded using one of several forms, depending on your preference. For example, a purchase with payment made in full at the time of the purchase could use either Cash Purchase or Record Expenses.

ENTER BILLS

Enter a vendor bill in Express when you receive an invoice from the vendor. Record the vendor bill using the Vendor Bill form, and later pay the bill. Express calls it a vendor *bill* instead of a vendor *invoice* to prevent confusion with customer invoices.

Express does not require you to enter vendor bills in order to pay a vendor. If a vendor presents a bill and is paid immediately, you can write a check and record the expense without entering a bill.

> ⟶ For more information, see "Record Expenses" on page 205 or "New Cash Purchase" on page 178 in this chapter.

On the Vendors screen, click the **Enter Bills** button, as shown in Figure 6.46. A new Vendor Bill form appears.

Alternatively, on the Vendors screen, under **Start a Task**, click the **Enter Bills** link.

Or, on the Vendors screen, under either **Find** heading, click the **Bills** link. The Bill list shows. Click the **Add a New Bill** link.

Or, click the **Vendors** menu, **Enter Bills**.

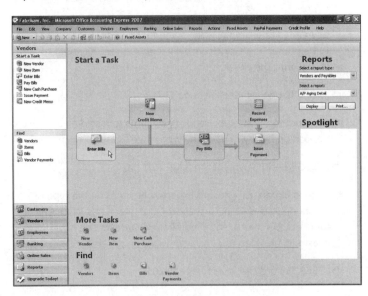

FIGURE 6.46 Create a new vendor bill when the company owes money to a vendor.

To add a bill, enter the following information, as shown in Figure 6.47:

1. **Current Layout**—Choose the default bill form layout or one of the bill forms that you design yourself. Click **Modify Layout** to edit the form to your unique needs by adding or deleting fields or moving fields to a different position on the form.

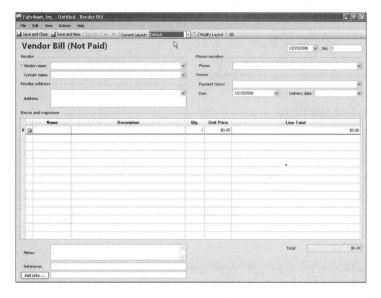

FIGURE 6.47   Enter the Vendor Bill information.

2. **Date**—The date of the bill is automatically entered using today's date. If a different date is needed, type the date or click the drop-down arrow to select a date from the calendar.

3. **Bill No.**—The bill number is automatically incremented and the next available number appears. You can type in a different number. If the company preferences do not allow duplicate document numbers, the bill number must be a unique number.

See "Company Preferences" on page 80.

4. **Vendor Name**—The Vendor Name field is required. Do one of the following:

   - Click the drop-down list arrow and choose the correct vendor from the list. If the vendor is new, click the first line in the list, **Add a New Vendor**.

- Start typing the vendor name and the full name will appear if the name has already been added as a vendor. When you are finished, press the **Enter** or **Tab** key. If the vendor is new, a window will appear asking whether you would like to add the vendor.

If the new vendor warning window appears, you have several available options:

- Click the **Set Up** button to add the vendor and as much information as you can about them. From that point on, Express will enter the vendor's information on new bills. This saves time.

- Alternatively, click the **Fast Add** button to add only the name of the vendor. Later, when you save the bill, Express tells you that the information about the vendor has changed (for example, the address and payment terms), and asks whether you would like to save the new information permanently in the vendor file.

- Click **No** if you made a spelling error. Then either correct the spelling of the vendor's name or choose the vendor using the drop-down list arrow.

5. **Contact Name**—The Contact Name field is filled in from the primary contact entered when the vendor was added. If a different vendor contact is needed, choose it using the drop-down list arrow. Express will not permit a contact that is not in the vendor's Contacts list.

6. **Vendor Address**—The Vendor Address field is filled in from when the vendor was added. If a different address is needed, choose it using the drop-down list arrow or type in the address.

7. **Phone Number**—The Phone Number field is filled in from the phone number entered when the vendor was added. If a different phone number is needed, choose it using the drop-down list arrow or type in the phone number.

8. **Payment Terms**—The Payment Terms field is filled in from the payment term entered when the vendor was added. If a different payment term is needed, do one of the following:

- Click the drop-down list arrow and choose the correct payment term from the list of all payment terms. If the payment term is new, click the first line in the list, **Add a New Payment Term**.

- Start typing the payment term and the full name will appear. When you're finished, press the **Enter** or **Tab** key. If the payment term is new, a window will appear asking whether you would like to add the term to the Payment Terms list.

9. **Due**—The Due date field is the last date to pay the bill without being late. Express fills in the due date based on the Bill Date and the Payment Terms fields. To change the due date, type the date or click the drop-down arrow to select a date from the calendar.

10. **Delivery Date**—The Delivery Date field is the date the company received the product or service. Type the date, or click the drop-down arrow to select a date from the calendar.

In the Items and Expenses section, enter the following:

11. **Name**—Click the drop-down list arrow, and then click one of the following, as shown in Figure 6.48:

    - **Expense**—A financial account.

    - **Item**—A product or service.

    - **Comment**—A multiline comment in the description column. A comment can also be a blank line.

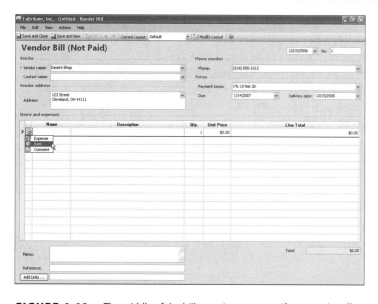

FIGURE 6.48 The middle of the bill contains expenses (for example, office supplies), line items (products and services), and comments.

12. **Description**—Multiple lines of text.

13. **Qty.**—Quantity, required. The quantity can be a positive number, a negative number, or 0.

14. **Unit Price**—Optional; the Unit Price can be only a positive number or 0.

15. **Line Total**—A calculated total. Line total equals quantity multiplied by price. Editing the line total will change the unit price.

16. **Memo**—Not typically printed. You might want to use the Memo field to detail any changes made to the bill and why.

17. **Reference**—You might want to enter your purchase order number.

18. **Add Links button**—Used to attach one or more files. For example, scan in the purchase order, save the file(s), and click the **Add Links** button. Then locate the file(s) on the computer and click the **OK** button. The filename appears in **Add Links**.

The Total field cannot be edited.

When a bill is complete, click the **Save and Close** button. The information is saved and the window closes. Alternatively, click the **Save and New** button. The information saves and the form clears, ready for a new bill.

If the bill contains new or edited vendor information, a window appears asking whether the information should be permanently saved, updating any previous information. Typically, you should answer **Yes**. The changed information is saved in the vendor's file and is available for future bills. Answering **No** only saves the information with the bill and does not update the vendor's file.

After completing a bill, click the **Actions** menu, and then choose to create a new bill or a credit memo for this bill. Or you can pay, edit, or void (but not delete) the bill.

NEW CASH PURCHASE

Use New Cash Purchase to record the purchase of an item or service with a handwritten check, credit card, or cash payment at the time the purchase is made.

Add a cash purchase using multiple methods:

On the Vendors screen, under **Start a Task**, click the **New Cash Purchase** link on the left, as shown in Figure 6.49. A Cash Purchase form appears.

Alternatively, click the **Vendors** menu, **New**, **New Cash Purchase**.

Or, on the Vendors screen, click the **New Cash Purchase** link under **More Tasks**.

Finally, also on the Vendors screen, you can click the **Record Expenses** button, and then click an expense type of **Cash**.

⇨   See "Record Expenses" on page 205.

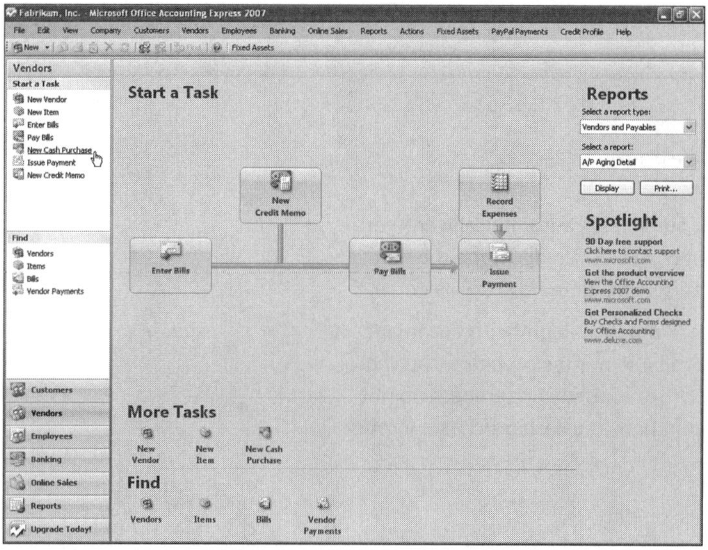

FIGURE 6.49   Record a purchase with a handwritten check, credit card, or cash payment made at the time of purchase.

To add a cash purchase, as shown in Figure 6.50, enter the following information:

1. **Current Layout**—Choose the default cash purchase form layout or one of the cash purchase forms that you design yourself. Click **Modify Layout** to edit the form to your unique needs by adding or deleting fields or moving fields to a different position on the form.

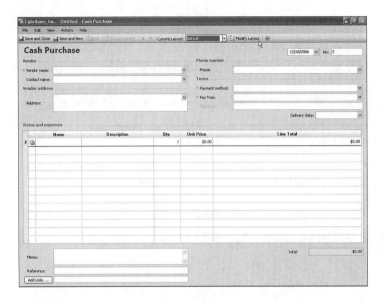

FIGURE 6.50   Record the purchase of items or services.

2. **Date**—The date of the cash purchase is automatically entered using today's date. If a different date is needed, type the date, or click the drop-down arrow to select a date from the calendar.

3. **Cash Purchase No.**—The cash purchase number is automatically incremented and the next available number appears. You can type in a different number. If the company preferences do not allow duplicate document numbers, the cash purchase number must be a unique number.

⟹   See "Company Preferences" on page 80.

4. **Vendor Name**—The Vendor Name field is required. Do one of the following:

   - Click the drop-down list arrow and choose the correct vendor from the list. If the vendor is new, click the first line in the list, **Add a New Vendor**.

   - Start typing the vendor name and the full name will appear if the name has already been added as a vendor. When you are finished, press the **Enter** or **Tab** key. If the vendor is new, a window will appear asking whether you would like to add the vendor.

If the new vendor warning window appears, do one of the following:

- Click the **Set Up** button to add the vendor and as much information as you can about them. From that point on, Express will enter the vendor's information on new cash purchases and bills. This saves time.

- Click the **Fast Add** button to add only the name of the vendor. Later, when you save the cash purchase, Express tells you that the information about the vendor has changed (for example, the address and payment method), and asks whether you would like to save the new information permanently in the vendor file.

- Click **No** if you made a spelling error. Then either correct the spelling of the vendor's name or choose the vendor using the drop-down list arrow.

5. **Contact Name**—The Contact Name field is filled in from the primary contact entered when the vendor was added. If a different vendor contact is needed, choose it using the drop-down list arrow. Express will not permit a contact that is not in the vendor's Contacts list.

6. **Vendor Address**—The Vendor Address field is filled in from when the vendor was added. If a different address is needed, choose it using the drop-down list arrow or type in the address.

7. **Phone Number**—The Phone Number field is filled in from the phone number entered when the vendor was added. If a different phone number is needed, choose it using the drop-down list arrow or type in the phone number.

8. **Payment Method**—The Payment Method field is required. Cash is shown. If a different payment term is needed, do one of the following:

- Click the drop-down list arrow and choose **Check** or **Credit Card**.

- Start typing the payment method, and the full name will appear. When you're finished, press the **Enter** or **Tab** key.

9. **Payment From**—Payment From is required. Enter the financial account. Click the drop-down list and choose the correct bank, credit card, or cash account; or start typing the financial account name or number and the full name will appear. When you're finished, press the **Enter** or **Tab** key.

10. **Check No.**—Check No. appears only if you choose **Check** as the payment method. Enter the check number for the manual check.

11. **Delivery Date**—Delivery Date is the date the company received the product or service. Type the date or click the drop-down arrow to select a date from the calendar.

    In the Items and Expenses section, enter the following:

12. **Name**—Click the drop-down list arrow, and then click one of the following, as shown in Figure 6.51:

    - **Expense**—A financial account.

    - **Item**—A product or service.

    - **Comment**—A multiline comment in the description column. A comment may also be a blank line.

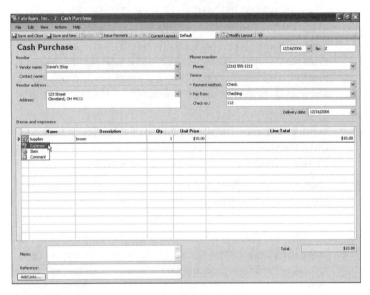

FIGURE 6.51 The middle of the form contains expenses (for example, office supplies), line items (products and services), and comments.

13. **Description**—Multiple lines of text.

14. **Qty.**—Quantity is required for an expense or item. Quantity can be a positive number, a negative number, or 0.

15. **Unit Price**—Unit Price is optional. It can be only a positive number or 0.

16. **Line Total**—A calculated total. Line total equals quantity multiplied by price. Editing the line total will change the unit price.

17. Memo—Memo is not typically printed. You might want to use the Memo field to detail any changes made to the cash purchase form and why.

18. Reference—You might want to enter your purchase order number.

19. Add Links button—Used to attach one or more files. For example, scan in the purchase order, save the file(s), and click the **Add Links** button. Then locate the file(s) on the computer and click the **OK** button. The filename appears in Add Links.

The Total field cannot be edited.

When a cash purchase is complete, click the **Save and Close** button. The information is saved and the window closes. Alternatively, click the **Save and New** button. The information saves and the form clears, ready for a new cash purchase.

If the cash purchase contains new or edited vendor information, a window appears asking if the information should be permanently saved, updating any previous information. Typically, answer **Yes**. The changed information is saved in the vendor's file and is available for future cash purchases and bills. Answering **No** only saves the information with the cash purchase and does not update the vendor's file.

After completing a cash purchase, you can issue payment, as shown in Figure 6.52, create a new cash purchase or a credit memo for this cash purchase, or you can edit or void (but not delete) the cash payment. The payment can be reissued for a handwritten check only. This means the previous check is voided and a new check is written.

NEW VENDOR CREDIT MEMO

A credit memo reverses a previous vendor transaction, indicating that the vendor owes your company. After a credit memo is issued, the credit memo can be applied against an outstanding current or future vendor bill, or money is refunded by the vendor.

Add a credit memo using multiple methods:

On the Vendors screen, under Start a Task, click the **New Credit Memo** button, as shown in Figure 6.53. The Vendor Credit Memo form opens.

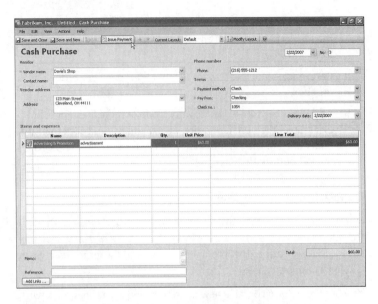

FIGURE 6.52   You can issue or reissue payment for the cash purchase.

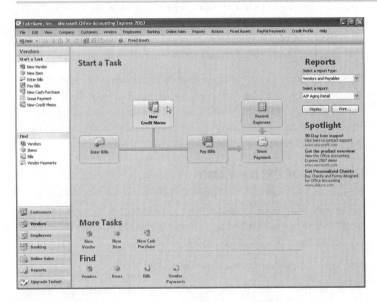

FIGURE 6.53   You use credit memos when you owe less than the bill; for example, when an item is returned or a service is not used, or when there is a problem and you receive a partial credit.

Alternatively, follow this procedure:

1. Click the **Vendors** menu.

2. Click the **New** menu item.

3. Click **New Credit Memo**.

Or, to create a vendor credit memo from an existing bill, do the following:

1. From a bill, click the **Actions** menu.

2. Click the **Create Vendor Credit Memo** menu item. The Vendor Credit Memo form opens, filled with the bill information.

Or, on the Vendors screen, do the following:

1. Under either **Find** heading, click the **Bills** link. The Bill list appears.

2. Right-click a bill, and then choose **New Credit Memo**. The Vendor Credit Memo form opens.

Or, open a new vendor credit memo using one of the preceding methods, and then click the **Create From** button, as shown near the top in Figure 6.54. The Select a Bill window opens. Click a vendor bill to choose it, and then click **OK**.

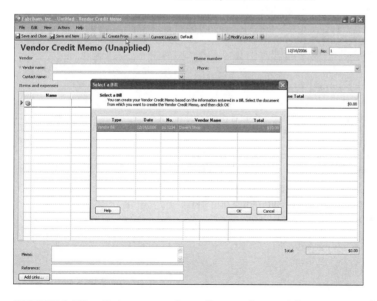

FIGURE 6.54   Open a new vendor credit memo form, and then create a vendor credit memo from a bill.

To add a vendor credit memo, as shown in Figure 6.55, enter the following information:

1. **Current Layout**—Choose the default cash purchase form layout or one of the cash purchase forms that you design yourself. Click **Modify Layout** to edit the form to your unique needs by adding or deleting fields or by moving fields to a different position on the form.

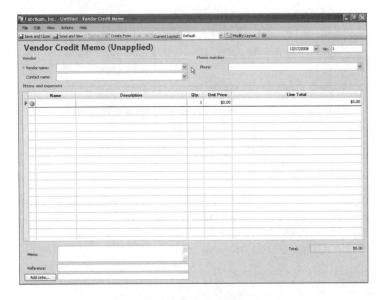

FIGURE 6.55 Complete the Vendor Credit Memo form.

2. **Date**—The date of the credit memo is automatically entered using today's date. If a different credit memo date is needed, type the date or click the drop-down arrow to select a date from the calendar.

3. **Credit Memo No.**—The credit memo number is automatically incremented and the next available number appears. You can type in a different number. If the company preferences do not allow duplicate document numbers, the credit memo number must be a unique number.

⇨ See "Company Preferences" on page 80.

4. **Vendor Name**—The Vendor Name field is required. Do one of the following:

   - Click the drop-down list arrow and choose the correct vendor from the list.

   - Start typing the vendor name and the full name will appear. When you're finished, press the **Enter** or **Tab** key.

5. **Contact Name**—The Contact Name field is filled in from the primary contact entered when the vendor was added. If a different vendor contact is needed, choose it using the drop-down list arrow. Express will not permit a contact that is not in the vendor's Contacts list.

6. **Phone Number**—The Phone field is filled in from the phone number entered when the vendor was added. If a different phone number is needed, choose it using the drop-down list arrow or type in the phone number.

In the Items and Services section, enter the following information:

7. **Name**—Click the drop-down list arrow, and then click one of the following:

   - **Expense**—A financial account to which to post; for example, the Freight expense account.

   - **Item**—A product or service.

   - **Comment**—A multiline comment in the Description column. A comment can also be a blank line.

8. **Description**—Multiple lines of text.

9. **Qty.**—Quantity, a required field for Item and Expense line items. Quantity can be a positive number, a negative number, or 0.

10. **Unit Price**—Used for Item and Expense line items. Unit Price can be only a positive number or 0.

11. **Line Total**—A calculated total. Line total equals quantity multiplied by price. The line total can be edited and affects the unit price.

12. **Memo**—Comments. For example, use the Memo field to detail any changes made when editing the credit memo and why.

13. **Reference**—You might want to enter the original document number the credit memo references.

14. **Add Links button**—Used to attach one or more files. For example, scan in the documentation to defend the decision to issue a credit memo, save the file(s), and click the **Add Links** button. Then locate the file(s) on the computer and click **OK**. The filename shows in Add Links.

The Total field cannot be edited.

When a credit memo is complete, click the **Save and Close** button. The information is saved and the window closes. Alternatively, click the **Save and New** button. The information saves and the form clears, ready for a new credit memo.

After a credit memo is saved, the following options are available to you:

- Click the **Edit** button to make changes to the saved information.
- Click the **Previous** button to see the previous invoice.
- Click the **Next** button to see the next invoice.
- Click the **Current Layout** drop-down list arrow to choose the form layout.
- Click **Modify Layout** to edit the form. Add or delete fields on the form or move fields to a different position on the form.
- Click the **Actions** menu, and then click **Void** to void the vendor credit memo. It cannot be deleted.

A check refund against the credit memo is applied when the refund is received from the vendor.

For example, create a vendor credit memo of $5 for damaged merchandise from an open bill for $10, and then save the vendor credit memo. In the Bill list, the bill will be reduced by the amount of the vendor credit memo, showing a bill balance of $5 and a credit memo balance of $0, indicating that it has been applied to the bill.

On the Vendors screen, click the **Bills** link under the Find heading. The Bill List opens, as shown in Figure 6.56. Notice that the credit memo has been applied to the bill.

⇨ See "Make Deposits" on page 233 in this chapter.

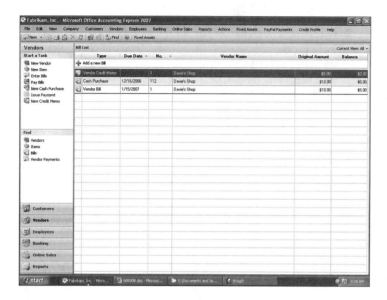

FIGURE 6.56 The credit memo has been applied to the bill.

PAY BILLS

Pay Bills enables you to pay one or more vendors and one or more bills. After recording a vendor bill, make a full or partial payment at any time.

Pay a bill using the following methods:

On the Vendors screen, click the **Pay Bills** button, as shown in Figure 6.57.

Alternatively, click the **Vendors** menu, **Pay Bills** menu item.

Or, on the Vendors screen, under either **Find** heading, click the **Bills** link. The Bill list appears. Right-click a bill. Click the **Pay Bill** menu item. The Pay Bill form opens with the bill information.

To pay a bill on an existing vendor bill, open a bill, click the **Actions** menu, and then the **Pay Bill** menu item, as shown in Figure 6.58. The Pay Bill form opens, filled with the bill information.

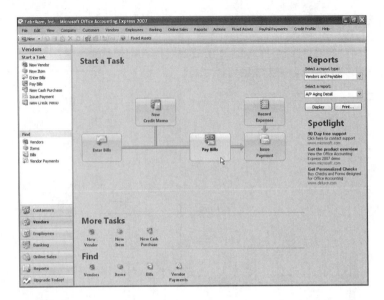

FIGURE 6.57   Pay a bill from a vendor.

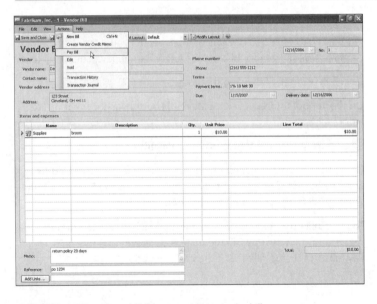

FIGURE 6.58   Pay a bill from an existing vendor bill.

To pay bills, as shown in Figure 6.59, enter the following information:

1. The date of the payment is automatically entered with today's date. If a different payment date is needed, type the date or click the drop-down arrow to select a date from the calendar.

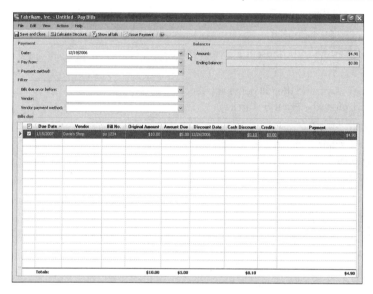

FIGURE 6.59 Complete the Pay Bill form when paying one or more vendor bills.

2. The Pay From field is required. The payment type is a cash, bank, or credit card financial account. Do one of the following:

   ■ Click the drop-down list arrow and choose the correct financial account from the list.

   ■ Start typing the financial account. Type the name, or type the account number and the name will appear. When you're finished, press the **Enter** or **Tab** key.

3. The Payment Method field is required. Choose the payment method by typing **Cash**, **Check**, or **Credit Card**; or use the drop-down list arrow and then click the correct payment method. If online banking is enabled, Electronic Payment is also available.

Bills can remain unfiltered, displaying all bills owed, or they can be filtered to display only those bills with the following:

4. **Bill Due On or Before**—Automatically entered with today's date. If a different date is needed, type the date or click the drop-down arrow to select a date from the calendar.

5. **Vendor**—Take one of the following actions:

   ■ Click the drop-down list arrow and choose the correct vendor from the list.

   ■ Start typing the vendor name and the full name appears. When you are finished, press the **Enter** or **Tab** key.

6. **Vendor Payment Method**—Cash, Check, or Credit Card. Electronic Payment is an option if online banking is enabled. Express compares this to the preferred vendor payment method previously entered on the vendor form when the vendor was added.

In Balances, the Amount field cannot be edited. It shows the total amount to be paid, including credits and discounts.

The Ending Balance field cannot be edited. It shows the ending balance in the Pay From financial account chosen earlier. This balance changes when a bill is checkmarked or uncheckmarked, or a credit, discount, or payment amount is changed on a bill in the Bills Due section.

To see all bills, click the **Show All Bills** button, as shown in Figure 6.60. The Bills Due section shows one open bill on each line. Change how the bills sort by clicking a column heading. A small Sort By arrow appears next to the column name and the bill rows sort by that column. Click the arrow again to change the sort order of the column from A–Z to Z–A.

Click the **Select All** check box to select all bills for payment. The bills to be paid have a checkmark. Uncheck a specific bill to not pay it or checkmark a bill to pay it.

In the Bills Due section, as shown in Figure 6.61, for each invoice, the Due Date, Vendor, Bill No., Original Amount, Amount Due, and Discount Date fields are not editable. You can change the following:

7. **Cash Discount**—The amount the bill is reduced because of an early payment made by a specific date. For example, 1%/10 Net 30 allows a 1% cash discount if payment is made within 10 days of the bill date. For a $500 bill, the cash discount would be $5. The amount owed if paid within 10 days of the bill date would be $495; otherwise, $500 is owed within 30 days.

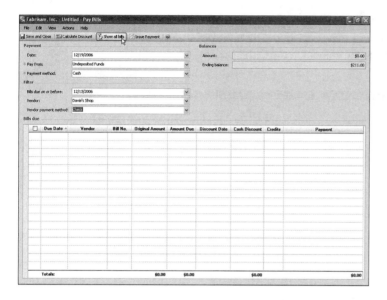

FIGURE 6.60   Click the Show All Bills button to remove all filters. All bills will appear in the Bills Due section.

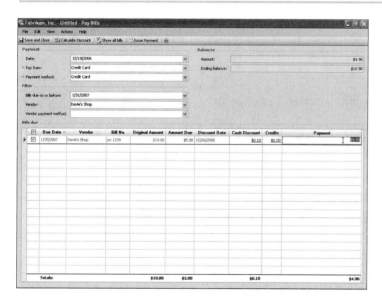

FIGURE 6.61   If you want to distribute the payment differently, change the cash discount, credits, or payment amounts for each bill.

The discount can be calculated automatically by clicking the **Calculate Discount** button, as shown in Figure 6.62. If the discount is off a penny, change the amount in the Cash Discount field.

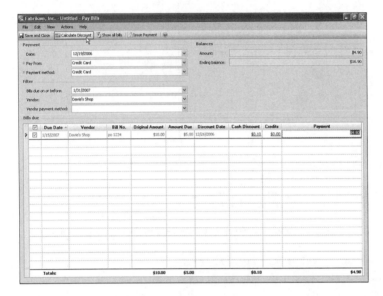

FIGURE 6.62   Click the Calculate Discount button to calculate the discount automatically.

8. **Cash Discount**—Shows the discount taken. To change the account or amount:

   ■ Click the **Cash Discount** amount, as shown in Figure 6.63. The Cash Discount window opens.

   ■ Change the cash discount account or amount.

   ■ Click the **OK** button. The window closes.

9. **Applied Credits and Payments**—Shows applied credits, as shown in Figure 6.64. To use some of or all the credit:

   ■ Change the **Amount to Use** field if the full amount of the credit is not applied against this bill.

   ■ Click the **Adjust** button to save the changes and close the Applied Credits and Payments window.

10. **Payment**—Enter the payment for this bill.

The Total field calculates automatically and cannot be edited.

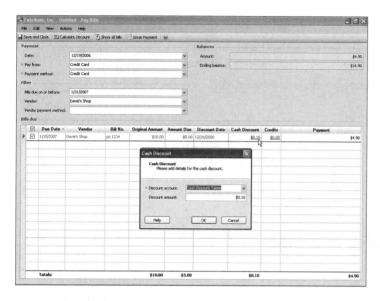

FIGURE 6.63 Click the Cash Discount amount to open the Cash Discount window, and then change the cash discount account or amount.

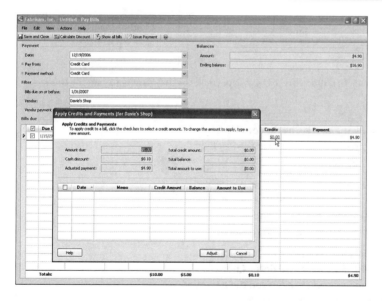

FIGURE 6.64 Click the Credits amount to open the Apply Credits and Payments window, and then change the amount to use.

After completing the Pay Bills form, you have several options:

- Click the **Save and Close** or the **Save and New** button to record a handwritten check or issue payment for one or more bills later.

- Click the **Issue Payment** button, as shown in Figure 6.65. A window opens.

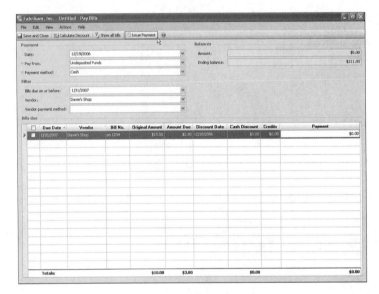

FIGURE 6.65   Click the Issue Payment button to record a cash or credit card payment or to start the check-printing process.

To issue payment, checkmark the **Mark Checks for Printing** field. Click **OK**. Express automatically asks to save the Pay Bills information before issuing payment.

If you do not choose to issue payment at this time, uncheck **Mark Checks for Printing**, and then click **OK**. The information is saved and the window closes. The payment is shown as Unissued in the Vendor Payments list, and can be issued later.

To enter a manual check, click the **Issue Payment** button and checkmark the **Write Checks Manually and Enter Check Numbers** field to record handwritten checks. Type the handwritten check number, or click the **Prefill Check Numbers** button, as shown in Figure 6.66, to use the next available check number.

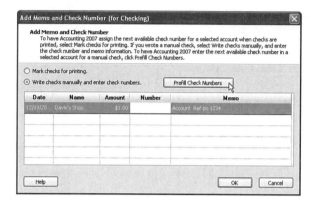

FIGURE 6.66   Use the Prefill Check Numbers button to automatically enter the next check number.

ISSUE PAYMENT

After you enter a bill it can be paid in full, or partial payments can be made. A check payment remains Not Issued until printed, and changes to Issued when printed.

Checks that are not printed or handwritten are recorded as Not Issued, as shown in Figure 6.67. This happens when payment is recorded on Pay Bills, Vendor Payment, Customer Refund, Employee Payment, or Checks and the checks are not printed at that time. Payments marked as Not Issued appear in the Vendor Payments list. Checks may be printed at any time using Issue Payments.

Open the Select Payments to Issue form using one of the following methods:

- On the Vendors screen, click the **Issue Payment** button, as shown in Figure 6.68.

- Click the **Vendors** menu, **Issue Payments** menu item.

- Click the **Issue Payment** link.

- Under the **Find** heading, click **Vendor Payments**. The Vendor Payments list appears. Right-click the vendor payment and click **Issue Payment**, as shown in Figure 6.69.

- On the Vendor Payment screen, click the **Issue Payment** button, as shown in Figure 6.70.

- On the Vendor Payment screen, click the **Actions** menu, **Issue Payment**.

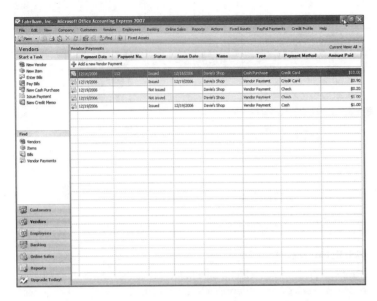

FIGURE 6.67 The Vendor Payments list shows the status of each vendor payment (issued or unissued); the payment method (check, credit card, cash, or electronic payment); and the amount of the payment.

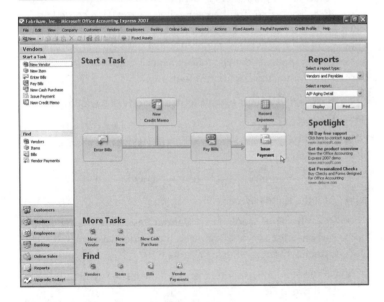

FIGURE 6.68 Issue payments to vendors.

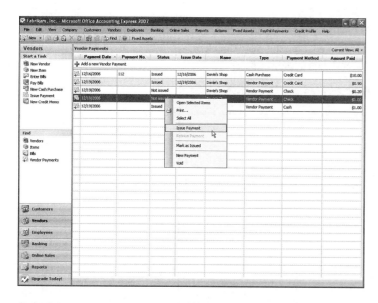

FIGURE 6.69   Print a check from the Vendor Payments list.

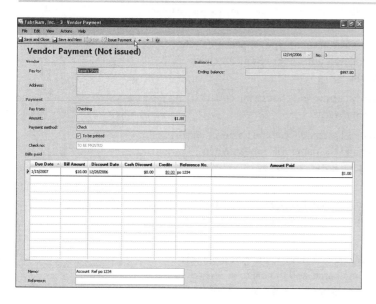

FIGURE 6.70   Pay a bill from an existing vendor payment.

To print checks, enter the following information, as shown in Figure 6.71:

1. The Payment Method field is required. Type the word **Check** or use the drop-down list arrow and then click **Check**.

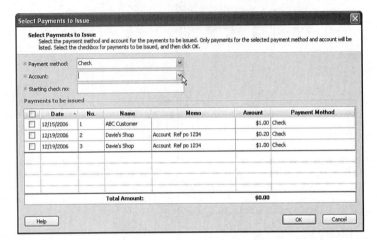

FIGURE 6.71   Complete the Select Payments to Issue form when making payments.

2. The Account field is required. The account types shown are Cash, Bank, or Credit Card Financial Account. Choose **Bank** for check printing. Do one of the following:

   - Click the drop-down list arrow and choose the correct financial account from the list.

   - Start typing the financial account. Type the name, or type the account number and the name will appear. When you're finished, press the **Enter** or **Tab** key.

The Payments to Be Issued section shows one row per payment. The Date, Vendor, No., Name, Memo, Amount, and Payment Method cannot be edited on this form.

Change how payments sort by clicking a column heading. A small Sort By arrow appears next to the column name, and the bill rows sort by that column. Click the arrow again to change the sort order of the column from A–Z to Z–A.

Click the **Select All** check box in the column heading to select all payments to print. Each payment to print has a check box. Uncheck a specific payment to stop paying it. Checkmark a payment to pay it.

Click **OK** to begin printing the checks.

⇨ See "Print Checks" on page 225.

VENDOR PAYMENT

A vendor payment is used to prepay a vendor before a vendor bill is received, or to view, edit, void, or issue a vendor payment that has already been recorded.

On the Vendor screen, under the **Find** heading, click **Vendor Payments**. The Vendor Payments list appears.

To add a new vendor payment, click the **Add a New Vendor Payment** link.

Or, in the **Vendors** menu, click the **New Vendor Payment** menu.

To edit a vendor payment, double-click the previously entered vendor payment to open it, as shown in Figure 6.72. The Vendor Payments form opens with the payment information.

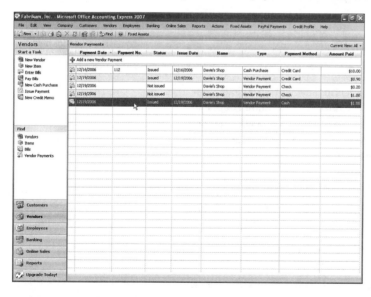

FIGURE 6.72   View an existing vendor payment.

To add a vendor payment, as shown in Figure 6.73, enter the following information:

1. **Date**—The date of the payment is automatically entered with today's date. If a different payment date is needed, type the date or click the drop-down arrow to select a date from the calendar.

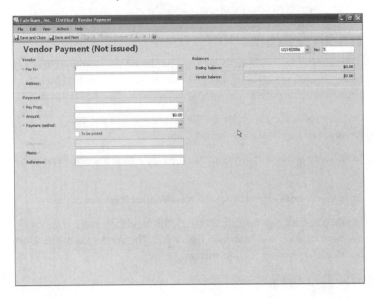

FIGURE 6.73 Complete the Vendor Payment form when prepaying a vendor, or when paying a vendor before the invoice is received.

2. **Vendor Payment No.**—The Vendor Payment No. field is automatically incremented and the next available number appears. You can type in a different number. If the company preferences do not allow duplicate document numbers, the vendor payment number must be a unique number.

⇨ See "Company Preferences" on page 80.

3. **Pay To**—The Pay To field is required. Do one of the following:

   - Click the drop-down list arrow and choose the correct vendor from the list. If the vendor is new, click the first line in the list, **Add a New Vendor**.

   - Start typing the vendor name and the full name will appear if the name has already been added as a vendor. When you are finished, press the **Enter** or **Tab** key. If the vendor is new, a window will appear asking whether you would like to add the vendor.

If the new vendor warning window appears, do one of the following:

- Click the **Set Up** button to add the vendor and as much information as you can about them. From that point on, Express will enter the vendor's information on new cash purchases and bills. This saves time.

- Click the **Fast Add** button to add only the name of the vendor. Later, when you save the cash purchase, Express tells you that the information about the vendor has changed (for example, the address and payment method), and asks whether you would like to save the new information permanently in the vendor file.

- Click the **No** button if you made a spelling error. Then either correct the spelling of the vendor's name or choose the vendor using the drop-down list arrow.

4. **Address**—The vendor Address field is filled in from when the vendor was added. If a different address is needed, choose it using the drop-down list arrow or type in the address.

5. **Payment From**—The Payment From field is required. The payment type is a cash, bank, or credit card financial account. Take one of the following actions:

- Click the drop-down list arrow and choose the correct financial account from the list.

- Start typing the financial account. Type the name, or type the account number and the name will appear. When you're finished, press the **Enter** or **Tab** key.

6. **Amount**—The Amount field is required. Enter the amount of the payment.

7. **Payment Method**—The Payment Method field is required. Choose the payment method by typing **Cash**, **Check**, or **Credit Card**; or use the drop-down list arrow and click the correct payment method. If online banking is enabled, Electronic Payment is also available.

8. **To Be Printed**—If a check is to be printed, checkmark the To Be Printed check box.

9. **Check No.**—The Check No. field is filled in only if a handwritten check is used.

10. **Memo**—Use this for comments.

11. **Reference**—You might want to enter the original document number the payment references.

The Ending Balance field cannot be edited. It shows the ending balance in the Pay From financial account chosen earlier. This balance changes when a bill is checkmarked or uncheckmarked, or a credit, discount, or payment amount is changed on a bill in the Bills Due section.

The Vendor Balance field cannot be edited. It shows the vendor's current balance and updates when the amount changes.

When a payment is complete:

■ Click the **Issue Payment** button, as shown in Figure 6.74, unless a handwritten check is used or the payment is to be paid later.

Express automatically asks to save the payment information before issuing payment. Click **OK**.

Express displays a window saying payment has been issued. Click **OK**.

■ Alternatively, click the **Save and Close** button to record hand-written checks or to issue payment later.

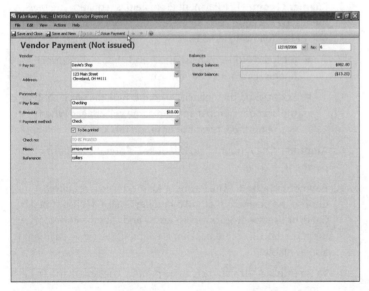

FIGURE 6.74   Click the Issue Payment button to record a cash or credit card payment or to start the check-printing process.

Click the **Credits** link to edit the credit amount, as shown in Figure 6.75. The Apply Credits and Payments window opens.

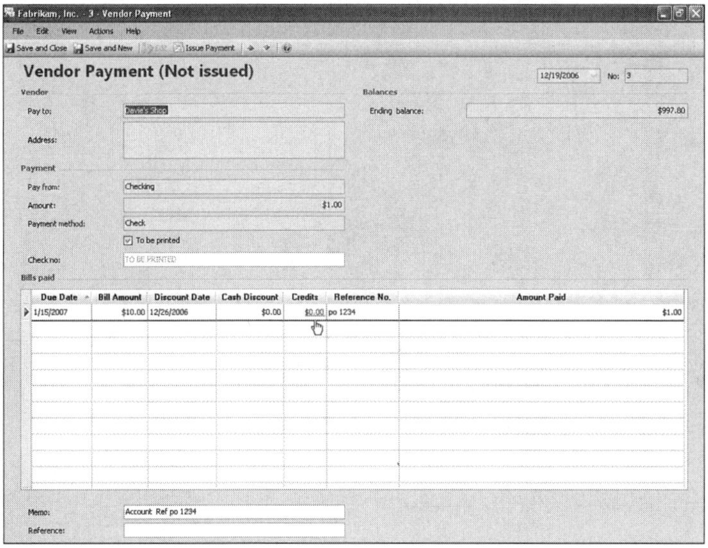

FIGURE 6.75 Edit an existing vendor payment, adding a vendor's credit memo, and then issue payment for the reduced amount.

RECORD EXPENSES

Record Expenses is used to record any type of expense payment—cash, manual or printed check, or credit card.

Open the Record Expense form using multiple methods:

On the Vendors screen, click the **Record Expenses** button.

Alternatively, on the Vendors screen, do the following:

1. Click the **Vendors** menu.
2. Click the **Record Expenses** menu item, as shown in Figure 6.76. A window opens asking the payment type, as shown in Figure 6.77.

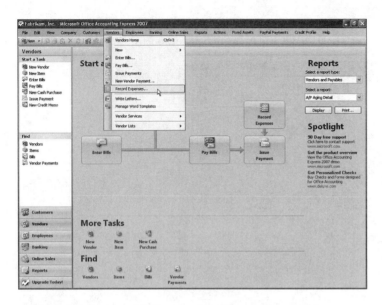

FIGURE 6.76 Record a cash, manual check, or credit card expense.

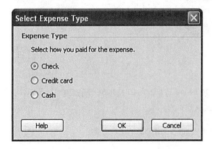

FIGURE 6.77 Select how the expense was paid.

Checkmark either Check, Credit Card, or Cash, and then click the **OK** button.

- Check expenses use Banking—Write Checks.

⇨ See "Write Checks" on page 220.

- Credit Card expenses use Banking—Credit Card Charge.

⇨ See "Credit Card Charge" on page 229.

- Cash expenses use Cash Purchase.

⇨ See "New Cash Purchase" on page 178.

Employees

The Employees section covers typical employee transactions:

- **Time Entry**—Time Entry is used to record one employee's time record for one activity during one time period.

  ⇨ See "New Time Entry" on this page.

- **Timesheet**—Timesheet records one week of time entries for an employee. All previously entered Time Entry records for that week also appear on the Timesheet. Use the Time Entry list to select multiple time entries to create a customer invoice.

  ⇨ See "New Timesheet" on page 211.

- **Employee Payment**—Employee Payment records employee advances and expenses.

  ⇨ See "Employee Payments" on page 215.

Express integrates with ADP Payroll.

  ⇨ See "ADP Payroll" on page 352.

Alternatively, ask your accountant how to record journal entries and print checks for manual payroll.

NEW TIME ENTRY

Time entry is used to record billable or nonbillable hours.

Add a time entry using multiple methods:

On the Employees screen, click the **New Time Entry** button, as shown in Figure 6.78.

Alternatively, open a time entry through the **Employee** menu, **New Time Entry** menu item.

Or, on the Employees screen:

1. Under either **Find** heading, click the **Time Entries** link. The Time Entry list appears.

2. Click the **Add a New Time Entry** link. A new Time Entry form appears.

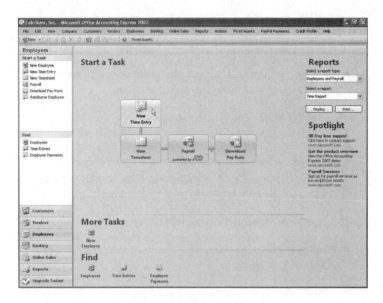

FIGURE 6.78   Open a time entry on the Employees screen by clicking the New Time Entry button or link.

To add a new time entry, as shown in Figure 6.79, enter the following information:

1. **Current Layout**—You can create your own time entry form or use the default form.

    ⇨   See "Modifying Entry Forms" on page 340 in Chapter 9 to create a custom data entry form.

2. **Date**—The date of the time entry is automatically entered using today's date. If a different time entry date is needed, type the date or click the drop-down arrow to select a date from the calendar.

3. **Time Entry No.**—The Time Entry No. field is automatically incremented and the next available number appears. You can type in a different number. If the company preferences do not allow duplicate document numbers, the time entry number must be a unique number.

    ⇨   See "Company Preferences" on page 80.

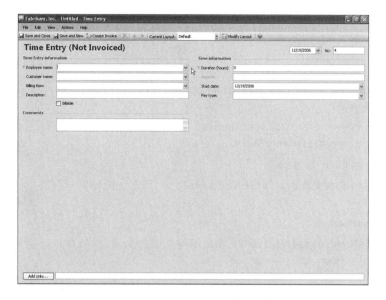

FIGURE 6.79   Enter the employee time information.

4. **Employee Name**—The Employee Name field is required. Do one of the following:

   - Click the drop-down list arrow and choose the correct employee from the list. If the employee is new, click the first line in the list, **Add a New Employee**.

   - Start typing the employee name and the full name appears. When you are finished, press the **Enter** or **Tab** key.

5. **Customer Name**—If the time is billable to the customer, enter the customer name. Do either of the following:

   - Click the drop-down list arrow and choose the correct customer from the list. If the customer is new, click the first line in the list, **Add a New Customer**.

   - Start typing the customer name, and the full name will appear if the name has already been added as a customer. When you're finished, press the **Enter** or **Tab** key.

6. **Billing Name**—The time is billable as a specific type of service item, depending on what service the employee provided. Do either of the following:

   - Click the drop-down list arrow and choose the correct item from the list. If the item is new, click the first line in the list, **Add a New Item**.

   - Start typing the item name and the full name appears. When you are finished, press the **Enter** or **Tab** key.

7. **Description**—Enter a description of the time.

8. **Billable**—Checkmark the **Billable** check box if the customer will be billed for this time.

9. **Comments**—Enter a multiline comment.

10. **Duration (hours)**—The time is required. It must be less than 24 hours per day and is entered as hours. For example, 2.25 would be 2 hours and 15 minutes.

11. **Amount**—Available only for ADP Payroll; the amount is equal to the hours times the pay rate.

12. **Start Date**—The date the time started; this is automatically filled with today's date. To change the start date, type the date, or click the drop-down arrow to select a date from the calendar.

13. **Pay Type**—Click the drop-down list arrow to choose from Overtime, Regular, Sick, or Vacation. Start typing the pay type and the full name will appear. Additional options are available for ADP Payroll.

14. **Add Links button**—Used to attach one or more files. For example, scan in the employee's handwritten time slip(s), save the file(s), and click the **Add Links** button. Then locate the file(s) on the computer and click **OK**. The filename appears in Add Links.

15. Click the **Save and Close**, **Save and New**, or **Create Invoice** button. The **Create Invoice** button uses the time entry to create a customer invoice.

Create a customer invoice containing specific time entries. On the Employees screen, under the Find heading, click the **Time Entries** link. The Time Entry list opens. Select entries by holding down the Ctrl key while clicking on each time entry to be included. Then right-click a highlighted entry to open the menu, as shown in Figure 6.80. Click the **Convert Time Entry to Invoice** menu item to bill the customer for the selected entries.

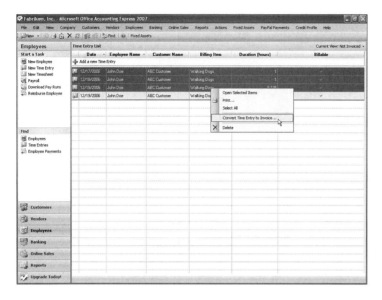

FIGURE 6.80 After completing time entries, select time entries from the Time Entry list to bill time to the customer.

The Invoice form opens with the selected time entries already showing, as shown in Figure 6.81. Complete the Invoice form and add additional products and services as needed.

⇨ See "New Invoice" on page 133.

NEW TIMESHEET

A timesheet is used to record an employee's billable or nonbillable hours for a week.

Add a timesheet using multiple methods:

On the Employees screen, click the **New Timesheet** button, as shown in Figure 6.82.

Alternatively, open a timesheet through the **Employee** menu, **New Timesheet** menu item.

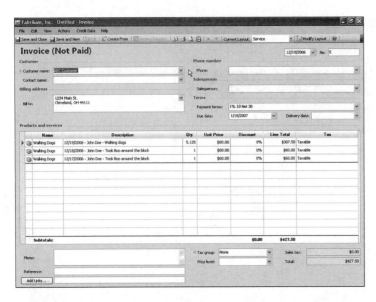

FIGURE 6.81   The selected time entries appear as line items on the customer invoice.

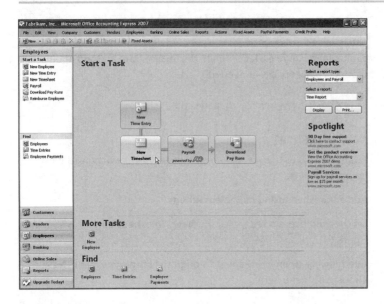

FIGURE 6.82   Open a timesheet on the Employees screen by clicking the New Timesheet button or link.

Timesheet entries are edited using Time Entry.

⇨ See "New Time Entry" on page 207 in this chapter to add or edit individual time entries.

Enter the following information on the timesheet, as shown in Figure 6.83:

1. **Current Layout**—Select the default form or create your own timesheet form.

   ⇨ See "Modifying Entry Forms" on page 340 in Chapter 9 to create a custom data entry form.

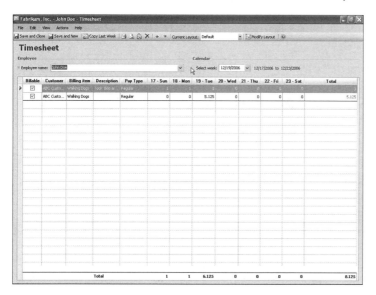

FIGURE 6.83 All previously entered time entries for an employee on a specific week appear on the timesheet.

2. **Time Entry No.**—The Time Entry No. field is automatically incremented and the next available number appears. You can type in a different number. If the company preferences do not allow duplicate document numbers, the time entry number must be a unique number.

   ⇨ See "Company Preferences" on page xxx. [Chapter 5]

3. **Employee Name**—The Employee Name is required. Do one of the following:

   - Click the drop-down list arrow and choose the correct employee from the list. If the employee is new, click the first line in the list, **Add a New Employee**.

   - Start typing the employee name and the full name appears. When you are finished, press the **Enter** or **Tab** key.

4. **Select Week**—Select Week automatically shows today's date and the week. If a different week is needed, type the date or click the drop-down list arrow to select a date from the calendar.

The timesheet contains one customer and billing item per line. For each line, the following can be changed:

5. **Billable**—Check the check box if the time can be billed to a customer.

6. **Customer Name**—Enter the customer name if the time can be billed to the customer. Do one of the following:

   - Click the drop-down list arrow and choose the correct customer from the list. If the customer is new, click the first line in the list, **Add a New Customer**.

   - Start typing the customer name and the full name will appear if the name has already been added as a customer. When you're finished, press the **Enter** or **Tab** key.

7. **Billable Item**—The time can be billed as a specific type of service item, depending on what service the employee provided. Do one of the following:

   - Click the drop-down list arrow and choose the correct item from the list. If the item is new, click the first line in the list, **Add a New Item**.

   - Start typing the item name and the full name appears. When you are finished, press the **Enter** or **Tab** key.

8. **Description**—Enter a description of the time.

9. **Pay Type**—Click the drop-down list arrow to choose from Overtime, Regular, Sick, or Vacation. Start typing the pay type and the full name will appear. Additional options are available for ADP Payroll.

10. **Days**—Enter the number of hours worked for each day. For example, 2.25 is 2 hours and 15 minutes. Be sure that all hours on a line are either billable or nonbillable. If billable and nonbillable hours exist, use two or more lines.

The total automatically recalculates as time is entered.

11. Click either the **Save and Close** button to save the information and close the window, or click the **Save and New** button to save the information and start a new timesheet.

To print a blank employee timesheet, click the **Actions** menu, **Print Blank Timesheet** menu item, as shown in Figure 6.84. A blank timesheet prints, as shown in Figure 6.85.

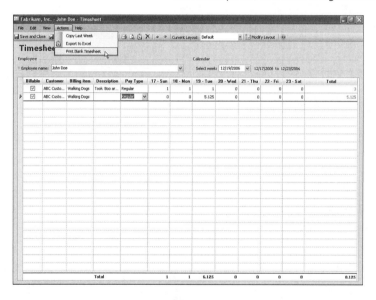

FIGURE 6.84 Print a blank timesheet.

EMPLOYEE PAYMENTS

Employee Payment is used to reimburse an employee or provide an advance.

Open the Employee Reimbursement form using multiple methods:

On the Employees screen, under the Start a Task heading, click **Reimburse Employee**, as shown in Figure 6.86.

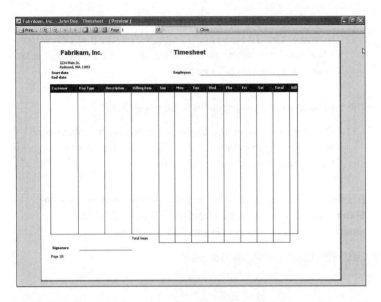

FIGURE 6.85   A blank timesheet, ready for an employee to complete.

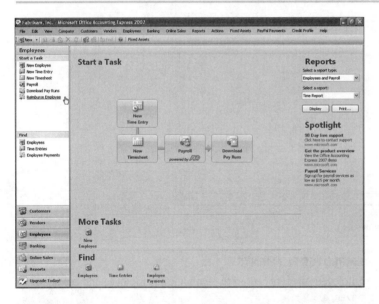

FIGURE 6.86   Reimburse an employee by clicking the Reimburse Employee link.

On the Employees screen, in the **Employee** menu, click the **Reimburse Employee** menu item to record a payment to an employee.

Alternatively, on the Employees screen:

1. Under either **Find** heading, click the **Employee Payments** link. The Employee Payment list appears.

2. Click the **Add a New Employee Payment** link. The Employee Reimbursement form opens.

To add an employee payment, as shown in Figure 6.87, enter the following information:

1. **Date**—The date of the payment is automatically entered with today's date. If a different payment date is needed, type the date or click the drop-down arrow to select a date from the calendar.

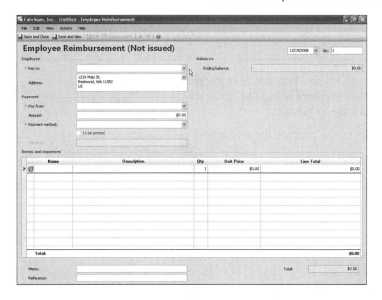

FIGURE 6.87 Complete the Employee Reimbursement form when reimbursing an employee or paying an advance.

2. **Employee Reimbursement No.**—The Employee Reimbursement No. field is automatically incremented and the next available number appears. You can type in a different number. If the company preferences do not allow duplicate document numbers, the employee reimbursement number must be a unique number.

See "Company Preferences" on page 80.

3. **Pay To**—The Pay To field is required. Do one of the following:

   - Click the drop-down list arrow and choose the correct employee from the list. If the employee is new, click the first line in the list, **Add a New Employee**.

   - Start typing the employee name and the full name will appear if the name has already been added as an employee.

4. **Employee Address**—The Employee Address field is filled in from when the employee was added. If a different address is needed, choose it using the drop-down list arrow or type in the address.

5. **Pay From**—The Pay From field is required. The payment type is a cash, bank, or credit card financial account. Do one of the following:

   - Click the drop-down list arrow and choose the correct financial account from the list.

   - Start typing the financial account. Type the name, or type the account number and the name will appear. When you are finished, press the **Enter** or **Tab** key.

6. **Amount**—The Amount field is required. Enter the amount of the payment.

7. **Payment Method**—The Payment Method field is required. Choose the payment method by typing **Cash**, **Check**, or **Credit Card**; or use the drop-down list arrow and click the correct payment method. If online banking is enabled, Electronic Payment is also available.

8. **To Be Printed**—If the check is to be printed, checkmark the **To Be Printed** check box.

9. **Check No.**—The Check No. field is filled in only if a handwritten check is used.

The Ending Balance field cannot be edited. It shows the ending balance in the Pay From *financial account* field chosen earlier. This balance updates when the Amount field changes.

In the Items and Expenses section, enter the following information:

10. **Name**—Click the drop-down list arrow, and then click one of the following:

    - **Expense**—A financial account. For example, the Postage account if the employee purchased stamps for the office.

- **Item**—A product or service.

- **Comment**—A multiline comment in the Description column. A comment can also be a blank line.

11. **Description**—Multiple lines of text.

12. **Qty.**—Quantity, a required field. Quantity can be a positive number, a negative number, or 0.

13. **Unit Price**—Can be only a positive number or 0.

14. **Line Total**—A calculated total. Line total = quantity multiplied by price. The line total can be edited and affects the unit price.

15. **Memo**—Use this for comments.

16. **Reference**—You might want to enter the original document number the payment references.

17. When a payment is complete, click the **Save and Close** button to record handwritten checks or to issue payment later, or click the **Save and New** button to start a new employee payment.

    Alternatively, click the **Issue Payment** button to record the cash, credit card, or handwritten check, or to open the Print Checks window to print the check.

To view employee payments, do the following:

On the Employees screen, under either **Find** heading, click the **Employee Payments** link. The Employee Payment list appears.

Alternatively, follow this procedure:

1. Click the **Employees** menu.

2. Click the **Employee Lists** menu item.

3. Click the **Employee Payments** menu item.

The Employee Payments list indicates whether an employee payment has been issued. To issue an employee payment that was previously saved, right-click the employee payment and click **Issue Payment**.

Banking

The Banking section covers typical bank transactions:

- **Write Checks**—Write Checks records handwritten or printed checks. However, Vendor Bills should be used instead of Write

Checks to pay previously recorded bills. Checks can be printed or saved and printed later.

☞ See "Write Checks" on this page.

- **Print Checks**—Print Checks aligns and prints checks that were previously recorded and saved but not printed.

☞ See "Print Checks" on page 225.

- **Payments**—Payments records payments for prepayments and expenses for vendors, customer refunds, and employee reimbursements and advances. However, Vendor Bills should be used instead of Write Checks to pay previously recorded bills.

☞ See "Enter Payments" on page 227.

- **Credit Card Charge**—Credit Card Charge records purchases made by credit card.

☞ See "Credit Card Charge" on page 229.

- **Deposits**—Deposits records, and optionally prints, a bank deposit slip for checks and cash received. Cash received back from the bank deposit can also be recorded.

☞ See "Make Deposits" on page 233.

- **Transfer Funds**—Transfer Funds records money moved from one financial account to another.

☞ See "Transfer Funds" on page 236.

WRITE CHECKS

Use Write Checks to record payment—either a handwritten or printed check—except when paying previously recorded vendor bills. Pay vendor bills previously entered in Express using the Pay Bills form. If the Write Checks form is used to pay a previously entered vendor bill, the check does not offset the bill and the bill still shows as unpaid.

☞ See "Pay Bills" on page 189 to pay vendor bills.

Write a check using multiple methods:

On the Banking screen, click the **Write Checks** button. A check form opens.

Alternatively, on the Banking screen, under Start a Task, click **Write Checks**, as shown in Figure 6.88.

Or, click the **Banking** menu, **Write Checks**.

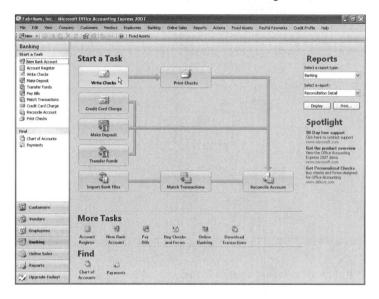

FIGURE 6.88   Click the Write Checks button to record a purchase made by check.

To add a check, as shown in Figure 6.89, enter the following information:

1. **Current Layout**—Choose the default check form layout or one of the check forms that you design yourself. Click **Modify Layout** to edit the form to your unique needs. Add or delete fields on the form, or move fields to a different position on the form.

2. **Bank Account**—The Bank Account field is required. Enter the financial account. Click the drop-down list and choose the correct bank, credit card, or cash account; or start typing the financial account name or number and the full name will appear. When you're finished, press the **Enter** or **Tab** key.

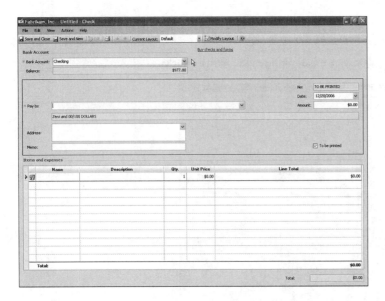

FIGURE 6.89 Enter the check information, and then click the Print button to print the check.

The Balance field cannot be edited. It shows the ending balance in the Pay From *financial account* field chosen earlier. This balance updates when the amount of the check changes.

3. **Pay To**—The Pay To field is required. Do one of the following:

   - Click the drop-down list arrow and choose a customer, vendor, employee, or tax agency from the list.

     If the payee is new, click the first line in the list, **Add a New Payee**. A window appears, as shown in Figure 6.90, asking which type of payee: customer, vendor, or employee. Choose one, and then click **OK**. Enter the information, and then return to the check form.

   - Start typing the name, and the full name will appear if the name has already been added. When you are finished, press the **Enter** or **Tab** key.

   To write a check to cash, create a vendor named Cash. To pay the bank or credit card company, create a vendor.

4. **Address**—The Address field is filled in from when the payee was added. If a different address is needed, choose it using the drop-down list arrow or type the address.

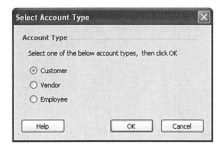

FIGURE 6.90   Add a new customer, vendor, or employee.

5. **Memo**—Use the Memo field for comments or for your account number so that the payee knows where to record the payment.

6. **To Be Printed**—The To Be Printed check box is checked to print the check or unchecked for a handwritten check.

7. **Check No.**—The Check No. field shows TO BE PRINTED unless the check is handwritten.

    A handwritten check number is automatically incremented and the next available number appears. You can type in a different number. If the company preferences do not allow duplicate document numbers, the check number must be a unique number.

    ⇨   See "Company Preferences" on page 80.

8. **Date**—The Date field is automatically entered using today's date. If a different date is needed, type the date or click the drop-down list arrow to select a date from the calendar.

9. **Amount**—The total amount of the check.

In the Items and Expenses section, enter the following information:

10. **Name**—Click the drop-down list arrow, as shown in Figure 6.91, and then click one of the following:

    - **Item**—A product or service.
    - **Comment**—A multiline comment in the description column. A comment can also be a blank line.
    - **Sales Tax**
    - **Account**—A financial account.

11. **Description**—Multiple lines of text.

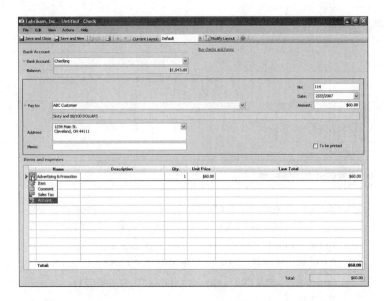

FIGURE 6.91 The middle of the check form contains expenses (for example, office supplies), line items (products and services), and comments.

12. **Qty.**—Quantity, a required field. Quantity can be a positive number, a negative number, or 0.

13. **Unit Price**—An optional field, Unit Price can be only a positive number or 0.

14. **Line Total**—A calculated total. Line total equals quantity multiplied by price. Editing the line total will change the unit price.

The Total field cannot be edited.

When the check is complete, do one of the following:

Click the **Save and Close** button. The information is saved and the window closes.

Alternatively, click the **Save and New** button. The information saves and the form clears, ready for a new check.

Or, click the **Printer** icon to print the check, as shown in Figure 6.92.

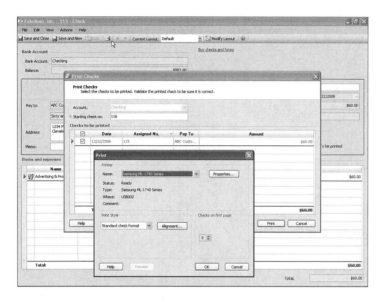

FIGURE 6.92 After completing a check, click the Printer icon button to print a check. You will be asked to save the check information before printing.

PRINT CHECKS

Print Checks allows you to pay one or more checks. There are options to accommodate different printers and check formats.

Print a check using multiple methods:

When finished with a check or payment form, a check can be printed immediately. Click the **Printer** icon button, as shown in Figure 6.92, or click the **File** menu and click the **Print** menu item.

Alternatively, on the Banking screen, click the **Print Checks** button, as shown in Figure 6.93. The Print Checks window opens, as shown in Figure 6.94.

Or, click the **Banking** menu, **Print Checks** menu item.

Or, on the Banking screen, under the Start a Task heading, click **Print Checks**.

Use the next check number entered by Express, or type in a different check number. Checkmark or uncheck checks to print, and then click the **Print** button. The Print window opens, as shown in Figure 6.95.

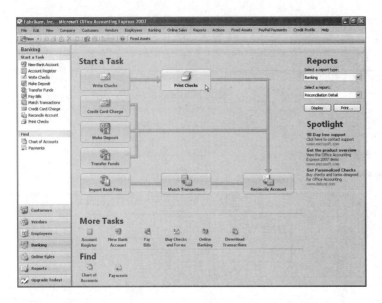

FIGURE 6.93 You can print a check any time, not only when the payment is recorded.

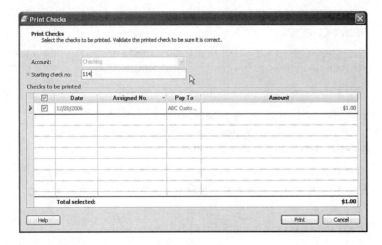

FIGURE 6.94 The Print Checks window gives you the opportunity to change the check number to print, and to uncheck any checks that are not printing now.

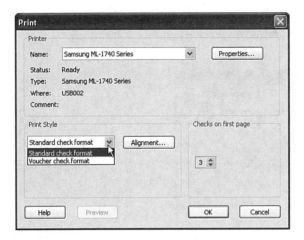

FIGURE 6.95   Choose a standard or voucher check style and how many checks print on a page. Use the Alignment button to assist in aligning the paper.

Enter the following:

1. **Printer Name**—Click the **Name** drop-down list arrow if the correct printer does not already appear.

2. **Print Style**—Use the Standard Check Format already shown, or click the Print Style drop-down list arrow and select the Voucher Check Format.

   ⟳   See "Preprinted Checks and Forms" on page xxx in Chapter 9 to purchase preprinted checks online.

3. **Alignment**—Click the Alignment button to align the check properly on the paper, if necessary.

4. **Checks on First Page**—Click the Checks on First Page arrow if the number of checks on a page is not correct.

Click the **OK** button to print the checks.

ENTER PAYMENTS

Enter Payments is used to pay anything other than a vendor bill previously entered in Express.

⟳   See "Enter Bills" on page 174 to enter a vendor bill.

⟳   See "Pay Bills" on page 189 to pay a vendor bill.

On the Banking screen, click the **Banking** menu, **Enter Payments** menu item, as shown in Figure 6.96. The Select Payment Type window opens, as shown in Figure 6.97.

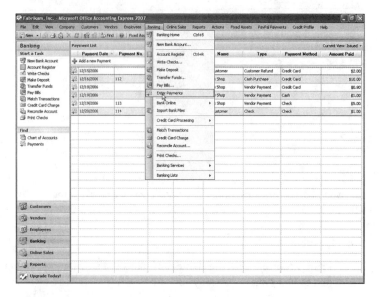

FIGURE 6.96   Open Enter Payments.

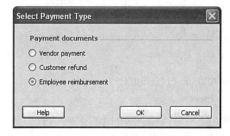

FIGURE 6.97   Use Enter Payments to pay anything other than a bill: prepayments and expenses for vendors, customer refunds, and employee reimbursements and advances.

Enter Payments uses the Vendor Payment form for prepayments and expenses, except vendor bill payments.

⇨ See "Vendor Payment" on page 201 to enter prepayments and expenses.

⇨ See "Enter Bills" on page 174 to enter a vendor bill.

⇨ See "Pay Bills" on page 189 to pay a vendor bill.

Customer Refund uses the Customer Refund form for customer refunds.

⇨ See "Customer Refund" on page 168.

Employee Reimbursement uses the Employee Reimbursement form for employee reimbursements and advances.

⇨ See "Employee Payments" on page 215.

CREDIT CARD CHARGE

Use Credit Card Charge to record the purchase of an item or service with a credit card at the time the purchase is made.

Add a credit card charge using multiple methods:

On the Banking screen, click the **Credit Card Charge** button, as shown in Figure 6.98. A Credit Card Charge form opens.

Alternatively, click the **Vendors** menu, **Record Expenses**. Click the **Credit Card** button, and then click **OK**. The Credit Card Charge form opens.

Or, click the **Banking** menu, **Credit Card Charge**. The Credit Card Charge form opens.

Or, on the Banking screen, under **Start a Task**, click **Credit Card Charge**.

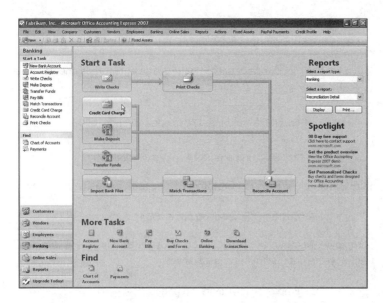

FIGURE 6.98   Open the Credit Card Charge form by clicking the Credit Card Charge button.

To add a credit card charge, as shown in Figure 6.99, enter the following information:

1. **Current Layout**—Choose the default credit card charge form layout or one of the credit card charge forms that you design yourself. Click **Modify Layout** to edit the form to your unique needs. Add or delete fields on the form, or move fields to a different position on the form.

2. **Date**—The date of the credit card charge is automatically entered using today's date. If a different date is needed, type the date or click the drop-down list arrow to select a date from the calendar.

3. **Credit Card Charge No.**—The Credit Card Charge No. field is automatically incremented and the next available number appears. You can type in a different number. If the company preferences do not allow duplicate document numbers, the credit card charge number must be a unique number.

   ⇨   See "Company Preferences" on page 80.

FIGURE 6.99   Enter the credit card charge.

4. **Vendor Name**—The Vendor Name field is required. Do one of the following:

- Click the drop-down list arrow and choose the correct vendor from the list. If the vendor is new, click the first line in the list, **Add a New Vendor**.

- Start typing the vendor name and the full name will appear if the name has already been added as a vendor. When you are finished, press the **Enter** or **Tab** key. If the vendor is new, a window will appear asking whether you would like to add the vendor.

If the new vendor warning window appears, do one of the following:

- Click the **Set Up** button to add the vendor and as much information as you can about them. From that point on, Express will enter the vendor's information on new credit card purchases. This saves time.

- Alternatively, click the **Fast Add** button to add only the name of the vendor. Later, when you save the credit card purchase, Express tells you that the information about the vendor has changed (for example, the address and payment method) and asks whether you would like to save the new information permanently in the vendor file.

231

- Click the **No** button if you made a spelling error. Then either correct the spelling of the vendor's name or choose the vendor using the drop-down list arrow.

5. **Contact Name**—The Contact Name field is filled in from the primary contact entered when the vendor was added. If a different vendor contact is needed, choose it using the drop-down list arrow. Express will not permit a contact that is not in the vendor's Contacts list.

6. **Vendor Address**—The Vendor Address field is filled in from when the vendor was added. If a different address is needed, choose it using the drop-down list arrow or type in the address.

7. **Phone Number**—The Phone Number field is filled in from the phone number entered when the vendor was added. If a different phone number is needed, choose it using the drop-down list arrow or type in the phone number.

8. **Payment Method**—The Payment Method field is required. The Credit Card option appears. If a different payment term is needed, do one of the following:

   - Click the drop-down list arrow and choose **Cash**, **Check**, or **Credit Card**.

   - Start typing the payment method and the full name will appear. When you are finished, press the **Enter** or **Tab** key.

9. **Payment From**—The Payment From field is required, so enter the financial account. You can click the drop-down list arrow and choose the correct bank, credit card, or cash account; or start typing the financial account name or number and the full name will appear. When you're finished, press the **Enter** or **Tab** key.

10. **Check No.**—The Check No. field appears only if you choose Check as the payment method. Enter the check number for a manual check.

11. **Delivery Date**—The Delivery Date field is the date the company received the product or service. Type the date or click the drop-down list arrow to select a date from the calendar.

In the Items and Expenses section, enter the following information:

12. **Name**—Click the drop-down list arrow, then click one of the following:

    - **Expense**—A financial account.

    - **Item**—A product or service.

- **Comment**—A multiline comment in the description column. A comment can also be a blank line.

13. **Description**—Multiple lines of text.

14. **Qty.**—Quantity, a required field. Quantity can be a positive number, a negative number, or 0.

15. **Unit Price**—An optional field, Unit Price can be only a positive number or 0.

16. **Line Total**—A calculated total. Line total equals quantity multiplied by price. Editing the line total will change the unit price.

17. **Memo**—You might want to use the Memo field to detail any changes made to the credit card charge form and why.

18. **Reference**—You might want to enter your purchase order.

19. **Add Links button**—Used to attach one or more files. For example, scan in the purchase order, save the file(s), and click the **Add Links** button. Then locate the file(s) on the computer and click the **OK** button. The filename appears in Add Links.

The Total field cannot be edited.

20. When a credit card charge is complete, click the **Save and Close** button. The information is saved and the window closes. Alternatively, click the **Save and New** button. The information saves and the form clears, ready for a new credit card charge.

If the credit card charge contains new or edited vendor information, a window appears asking whether the information should be permanently saved, updating any previous information. Typically, you should answer **Yes**. The changed information is saved in the vendor's file, available for future purchases and bills. Answering **No** saves only the information with the credit card charge and does not update the vendor's file.

After completing a credit card charge, you can create a new credit card charge, or it can be edited or voided (but not deleted).

MAKE DEPOSITS

Use Make Deposits when depositing checks into the bank and any cash received back from the deposit. Optionally, a bank deposit slip may be printed.

Add a deposit using multiple methods:

On the Banking screen, click the **Make Deposit** button, as shown in Figure 6.100. The Deposit form opens.

Alternatively, click the **Banking** menu, **Make Deposit**.

Or, on the Banking screen, under the Start a Task heading, click the **Make Deposit** link.

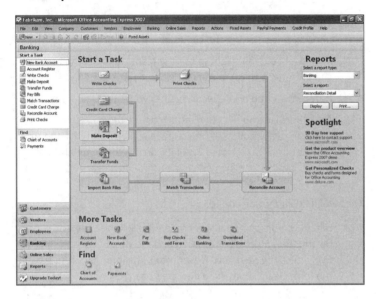

FIGURE 6.100   Open the Deposit form.

To add a deposit, as shown in Figure 6.101, enter the following information:

1. **Date**—The date of the deposit is automatically entered using today's date. If a different date is needed, type the date or click the drop-down list arrow to select a date from the calendar.

2. **Deposit In**—The Deposit In field is required. Enter the financial account. Click the drop-down list and choose the correct bank; or start typing the financial account name or number and the full name will appear. If the bank is new, click the first line in the list, **Add a New Bank**. When you're finished, press the **Enter** or **Tab** key.

3. **Memo**—Enter comments.

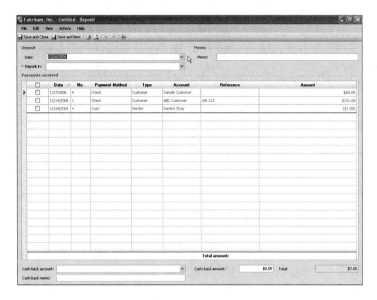

FIGURE 6.101   Deposit one or more checks.

The Payments Received section shows one row per undeposited check received. Change how the checks sort by clicking a column heading. A small Sort By arrow appears next to the column name, and the bill rows sort by that column. Click the arrow again to change the sort order of the column from A–Z to Z–A.

Click the **Select All** check box to select all checks for deposit. The checks to deposit have a checkmark. Uncheck a specific check to remove it from the deposit.

For each additional line item, enter the type, account, reference, and amount, as shown in Figure 6.102.

The total calculates automatically when a check is added or removed from the deposit and cannot be edited.

4. **Cash-Back Account**—Enter the financial account. Click the drop-down list and choose the correct financial account, or start typing the financial account name or number and the full name will appear. If the account is new, click the first line in the list, **Add a New Financial Account**. When you're finished, press the **Enter** or **Tab** key.

5. **Cash-Back Memo**—Enter comments.

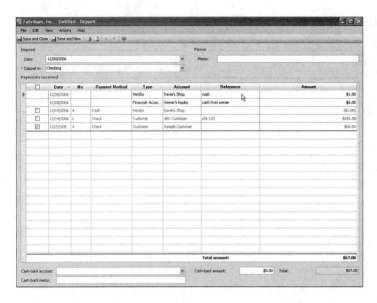

FIGURE 6.102   The Deposit form shows all transactions in the Undeposited Funds account. Click a blank line to add additional lines for additional deposit items.

6. **Cash-Back Amount**—Enter the amount of money that was received back from the deposit.

7. When a deposit is complete, do one of the following:

    - Click the **Save and Close** button. The information saves and the window closes.

    - Click the **Save and New** button. The information saves and the form clears, ready for a new deposit.

    - The deposit ticket can be printed immediately. Click the **Printer** icon button, or click the **File** menu and then click the **Print** menu item.

TRANSFER FUNDS

Use Transfer Funds to move money from one financial account to another financial account. Inventory accounts and sales tax agency accounts cannot transfer money.

Transfer funds using multiple methods:

On the Banking screen, click the **Transfer Funds** button, as shown in Figure 6.103. The Transfer Funds form opens.

Alternatively, click the **Banking** menu, **Transfer Funds**.

Or, on the Banking screen, under **Start a Task**, click the **Transfer Funds** link.

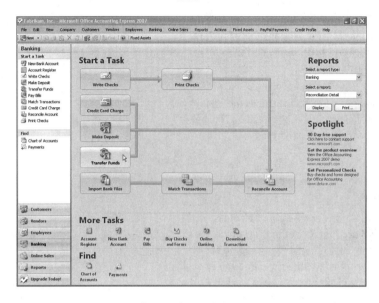

FIGURE 6.103   Open the Transfer Funds form by clicking the Transfer Funds button.

To add a transfer, as shown in Figure 6.104, enter the following information:

1. **Date**—The Transfer Date field is automatically entered using today's date. If a different date is needed, type the date or click the drop-down list arrow to select a date from the calendar.

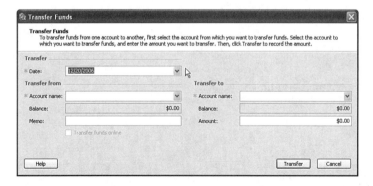

FIGURE 6.104   Transfer money between accounts.

2. **Transfer from Account Name**—The Transfer from Account Name field is required. Enter the financial account. Click the drop-down list and choose the correct financial account, or start typing the financial account name or number and the full name will appear. If the financial account is new, click the first line in the list, **Add a New Financial Account**. When you are finished, press the **Enter** or **Tab** key. Inventory accounts and sales tax agency accounts cannot transfer money.

The Transfer from Balance field cannot be edited. It shows the ending balance in the Transfer From *financial account* chosen earlier. This balance updates when the amount of the transfer changes.

3. **Memo**—Enter comments.

4. **Transfer Funds Online**—If online banking has been set up, the transfer may be made online.

5. **Transfer to Account Name**—Transfer to Account Name is required. Enter the financial account. Click the drop-down list and choose the correct financial account, or start typing the financial account name or number and the full name will appear. If the financial account is new, click the first line in the list, **Add a New Financial Account**. When you're finished, press the **Enter** or **Tab** key. Inventory accounts and sales tax agency accounts cannot transfer money.

6. **Transfer to Balance**—This field cannot be edited. It shows the ending balance in the Transfer To *financial account* field chosen earlier. This balance updates when the amount of the transfer changes.

7. **Amount**—Enter the amount of the transfer. It must be a positive amount.

When a deposit is complete, click the **Transfer** button. The information is saved and the window closes.

You can edit or void (not delete) account transfers from the Account Register.

Company

This section covers transactions that cannot be recorded using any other Express form:

- **Journal Entry**—Journal entries are typically used for corrections or end of period adjustments.

  ⇨ See the next section, "New Journal Entry."

- **Cash-Basis Journal Entry**—Cash-Basis Journal Entries are used to move entries from the Other Cash Income account or Other Cash Expense account to a more appropriate account.

  ⇨ See "New Cash-Basis Journal Entry" on page 242.

NEW JOURNAL ENTRY

You use a journal entry to record an end-of-period transaction or to correct a transaction in the unlikely event that it cannot be corrected using the normal customer, vendor, employee, and banking data entry forms.

A journal entry contains two or more lines, consisting of one or more debits and one or more credits. Each line contains a financial account affected by the transaction and an amount, called a debit or credit.

Use a journal entry to record a transaction only when another form is not available. It is easier to use another form because you do not need to understand debits and credits when using other forms; Express records the debits and credits for you.

Your accountant will usually make journal entries for you, if any are needed. However, if you record them, remember the following:

- Debits increase assets, credits decrease assets.
- Credits increase liabilities, debits decrease liabilities.
- Credits increase equity, debits decrease equity.
- Credits increase income, debits decrease income.
- Debits increase expenses, credits decrease expenses.
- The total of all debits must equal the total of all credits.
- Each journal entry should have a description explaining why it was created and who authorized it.

Create a journal entry by clicking the Company menu, New Journal Entry, as shown in Figure 6.105. The Journal Entry form opens.

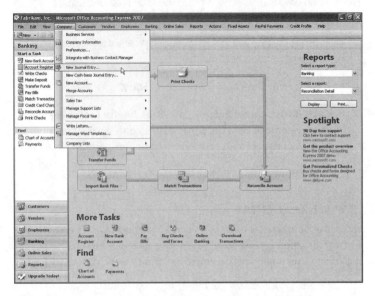

FIGURE 6.105   Open the Journal Entry window using the menu.

To add one or more journal entries, enter the following information, as shown in Figure 6.106:

1. **Journal Number**—The Journal Number field increments automatically but can be changed. However, changing the number is not recommended.

2. **Memo**—Enter comments.

One line appears for each debit or credit. Enter the following information:

3. **Voucher No.**—The first voucher number increments automatically from the previous one used. The second line and succeeding lines do not increment because they are assumed to be part of the same transaction. When the transaction balances (the debits total the credits), type a new voucher number on the next line for the next transaction.

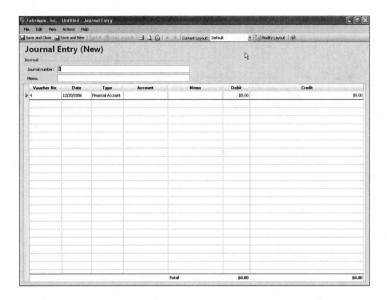

FIGURE 6.106   Record one or more journal entry transactions at one time.

4. **Type**—Click the drop-down list arrow and choose **Financial Account**, **Vendor**, **Customer**, or **Tax Code**. Choose Vendor for accounts payable transactions and Customer for accounts receivable transactions. Choose Tax Code to adjust sales tax balances due to discounts, errors, or payments.

5. **Account**—The Account field varies depending on the Type field. For the Financial Account type, choose an account; for the Customer type, choose a customer; for the Vendor type, choose a vendor; for the Tax Code type, choose a tax code. You can add new accounts by clicking on the first line in the drop-down list.

6. **Memo**—Enter comments.

7. **Debit**—Enter an amount.

8. **Credit**—Enter an amount.

When the journal entry is complete, do one of the following:

- Click the **Save and Close** button. The information is saved and the window closes.
- Click the **Save and New** button. The information saves and the form clears, ready for a new journal entry.

If the credits do not total the same amount as the debits, a warning window opens, as shown in Figure 6.107, and the transaction will not save until the error is fixed.

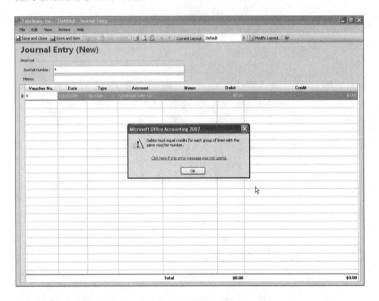

FIGURE 6.107   Credits *must* equal debits.

NEW CASH-BASIS JOURNAL ENTRY

Typically used only by your accountant, a cash-basis journal entry is used to move entries from the Other Cash Income account or Other Cash Expense account to a more appropriate account. The Cash-Basis Journal Entry window looks the same as a journal entry.

⇨   See "New Journal Entry" on page 239.

Create a cash-basis journal entry by clicking the Company menu, New Cash-Basis Journal Entry, as shown in Figure 6.108. The Cash-Basis Journal Entry form opens, as shown in Figure 6.109.

⇨   See "New Journal Entry" on page 239 for details. The forms are similar.

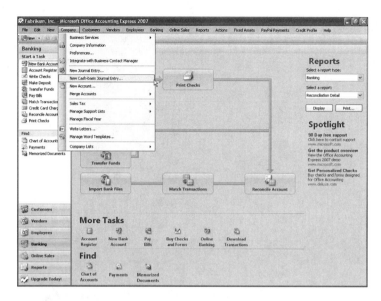

FIGURE 6.108 Open the Cash-Basis Journal Entry window using the menu.

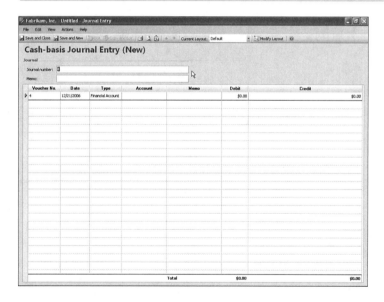

FIGURE 6.109 Record a cash-basis journal entry.

WHAT YOU'LL LEARN

- Discover Each Express Report and What It Does
- How to Customize Reports
- How to Send Reports to Excel and Email
- Graphing a Report

Accounting Reports

Express provides many useful reports. You can view a report on the screen, print, email, or export to Excel. In addition, you can display a graph of the report with the click of a button. Reports are fully customizable with a few mouse clicks.

Reports Overview

The following reports are available in Express:

Company and Financial

- Profit and Loss
- Balance Sheet
- Cash Flow Statement
- Trial Balance
- Transaction Detail by Account
- GL Report
- Transaction Journal
- Sales Tax Liability
- Transaction Detail by Tax Code
- Journal Entries
- Items
- Chart of Accounts

Customer and Receivables

- A/R Aging Detail
- Customer Transaction History
- Customers
- Quotes
- Invoices
- Received Payments
- Customer Refunds

Sales

- Sales by Customer Summary
- Sales by Customer Detail
- Sales by Item Summary
- Sales by Item Detail
- Online Sales by Customer Summary
- Online Sales by Item Summary
- Online Sales Items
- Online Orders
- Online Sales Receipts

Vendors and Payables

- A/P Aging Detail
- Vendor Transaction History
- Vendors
- Bills
- Vendor Payments

Banking

- Reconciliation Detail
- Payments
- Failed Payments

Employees and Payroll

- Time Report
- Employees
- Time Entries
- Employee Payments

A report can be modified, but it cannot be saved as a memorized report. Instead, export reports to Microsoft Excel version 10 or higher.

Individual Reports

Express reports are grouped into Company and Financials, Customers and Receivables, Sales, Vendors and Payables, Banking, and Employees and Payroll. Each report is shown and discussed in this chapter.

Company and Financial Reports

The Company and Financial reports are the basic reports showing the overall health of the business. They consist of Profit and Loss, Balance Sheet, Cash Flow Statement, and Trial Balance. Detailed reports showing transactions include Transaction Detail by Account, GL Report, Transaction Journal, Sales Tax Liability, and Transaction Detail by Tax Code.

PROFIT AND LOSS

The Profit and Loss report shows the company's net income or loss for a specific period.

To view the Profit and Loss report, shown in Figure 7.1, click the **Reports** menu, **Company and Financial**, **Profit and Loss**.

BALANCE SHEET

The Balance Sheet, shown in Figure 7.2, is a snapshot of what the company owns and owes on a specific date, plus the equity and retained earnings in the company.

Click the **Reports** menu, **Company and Financial**, **Balance Sheet** to view the Balance Sheet.

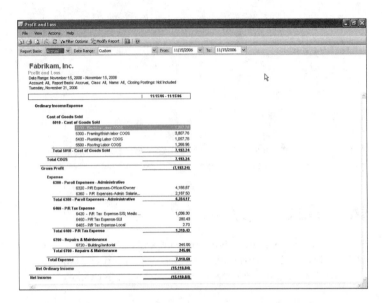

FIGURE 7.1 The Profit and Loss report includes all income, cost of goods sold, and expenses of the business.

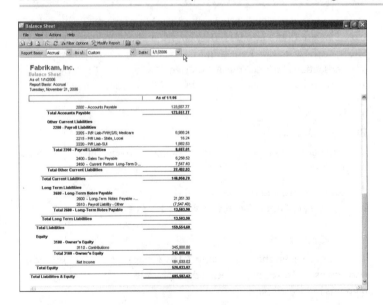

FIGURE 7.2 The Balance Sheet shows the company's assets, liabilities, and equity as of a specific date.

CASH FLOW STATEMENT

The Cash Flow statement, shown in Figure 7.3, shows the flow of cash through the company for a specific period. This report helps a small business manage cash flow timing and stay in business.

To view the Cash Flow statement, click the **Reports** menu, **Company and Financial**, **Cash Flow Statement**.

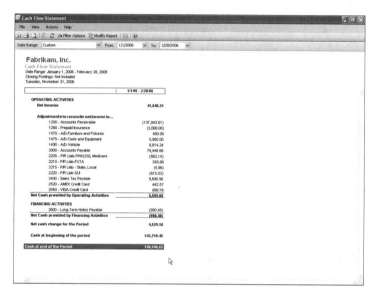

FIGURE 7.3   The Cash Flow statement shows cash moving into and out of a business over a period of time.

TRIAL BALANCE

The Trial Balance report, shown in Figure 7.4, verifies that debits equal credits, proving that both sides of a transaction were fully recorded in Express.

Click the **Reports** menu, **Company and Financial**, **Trial Balance** to view the Trial Balance report.

TRANSACTION DETAIL BY ACCOUNT

As seen in Figure 7.5, Transaction Detail by Account sorts transactions by account number. It is used to find errors when transactions are posted to the wrong account.

To view the Transaction Detail by Account report, click the **Reports** menu, **Company and Financial**, **Transaction Detail by Account**.

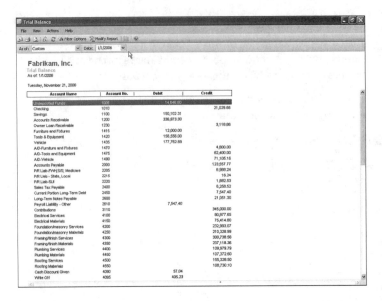

FIGURE 7.4 The Trial Balance report shows all general ledger accounts and their balances on a specific date. The left amount column shows debits, and the right amount column shows credits.

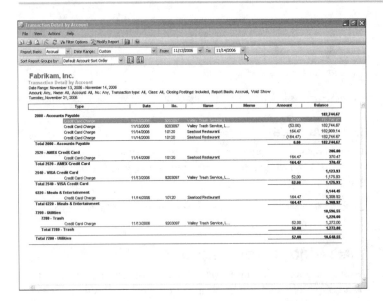

FIGURE 7.5 The Transaction Detail by Account report shows all account detail during a specific period.

GL (GENERAL LEDGER) REPORT

The GL Report, shown in Figure 7.6, is similar to the Transaction Detail by Account report, and also shows whether an amount is a debit or a credit.

Click the **Reports** menu, **Company and Financial**, **GL Report** to view the GL Report.

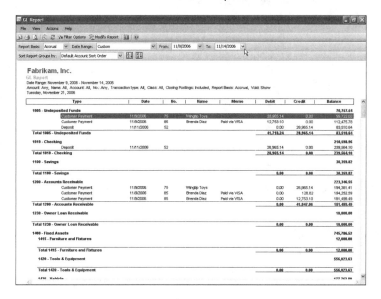

FIGURE 7.6   The GL Report shows transaction details for all accounts during a specific period.

TRANSACTION JOURNAL

The Transaction Journal, shown in Figure 7.7, shows each type of transaction and, when appropriate, also shows the payment status.

Click the **Reports** menu, **Company and Financial**, **Transaction Journal** to view the Transaction Journal report.

SALES TAX LIABILITY

The Sales Tax Liability report, shown in Figure 7.8, shows all sales taxes collected and owed to each taxing authority during a specific period.

Click the **Reports** menu, **Company and Financial**, **Sales Tax Liability** to view the Sales Tax Liability report.

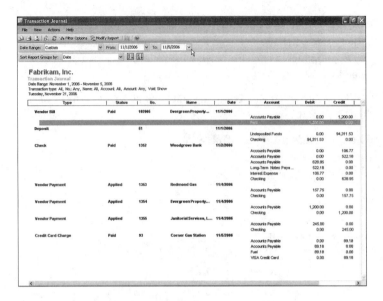

FIGURE 7.7   The Transaction Journal report shows all transactions, and their debits and credits, during a specific period, sorted by date and then by transaction.

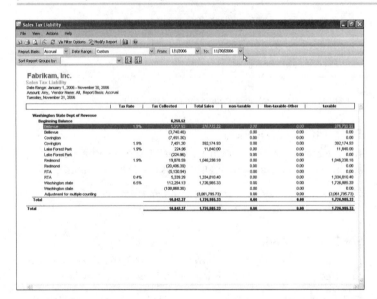

FIGURE 7.8   Quickly see which taxing authorities to pay and the amount to pay.

TRANSACTION DETAIL BY TAX CODE

The Transaction Detail by Tax Code report, shown in Figure 7.9, lists all transactions containing sales taxes collected during a specific period of time, sorted by taxing authority.

To view the Transaction Detail by Tax Code report, click the **Reports** menu, **Company and Financial**, **Transaction Detail by Tax Code**.

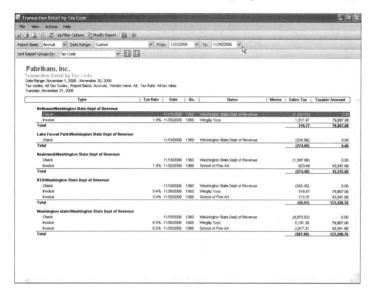

FIGURE 7.9 Use the Transaction Detail by Tax Code report to verify that taxes were correctly recorded.

JOURNAL ENTRY LIST

The Journal Entry List, shown in Figure 9.10, is a list of all journal entries or only voided, non-voided, cash basis, or voided cash basis journal entries. Click **Current View** to change which entries appear.

Click the **Company** menu, **Company Lists**, **Journal Entries** to see a listing of all journal entries. Optionally, click **Current View** to filter the list to show only non-voided, voided, cash basis, or voided cash basis journal entries.

ITEM LIST

The Item List, shown in Figure 7.11, is a list of all items or only active or inactive items. Click **Current View** to change which items appear.

Click the **Company** menu, **Company Lists**, **Items** to see a listing of all items. Optionally, click **Current View** to filter the list to show only active or inactive items.

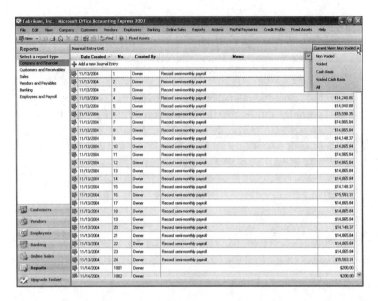

FIGURE 7.10   The Journal Entry List shows journal entries entered in Express.

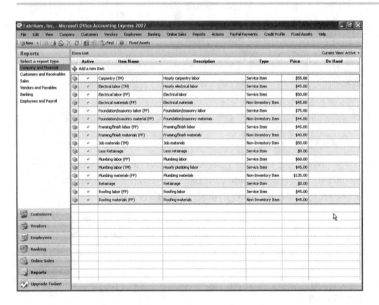

FIGURE 7.11   The Item List shows all service and non-inventory items entered in Express.

CHART OF ACCOUNTS

The Chart of Accounts, shown in Figure 7.12, is a list of all general ledger accounts or only active or inactive accounts. Click **Current View** to change which accounts appear.

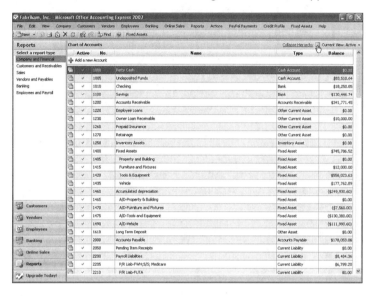

FIGURE 7.12 The Chart of Accounts lists general ledger accounts and their current balance.

Click the **Company** menu, **Company Lists**, **Chart of Accounts** to see a listing of general ledger accounts.

Optionally, click **Current View** to filter the list to show only active or inactive general ledger accounts. Click **Collapse Hierarchy** to see a summary of general ledger accounts or **Expand Hierarchy** to see both summary and detail accounts.

Customer and Receivable Reports

The Customer and Receivable reports show customer account status and purchase history. They consist of A/R Aging Detail and Customer Transaction Detail.

A/R (ACCOUNTS RECEIVABLE) AGING DETAIL

Use the A/R Aging Detail report, shown in Figure 7.13, to track how well customers are paying their invoices. Take action on late-paying customers before they become bad debts.

To view the A/R Aging Detail report, click the **Reports** menu,
Customers and Receivables, **A/R Aging Detail**. Optionally, enter the
Aging Interval Days and the **Through Days Past Due**. These change
the column headings and calculations on the aging portion of the
report.

Through Days Past Due

Aging, Interval Days

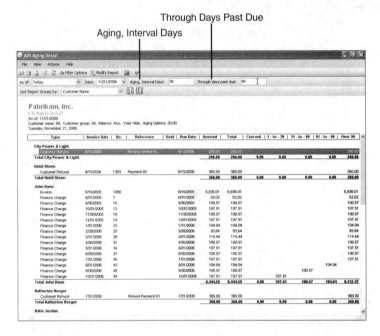

FIGURE 7.13 The A/R Aging Detail report shows outstanding invoices along with payments, finance charges,
and credit memos—sorted by customer and aging of the amounts over specific days.

CUSTOMER TRANSACTION HISTORY

The Customer Transaction History, shown in Figure 7.14, details all customer transactions by customer.

Click the **Reports** menu, **Customers and Receivables**, **Customer
Transaction History** to view the Customer Transaction History report.

CUSTOMER LIST

As shown in Figure 7.15, the Customer List show all customers or only
active or inactive customers. Click **Current View** to change which customers appear.

Click the **Customers** menu, **Customer Lists**, **Customer** to see a listing
of customers. Optionally, click **Current View** to filter the list to show
only active or inactive customers.

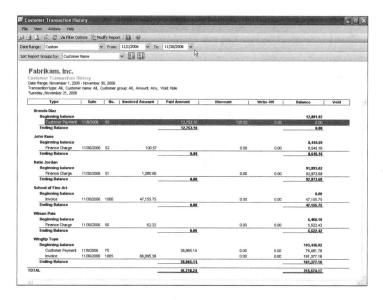

FIGURE 7.14   The Customer Transaction History report shows all transactions for a specific period, including invoices, credit memos, payments, and amounts written off.

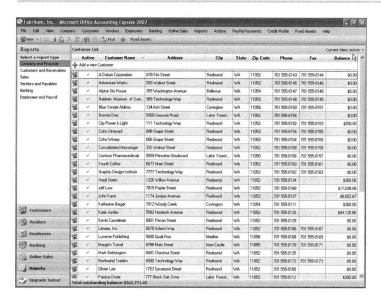

FIGURE 7.15   The Customer List shows all customers and their addresses, phone numbers, faxes, and balances.

QUOTE LIST

As shown in Figure 7.16, the Quote List shows all quotes or only accepted, rejected, expired, or open quotes. New quotes may be added, or existing quotes rejected or edited.

Click the **Customers** menu, **Customer Lists**, **Quotes** to see a listing of all quotes in Express. Optionally, click **Current View** to filter the list to show only open, accepted, rejected, or expired quotes.

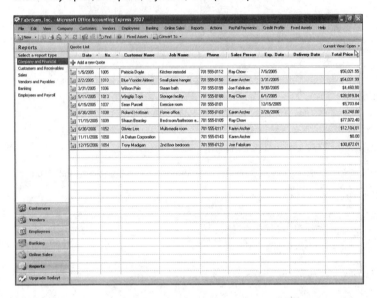

FIGURE 7.16   The Quote List shows quotes in Express. Each quote includes the salesperson, expected and actual delivery date, and the amount of the quote.

INVOICE LIST

The Invoice List, shown in Figure 7.17, shows all invoices or only open, overdue, or voided invoices. Invoices may be added, edited, printed, emailed, or voided.

Click the **Customers** menu, **Customer Lists**, **Invoices** to see a listing of all invoices in Express. Optionally, click **Current View** to filter the list to show overdue, open, or voided invoices.

RECEIVED PAYMENT LIST

Use the Received Payment List, shown in Figure 7.18, to verify the form of customer payment and amount.

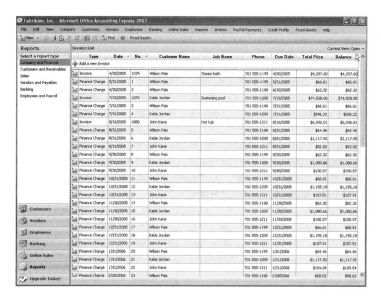

FIGURE 7.17   The Invoice List shows invoices, finance charges, and credit memos in Express.

Click the **Customers** menu, **Customer Lists**, **Received Payments** to see a listing of all payments received in Express. Optionally, click **Current View** to filter the list to show only open, fully applied, or voided payments.

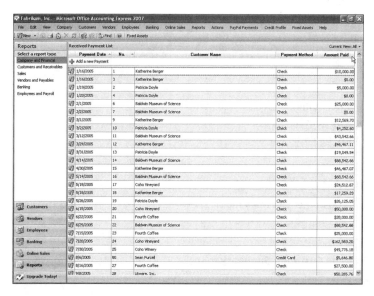

FIGURE 7.18   The Received Payment List shows customer payments entered in Express, the form of payment, and the amount.

CUSTOMER REFUNDS

The Customer Refunds list, shown in Figure 7.19, shows how the refund is paid, and the status and amount of the refund.

Click the **Customers** menu, **Customer Lists**, **Customer Refunds** to see a listing of all customer refunds in Express. Optionally, click **Current View** to filter the list to show only not issued, issued, or voided refunds.

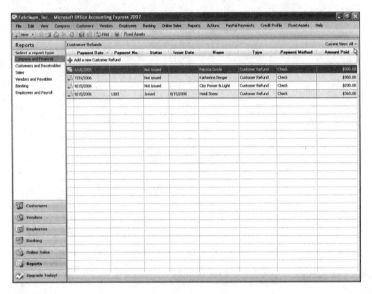

FIGURE 7.19   Customer Refunds shows refunds to customers entered in Express.

Sales Reports

Sales Reports include Sales by Customer Summary, Sales by Customer Detail, Sales by Item Summary, Sales by Item Detail, Online Sales by Customer Summary, Online Sales by Item Summary, and Online Orders List.

SALES BY CUSTOMER SUMMARY

As shown in Figure 7.20, the Sales by Customer Summary report shows each customer and summarizes the amount sold to them during a specific period.

Click the **Reports** menu, **Sales**, **Sales by Customer Summary** to see the Sales by Customer Summary report.

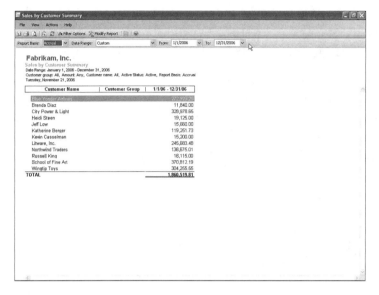

FIGURE 7.20   The Sales by Customer Summary report is a list of customers and their total purchases.

SALES BY CUSTOMER DETAIL

The Sales by Customer Detail report, shown in Figure 7.21, shows all customers, their invoices, and the items and services they purchased, along with the quantities and dollar amounts during a specific period.

Click the **Reports** menu, **Sales**, **Sales by Customer Detail** to view the Sales by Customer Detail report.

SALES BY ITEM SUMMARY

As shown in Figure 7.22, the Sales by Item Summary report shows each service and non-inventory item and summarizes the amount sold for a specific period.

Click the **Reports** menu, **Sales**, **Sales by Item Summary** to see the amount sold for each item.

SALES BY ITEM DETAIL

The Sales by Item Detail report, shown in Figure 7.23, shows invoices and invoice amounts for each non-inventory and service item for a specific period.

Click the **Reports** menu, **Sales**, **Sales by Item Detail** to see invoice amounts for each item.

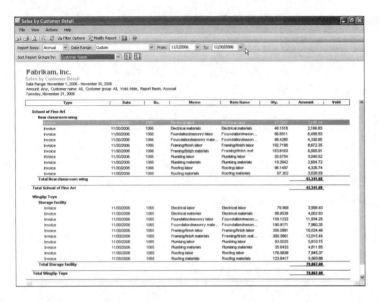

FIGURE 7.21 The Sales by Customer Detail report shows all transactions related to customers—sales, credit memos, refunds, and payments.

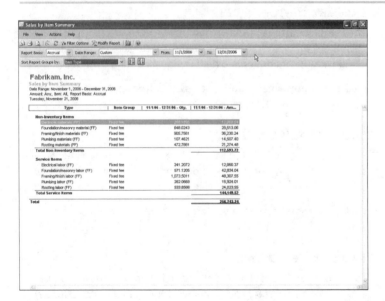

FIGURE 7.22 The Sales by Item Summary report shows the quantity and amount of items sold.

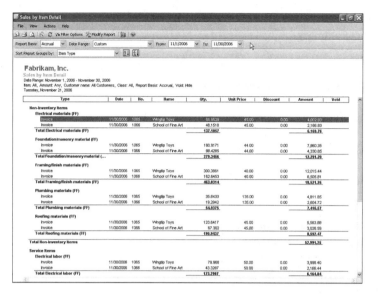

FIGURE 7.23 The Sales by Item Detail report shows transactions sorted by item.

ONLINE SALES BY CUSTOMER SUMMARY

The Online Sales by Customer Summary report shows each customer and their online sales total for a specific period.

The Online Sales by Customer Summary report is available only after the eBay add-in is enabled.

⇨ See "Sell Online" on page 328 for more information about the eBay add-in.

Click the **Reports** menu, **Sales**, **Online Sales by Customer Summary** to see a listing of customers and the dollar amounts sold for a specific period.

ONLINE SALES BY ITEM SUMMARY

The Online Sales by Item Summary report shows each service and non-inventory item and the dollar amount sold online during a specific period.

The Online Sales by Item Summary report summarizes online sales, one line per customer. The Online Sales by Item Summary report is available only after the eBay add-in is enabled.

⇨ See "Sell Online" on page 328 for more information about the eBay add-in.

To view the Online Sales by Item Summary report, click the **Reports** menu, **Sales**, **Online Sales by Item Summary**.

ONLINE ORDERS LIST

The Online Orders List is a list of all the purchases customers have made from eBay orders entered through Online Marketplace. The list contains the close date, order number, user ID, customer, description, payment method, status, and amount. The Online Order List is available only after the eBay add-in is enabled.

⇨ See "Sell Online" on page 328 for more information about the eBay add-in.

Click the **Online Sales** menu, **Online Sales Lists**, **Online Orders** to view the Online Orders List. Optionally, click **Current View** to filter the list to show only pending, converted, or cancelled online orders.

ONLINE SALES RECEIPTS LIST

The Online Sales Receipt List is a list of all the online orders that have been converted to online sales receipts by clicking the **Convert to Online Sales Receipt** button on an online sales order.

The Online Sales Receipts List shows all online payments for online sales. The Online Sales Receipts List is available only after the eBay add-in is enabled.

⇨ See "Sell Online" on page 328 for more information about the eBay add-in.

To view the Online Sales Receipt List, click the **Online Sales** menu, **Online Sales Lists**, **Online Sales Receipts**.

Vendor and Payable Reports

Vendor and Payable Reports include A/P Aging Detail, Vendor Transaction History, Vendor List, Bill List, and Vendor Payments.

A/P AGING DETAIL

The A/P Aging Detail report, shown in Figure 7.24, is used to see which vendor bills are outstanding. Use this report to match outstanding bills with credit memos and payments. If a payment or credit memo does not record the bill it is paying, the bill will still show as outstanding on this report.

Click the **Reports** menu, **Vendors and Payables**, **A/P Aging Detail** to view the A/P Aging Detail. Optionally, enter the **Aging Interval Days** and the **Through Days Past Due**. These change the column headings and calculations on the aging portion of the report.

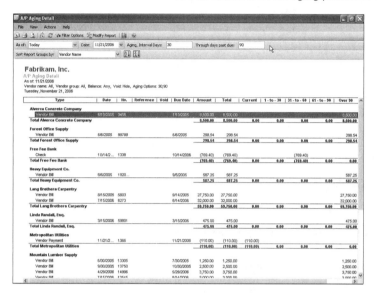

FIGURE 7.24 The A/P Aging Detail report shows outstanding bills to pay to vendors, along with check payments and credit memos—sorted by vendor, with aging of the bills over specific days.

VENDOR TRANSACTION HISTORY

The Vendor Transaction History report, shown in Figure 7.25, shows all vendor transactions for a specific period, including bills, credit card charges, and payments.

To view the Vendor Transaction History report, click the **Reports** menu, **Vendors and Payables**, **Vendor Transaction History**.

VENDOR LIST

Use the Vendor List, shown in Figure 7.26, when calling to collect outstanding payments. The Vendor List includes the vendor phone, fax, and balance owed.

Click the **Vendors** menu, **Vendor Lists**, **Vendors** to view the Vendor List. Optionally, click **Current View** to filter the list to show only active or inactive vendors.

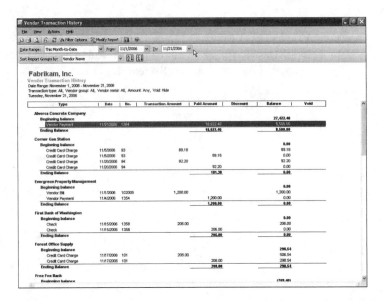

FIGURE 7.25 The Vendor Transaction History report shows all vendor transaction details.

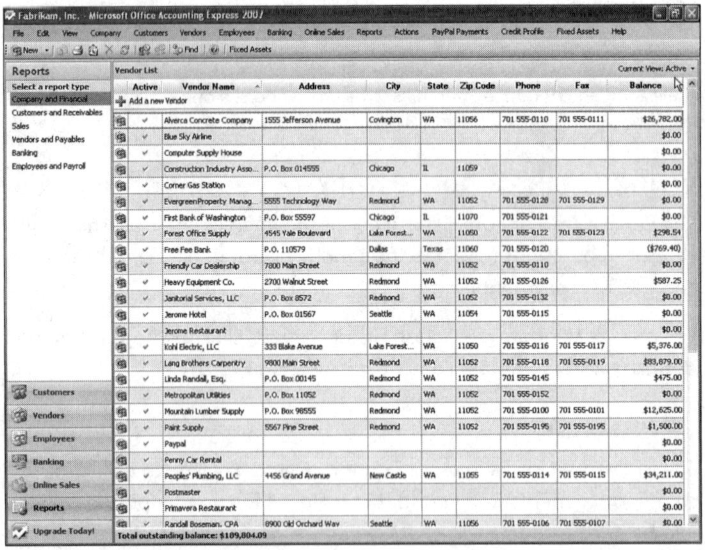

FIGURE 7.26 The Vendor List shows all vendors and their addresses, phone numbers, fax numbers, and balances owed.

BILL LIST

As shown in Figure 7.27, the Bills List not only shows the original amount and the balance due; you also can filter the list to show only overdue or open bills when deciding to pay bills.

Click the **Vendors** menu, **Vendor Lists**, **Bills** to see a listing of all bills in Express. Optionally, click **Current View** to filter the list to show overdue, open, or voided invoices.

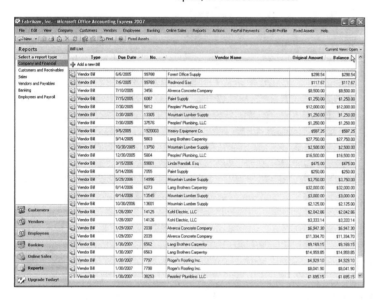

FIGURE 7.27 The Bill List shows all bills entered in Express, the original amount, and the balance due.

VENDOR PAYMENTS

The Vendor Payments list, shown in Figure 7.28, lists your payments and can be used to find a discrepancy between the amount the vendor shows and your records.

Click the **Vendors** menu, **Vendor Lists**, **Vendor Payments** to see a listing of all check, credit card, and cash payments in Express. Optionally, click **Current View** to filter the list to show only not issued, issued, or voided payments.

267

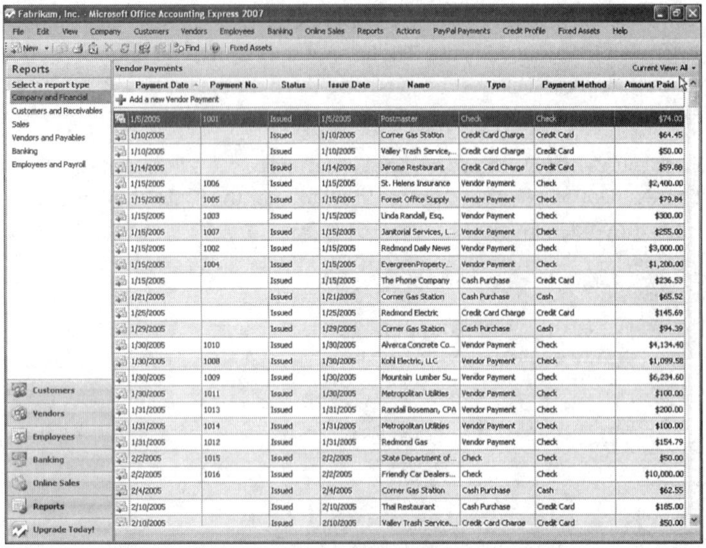

FIGURE 7.28 The Vendor Payments list shows all vendor payments entered in Express, the form of payment, and the amount.

Banking Reports

Banking reports include Reconciliation Detail and Failed Payments.

RECONCILIATION DETAIL

The Reconciliation Detail report, shown in Figure 7.29, should be printed each month when the account is reconciled. If a transaction changes on a previously reconciled report, the reconciliation will need to be redone and the report printed again. Repeat for all reconciliation reports after the changed report.

Click the **Reports** menu, **Banking**, **Reconciliation Detail** to see the cleared and uncleared deposits and withdrawals for a specific statement.

PAYMENTS

As shown in Figure 7.30, the Payments report shows checks, charges, and payments made to vendors.

Click the **Reports** menu, **Banking**, **Payments** to see the checks, charges, and vendor payments.

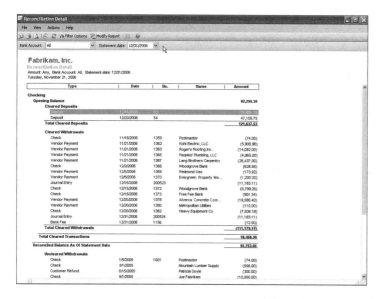

FIGURE 7.29 The Reconciliation Detail report shows the cleared and uncleared deposits and withdrawals for a specific statement date.

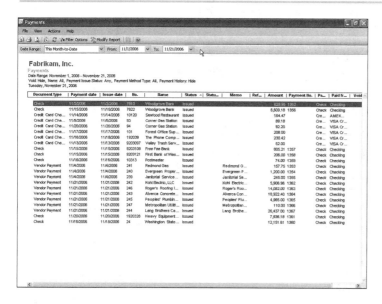

FIGURE 7.30 The Payments report shows all payments.

FAILED PAYMENTS

The Failed Payments report shows the detailed status of payments that failed to issue.

The Failed Payments report is available only after the PayPal add-in is enabled.

⇨ See "PayPal" on page 321 for more information about the PayPal add-in.

Click the **Reports** menu, **Banking**, **Failed Payments**.

Employee and Payroll Reports

Employee and Payroll reports include the Time report, Employee List, Time Entry List, and Employee Payments.

TIME REPORT

The Time report may be used before billing customers for employee time.

Click the **Reports** menu, **Employees and Payroll**, **Time Report** to see billable time for employees.

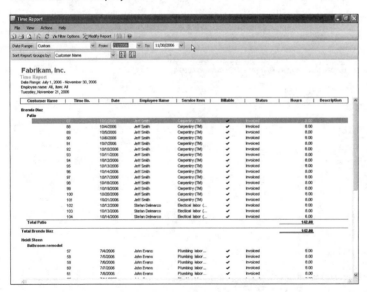

FIGURE 7.31   The Time report shows each customer and the date, employee name, billable hours, service, and billing status.

EMPLOYEE LIST

The Employee List shows all active or inactive employees.

Click the **Employees** menu, **Employee Lists**, **Employees**. Optionally, click **Current View** to filter the list to show only active or inactive employees.

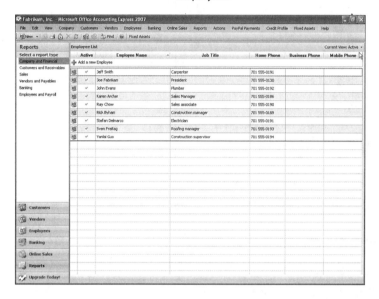

FIGURE 7.32   The Employee List shows all employees and their phone numbers.

TIME ENTRY LIST

The Time Entry List shows billable employee hours and indicates whether the hours have been invoiced.

Click the **Employees** menu, **Employee Lists**, **Time Entries**. Optionally, click **Current View** to filter the list to show only not invoiced, invoiced, or billable but not invoiced time entries.

EMPLOYEE PAYMENTS

Employee Payments shows issued, not issued, and voided employee payments.

Click the **Employees** menu, **Employee Lists**, **Employee Payments**. Optionally, click **Current View** to filter the list to show only not issued, issued, and voided employee payments.

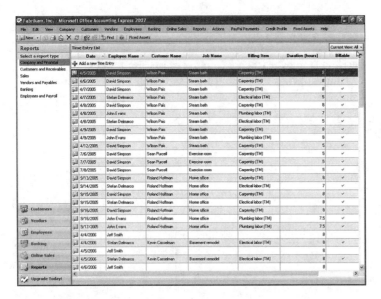

FIGURE 7.33   The Time Entry List shows the hours billed for each employee, job, and date.

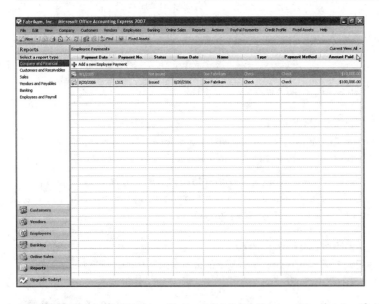

FIGURE 7.34   The Employee Payments list shows the amount and status of each payment to an employee.

Report Options

Report options include numerous ways to modify and use Express reports, as shown in Figure 7.35.

If the Toolbar is not showing, click the **View** menu, **Toolbar**.

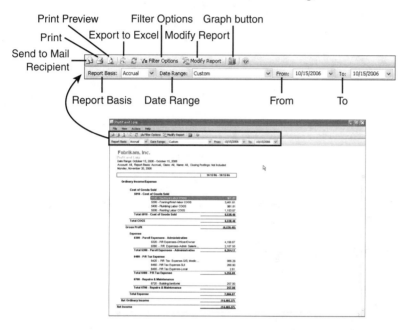

FIGURE 7.35   Email, print, send to Excel, or customize a report using the many options found on the Toolbar.

Send to Mail Recipient

The **Send to Mail Recipient** button, shown in Figure 7.36, sends an email with a report as an Excel attachment.

Print

Click the **Print** button to print the report. The Print window opens, as shown in Figure 7.37. Choose the appropriate options, and then click the **OK** button to send the report to the printer.

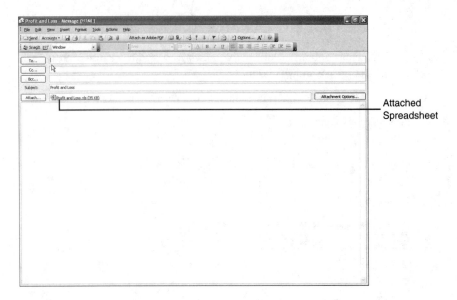

Attached
Spreadsheet

FIGURE 7.36   Click the Send to Mail Recipient (as an Excel attachment) button to create an email message with the report attached as an Excel spreadsheet.

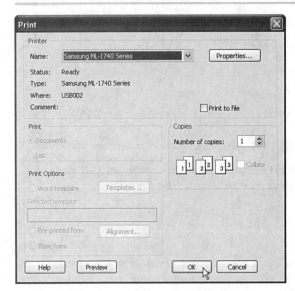

FIGURE 7.37   Select the printer and number of copies to print. Other options may appear depending on your specific printer.

To keep from wasting paper:

- Show only those items you need to see by filtering the report.

⮕ See how to filter in "Filter Options," page 277.

- As shown in Figure 7.35, click the **Print Preview** button instead of the **Print** button to check that the report fits properly on the paper before printing.

- Click the **File** menu, **Page Setup** to change paper margins or to change the orientation from Portrait to Landscape.

Print Preview

As shown in Figure 7.38, use Print Preview to save paper. View the report on the computer screen first before deciding whether to print it.

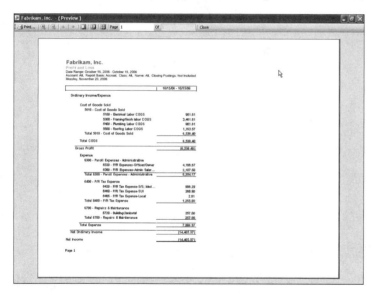

FIGURE 7.38   Click the Print Preview button to see how the report will look when printed.

Print Preview provides many ways to view a report on the screen:

- Click the **Zoom In** button to see a portion of the report magnified, or click the **Zoom Out** button to see the full page on the screen.

- Use the **Previous Page** and **Next Page** buttons to page through the report.

- Select how many pages to view on the screen at once by clicking the **View One Page**, **View Two Pages**, or **View Four Pages** buttons.

- View and print only specific pages of the report by entering the first page to view after **Page**, and the last page after **To**.

- Click the **Close** button to close the report and return to Express, or click the **Print** button to open the Print window.

Export to Excel

Send an Express report to Excel if you want to analyze the data further. Click the **Export to Excel** button, shown in Figure 7.35, to open and view the report in Excel, as seen in Figure 7.39.

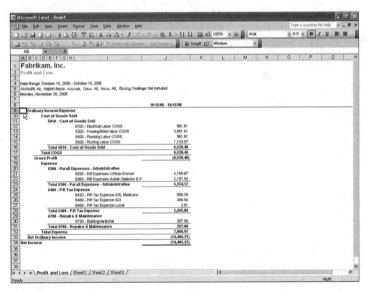

FIGURE 7.39   View and modify the report to Microsoft Excel if you have Excel Version 10 or newer on your computer.

Refresh Report

If the data has changed, the **Refresh Report** button updates the report, as shown in Figure 7.40.

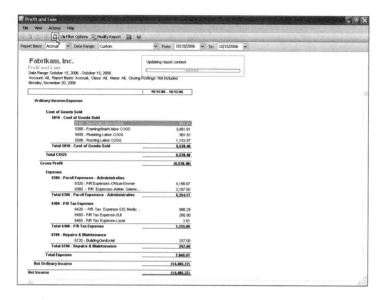

FIGURE 7.40   Make sure that the report data is up to date by clicking the Refresh Report button. The numbers on the screen change to reflect the current data.

Filter Options

View shorter reports by filtering the data to see only what you need in the report. Click the **Filter Options** button, shown in Figure 7.35, to open the Select Filter Options window, as seen in Figure 7.41.

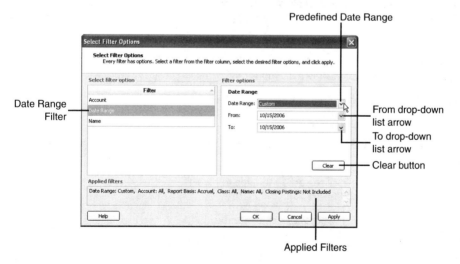

FIGURE 7.41   Filter the report to show only what you want to see.

Each report has different information and, therefore, different filters. A filter can also use multiple criteria. For example, to view a report showing only the bank account with dates between 10/1/2007 and 10/15/2007:

1. Click **Account**.

2. Click **Bank Account**.

3. Click **Date Range**.

4. Click **Custom**.

5. Click the **From** selection arrow.

6. Click **10/1/2007** on the calendar.

7. Click the **To** selection arrow.

8. Click **10/15/2007** on the calendar.

To see a report showing the bank account, but without specific dates:

1. Click the **Date Range** filter.

2. Click the **Clear** button to remove the 10/1/2007 to 10/15/2007 filter. Notice how the date range is removed from the Applied Filters area.

If filtering by date, choose a predefined date range by clicking the Date Range button, shown in Figure 7.35. There are 27 predefined date ranges including **All**, **Previous or Current Week**, **Month**, **Fiscal**, and **Calendar Year**. Or choose **Custom** and then enter the **From** and **To** dates.

If filtering by account, choose from 16 predefined group of accounts or select one or more specific accounts, as shown in Figure 7.42.

As shown in Figure 7.43, to select one or more accounts as filters:

1. In the **Account** filter, click **Selected Accounts**.

2. Click the **Show Selected** button to open the Select Accounts window.

3. In the Available Options area, click the account name to highlight it.

4. Click the **Add** button to move the account name into the Selected Options area.

5. When finished selecting accounts, click the **OK** button.

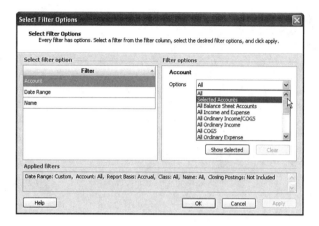

FIGURE 7.42 Select a predefined range of accounts.

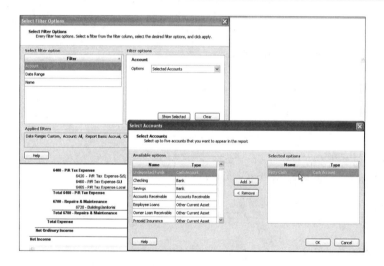

FIGURE 7.43 The Selected Accounts option enables you to choose one or more accounts.

As shown in Figure 7.44, if filtering by name, choose a predefined group of names:

- **All**
- **All Customers**
- **All Vendors**
- **Selected Names**—One or more specific customers and/or vendors

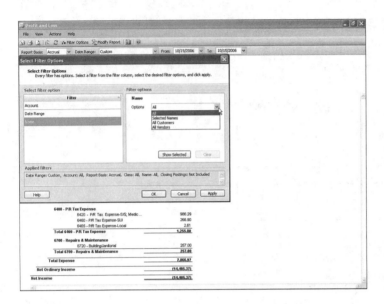

FIGURE 7.44   Select a predefined range of names or specific names.

As shown in Figure 7.45, to filter by specific customers and/or vendors:

1. Click **Name** in the Filter area.

2. Click the **Name Options** drop-down arrow.

3. Click **Selected Names** from the list.

4. Click the **Show Selected** button. The Select Names window appears.

5. In the Available Options area, click the vendor or customer to add to the filter.

6. Click the **Add** button to select the customer or vendor.

7. Continue adding customers or vendors.

8. To remove a customer or vendor from the filter, click the **Remove** button.

9. When done, click the **OK** button to return to the Select Filter Options screen.

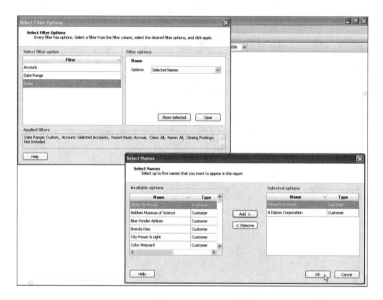

FIGURE 7.45   Choose one or more vendors and/or customers.

Modify Report

Modify Report is used to customize and improve the presentation of the report for your specific needs. Information filtering is the first choice. Choose to

- Not filter the report

- Use a predefined filter

- Open the Select Filter Options window (also see Figure 7.46)

As shown in Figure 7.47, click **Columns** in the Modify Report pane to change the columns displayed.

Display Column By determines the number of columns within the date range specified:

- **Totals Only** displays one column with the totals.

- **Monthly** displays one column for each month.

- **Quarter** displays one column for each calendar quarter.

- **Year** displays one column for each calendar year.

- **Fiscal Quarter** displays one column for each quarter.

- **Fiscal Year** displays one column for each fiscal year.

Modify Report button   Modify Report pane

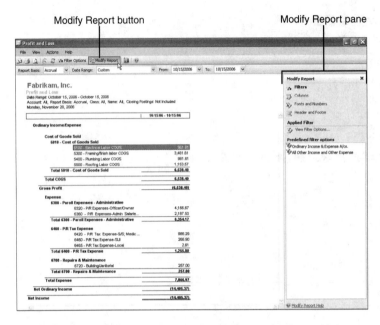

FIGURE 7.46 Clicking the Modify Report button makes the Modify Report pane visible. Select options in the Modify Report pane to change the filter, columns, fonts, number formatting, header, and footer.

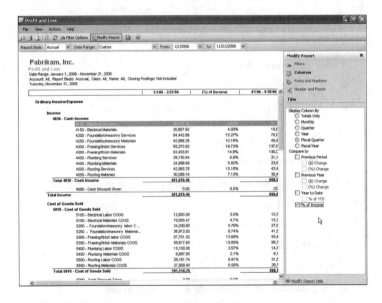

FIGURE 7.47 Select how the columns display.

Compare To shows twice as many columns, an additional column to the right of each display column for

- Previous Period Dollar Amount
- Previous Period Percent Change
- Previous Year Dollar Amount
- Previous Year Percent Change
- Percentage of Year-to-Date
- Percentage of Income

Checkmark a column check box to display a column, or uncheck the column check box to remove the column from the report.

1. As shown in Figure 7.48, click **Fonts and Numbers** in the Modify Report pane to change the look of the report.

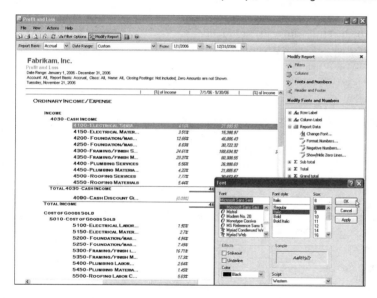

FIGURE 7.48   Improve the report by changing the fonts, styles, sizes, and colors.

2. Click the plus sign to the left of Row Label to expand the options.

3. Click **Change Font**.

4. Change the font, font style, size, effects, and color as desired. Your fonts might differ from this example.

Additional changes include

- Dividing all amounts by 1,000

- Hiding zeros

- Hiding amounts to the right of the decimal

- Hiding zero balance lines

- Formatting negative numbers

5. Click the **Apply** button to view your changes without closing the window.

6. Click the **OK** button when you are satisfied with the look of the report.

7. Repeat steps 2 through 6 for Column Label, Report Data, Sub Total, Total, and Grand Total.

8. Click **Close Modify Report**, and then view the finished report.

As shown in Figure 7.49, any column text box with a line around the outside can be modified. In this report, you may change the text used for the Company Name, Report Title, Subtitle, Notes, and Footer. Or, if you choose, remove it completely from the report by unchecking the appropriate check box.

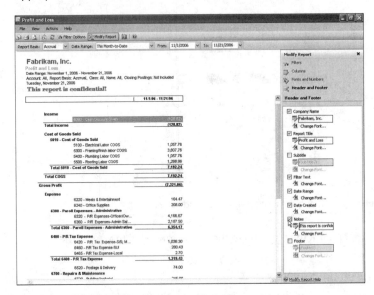

FIGURE 7.49   Add additional notes to a report, and then change the font to make it stand out.

To add a note:

1. Type text into the note.

2. Checkmark the check box to display the note in the report.

3. Click **Change Font**, and then change the type style, size, and color.

4. Click the **OK** button.

Show Chart

With one click a graph appears above the report, as shown in Figure 7.50. For more in-depth charting use Excel. Using either method, a chart provides for a quick visual grasp of the data.

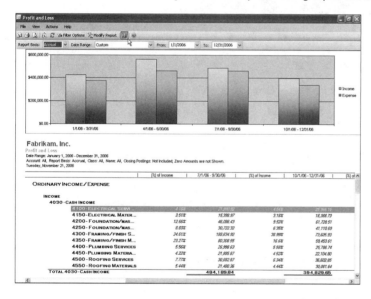

FIGURE 7.50   Displaying a graph is as easy as clicking the Show Chart button.

Report Basis

Choose between a Cash Basis or Accrual Basis report. Tell your accountant that the accounting reports can be printed on a cash or accrual basis and ask which method is best for your company.

A Cash Basis report shows income when money is received and expenses when money is paid. An Accrual Basis report shows income when earned and expenses when the services or items are used.

For example, if Ann worked in December 2007 but wasn't paid until January 2008, an Accrual Basis report would show her wages and the associated taxes in December 2007, whereas a Cash Basis report would show them in January 2008.

As shown in Figure 7.51, to change the report basis, click the **Report Basis** drop-down list arrow. Click either **Cash** or **Accrual**. The report changes to reflect your choice.

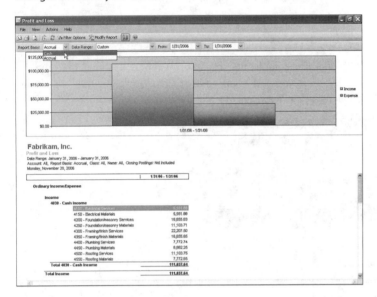

FIGURE 7.51   A change between Cash Basis and Accrual Basis is easily shown in the report.

Date Range

Use predefined date ranges, or enter the **From** and **To** dates to show only the needed data.

As shown in Figure 7.52, choose a predefined date range.

Or, type the date directly in **From** and **To**.

Or, click the selection arrows to the right of **From** and **To**, and then choose the date from the calendar.

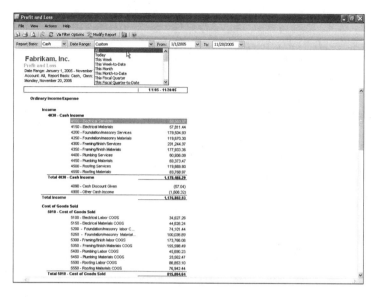

FIGURE 7.52 A frequently used option is the date range.

Sort Order

Most reports permit you to sort alphabetically or by groups.

Some reports can be sorted; for example, by date or by account, as shown in Figure 7.53. If this is the case, a sorting toolbar appears below the Report Basis and Date Range toolbar. To sort, follow these steps:

1. Click the drop-down list box arrow to the right of **Sort Report Groups By**.

2. Choose a sorting method.

3. Click either the **A to Z** button to sort in ascending order or the **Z to A** button to sort in descending order by your chosen method. The report re-sorts.

To sort a report by a specific column, as shown in Figure 7.54:

1. Click a column heading to select the column to sort.

2. Click to the right of the column heading text, on the small blue sorting arrow. This sorts the column alphabetically.

3. Optionally, click again on the sorting arrow to sort the column in reverse order.

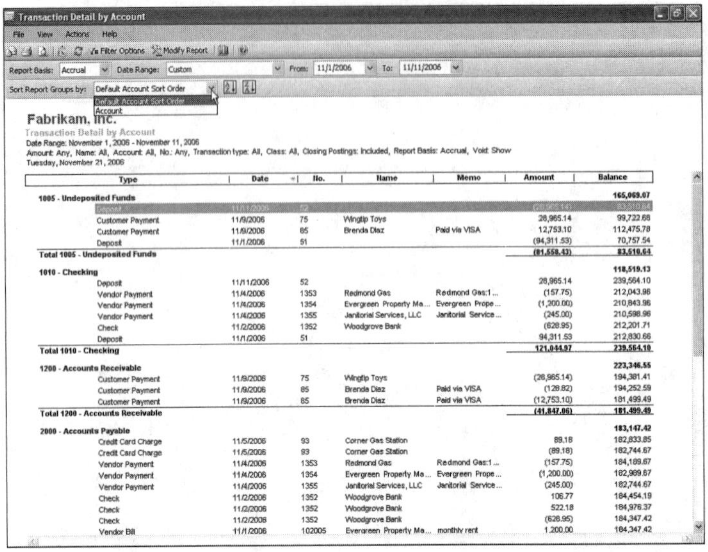

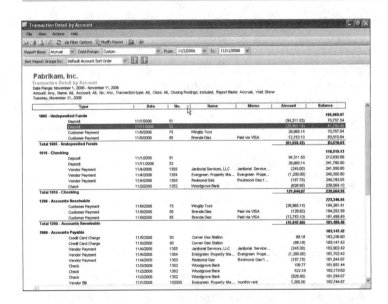

FIGURE 7.53   Some reports have a sorting capability.

FIGURE 7.54   Columns can be sorted alphabetically, ascending or descending.

Move Columns

Drag a column heading to move the column to another position, as shown in Figure 7.55. It's that easy!

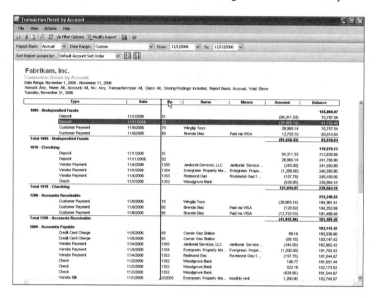

FIGURE 7.55 Columns can be repositioned. Drag the Name column heading to move it before the No. column. The dark vertical line indicates where the Name column will be placed.

Resize Columns

Resize columns to see all the data on the screen without scrolling, or to print within one page width, as shown in Figure 7.56.

View Detail

Double-click a transaction line to see the original transaction entry, as shown in Figure 7.57.

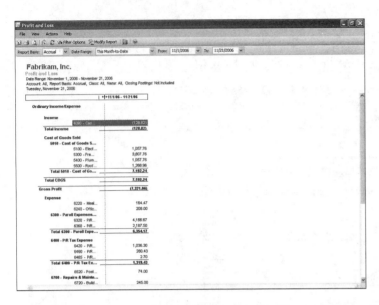

FIGURE 7.56   Resize a column by dragging the vertical line separating one heading from another heading.

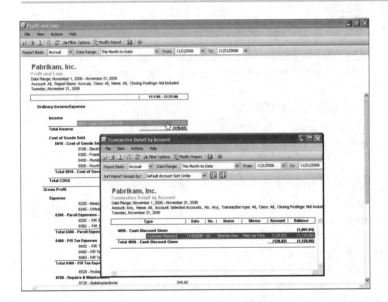

FIGURE 7.57   See the detailed transactions that make up an amount by double-clicking on the number. A second report window opens showing the detail.

- Create Customer Statements and Reconcile Accounts
- Audit Your Work for Accuracy
- View, Adjust, and Pay Sales Tax
- Send Your Books to the Accountant the Easiest Way

End of Period

You want to be sure everything is accurate and ready for the accountant at the end of the period. Don't worry, a check list is included in the book. You are guided through each step.

End of Month, Quarter, or Year

At the end of each month, quarter, and year you will need to do the following:

- Create customer statements

⇨   See "Create Statement," page 292.

- Reconcile accounts

⇨   See "Reconcile Account," page 295.

- Verify that account balances are accurate

⇨   See "Audit the Data," page 300.

- Pay sales tax

⇨   See "Pay Sales Tax," page 302.

- Back up

⇨   See "Backup," page 371.

- Send your accountant the financial information for taxes, closing entries, and financial reports

⇨   See "Accountant Review," page 306.

Optionally, you can close a fiscal year by clicking the **Company** menu, **Manage Fiscal Year**, then choosing a fiscal year and clicking the **Close Fiscal Year** button. This prevents problems posting to a previous fiscal year in error.

Create Statement

Send customer statements at the end of the period. This will make customers aware of their account balance so that they will pay it. If they disagree with the balance or transactions, they might call you to discuss their concerns.

To create a statement, click **Create Statement** at the bottom of the Customers screen in **More Tasks**, as shown in Figure 8.1. Or click the **Customers** menu, **Create Statement**.

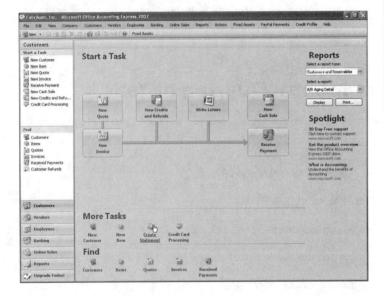

FIGURE 8.1 Print customer statements to remind customers to pay.

As Figure 8.2 shows, to create customer statements, enter the following information:

- **Statement Period From**—Type the date, or click the drop-down arrow to select a date from the calendar. Type a month, /, and day (for example, 6/1), and then press the **Enter** key; Express automatically enters the current year (6/1/2007). Any transactions before the Statement Period From date are summarized on the first line as a Balance Forward amount.

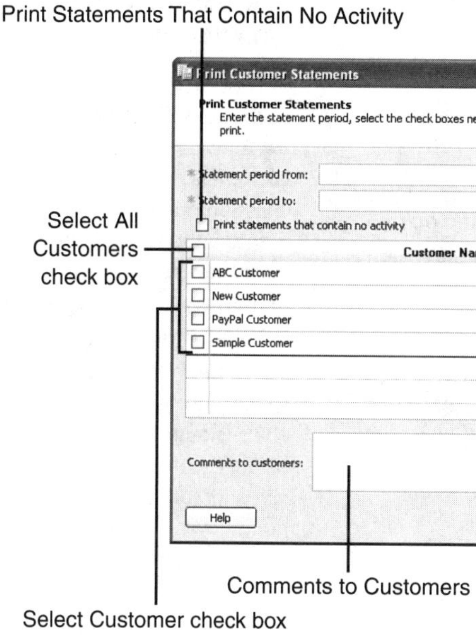

Print Statements That Contain No Activity

Select All Customers check box

Comments to Customers

Select Customer check box

FIGURE 8.2 Choose the statement dates and customers, and then print. Easy!

- **Statement Period To**—Type the date, or click the drop-down arrow to select a date from the calendar. Type a month, /, day (for example, 6/1), and then press the **Enter** key; Express automatically enters the current year (6/1/2007). Any transactions after this date are not shown on the statement or included in the amount due.

- **Print Statements That Contain No Activity**—Checkmark this check box to print statements for customers that have a balance owed, but no activity within the statement period.

- **Select All Customers**—Checkmark this option and Express quickly checkmarks each individual customer.

- **Comments to Customers**—Enter a comment. For example, **Thank you for speedy payment!**.

When the Print Customer Statements form is complete, click the **OK** button. The Print window opens.

To print customer statements, enter the following information, as shown in Figure 8.3:

- **Printer Name**—The default printer shows. To change the printer, click the drop-down list arrow, and then choose the correct printer.

- **Properties**—Click the **Properties** button to change the way the printer behaves. These properties are unique to each printer model.

- **Number of Copies**—Type a number or click the up and down arrows to choose how many copies of each customer statement will print.

TIP

HOW TO PRINT ALL CUSTOMERS WITH A BALANCE OWED

Be sure to checkmark **Print Statements That Contain No Activity**; otherwise, customers that did not purchase anything this statement period will not print, even though they owe money.

Checkmark the **Select All Customers** check box, for speed, and then uncheck any customers with a zero balance. Otherwise, a page will print for customers that do not owe money, wasting paper and time.

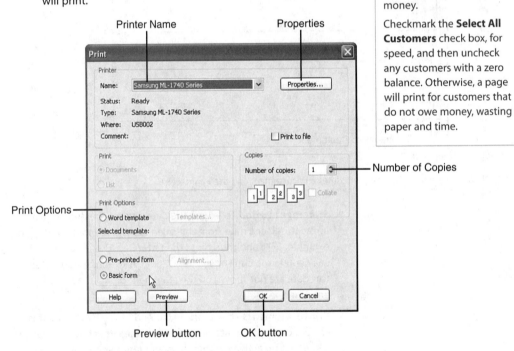

Printer Name   Properties

Print Options

Number of Copies

Preview button   OK button

FIGURE 8.3   Select the printer, number of copies, and form to use. Then preview or print.

- **Print Options**—Choose one of the following:
  - **Word Template**—Use if you have created your own statement form. Click **Word Template**, and then click the **Templates** button and choose the correct template or create a new template.
  - **Pre-Printed Form**—Use if preprinted statement paper is in the printer tray. Click **Company**, **Business Services**, and

then **Checks and Forms** to obtain preprinted forms. Click the **Alignment** button to align the paper correctly before printing statements.

- **Basic Form**—Uses blank paper; the statements print with data, along with headings and lines.

■ Click the **Preview** button to check your work. The Print Preview is shown in Figure 8.4. Then close the preview or click the **Print** button.

■ Click the **OK** button to begin printing the statements.

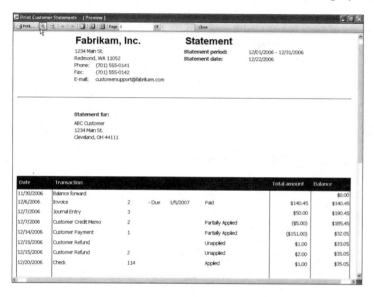

FIGURE 8.4   Click the Preview button to see the customer statements before printing.

Reconcile Account

When your bank and credit card statements arrive, reconcile the statements against the transactions in Express.

Open the reconciliation form using one of multiple methods:

■ On the Banking screen, click the **Reconcile Account** button, shown in Figure 8.5.

■ On the Banking screen, under **Start a Task**, click the **Reconcile Account** link.

■ Click the **Banking** menu, **Reconcile Account**.

To reconcile the bank statement, enter the following information, as shown in Figure 8.6:

- **Account**—Type the name or account number of a banking or credit card account, or click the drop-down list arrow to choose one from the list.

- **Statement Date**—Today's date shows. Type in the ending statement date, or click the drop-down arrow to select a date from the calendar. Type a month, /, day (for example, 6/1), and then press the **Enter** key; Express automatically enters the current year (6/1/2007).

- **Beginning Balance**—Type the amount shown as the beginning balance on the statement. This amount is the same as the ending balance shown on last month's statement.

- **Ending Balance**—Type the amount shown as the ending balance on the statement.

Click the **Next** button to continue.

TIP

RECONCILE AGAIN AFTER MAKING CORRECTIONS

"I'm positive I did that month's bank reconciliation. Here's the report I printed." Yes, you did the reconciliation. Then you went back and corrected a transaction affecting a reconciliation. Now Express undid the reconciliation affected by the correction, and all reconciliations after the correction. Don't throw out printed reconciliations—you might need them to reconcile again. In addition, bank statements and reconciliations are one of the first things an auditor might look at to make sure that fraud does not exist.

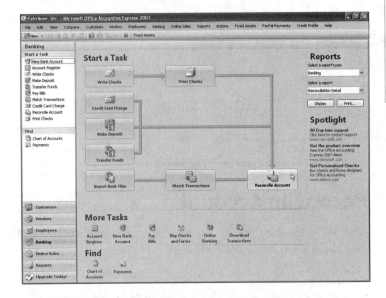

FIGURE 8.5   Open the reconciliation form.

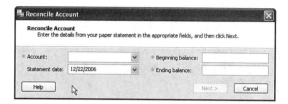

FIGURE 8.6 Reconcile a credit card or banking account.

The reconciliation form for checking can be seen in Figure 8.7.

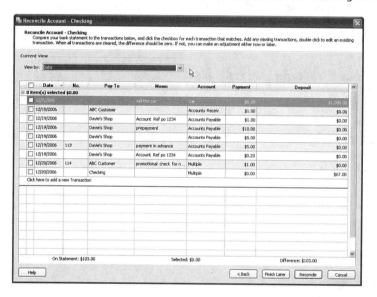

FIGURE 8.7 For checking accounts, the Reconcile Account - Checking window opens.

The reconciliation form for checking, savings, and credit cards look the same except for the name.

- **View By**—Sorts the transactions by date or by subcategories— payments and charges for credit card accounts, or checks and deposits for checking and savings accounts. Click the drop-down list arrow to choose the correct sorting for your statement.

- Click the + or – next to the subcategory heading to expand or collapse the detail.

- Change how the subcategory sorts by clicking a column heading. A small Sort By arrow appears next to the column name, and the transaction rows sort by that column. Click the arrow to change the sort order of the column from A–Z to Z–A.

- Click the **Select All** check box to select or unselect all transactions for payment.

- **Check or uncheck transactions**—A checkmarked transaction means that it shows on the statement. Transactions without a checkmark mean they are still outstanding; the financial institution has not yet received them.

- **Click Here to Add a New Transaction**—Used when a transaction is on the statement but has not yet been entered in Express. The Select Transaction window opens, as shown in Figure 8.8. Choose from **Write Check**, **Transfer Funds**, **Enter Bank Fee**, **Deposit Customer Payments**, and **Enter Interest Income**. Then click the **OK** button. The appropriate transaction entry form opens.

- To edit or void a transaction, double-click the transaction and it opens.

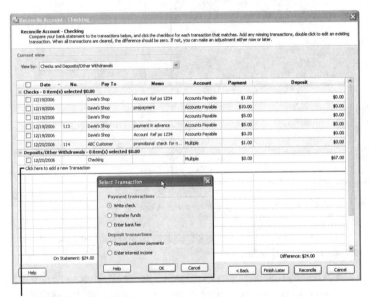

Add a New Transaction link

FIGURE 8.8   Add a new transaction without exiting from the reconciliation.

If you double-check the statement and the checked items, and everything seems okay but the difference total is not $0.00, click the **Back** button to check the beginning and ending statement balances.

If you can't finish the reconciliation at this time, click either **Cancel** (nothing is saved) or **Finish Later** (the transactions will still be check-marked when you return later).

Note the Difference total, shown in Figure 8.9. When it is $0.00 and all the items on the statement are checked off, the statement is reconciled. When it is reconciled

1. Click the **Reconcile** button. The Reconcile Complete window opens.

2. Click the **Display Report** button.

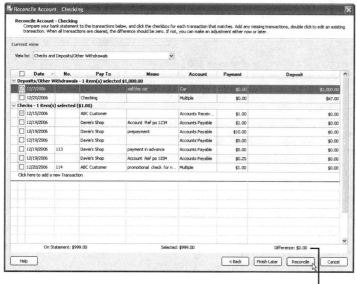

Difference total

FIGURE 8.9 The statement reconciles to the transactions in Express!

The Reconciliation Detail report, shown in Figure 8.10, can be emailed, printed, or modified to your needs.

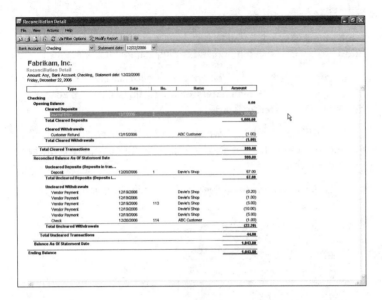

FIGURE 8.10 The reconciliation report displays—be sure to print and file it!

Audit the Data

Periodically verify that your balances and the transactions look right, especially before sending information to the accountant or a taxing authority. This can be done by printing reports and checking them, calling or emailing vendors and customers to verify balances, and reviewing old outstanding bank and credit card transactions to see whether they need to be voided. Does everything make sense? Use the Memo field in transactions to record why a transaction was done a specific way and who authorized it, so that you don't have to remember the details.

To write a vendor or customer letter to verify the balance, open the Write Letters Wizard using one of these methods:

- As seen in Figure 8.11, on the Customers screen, click the **Write Letters** button.

- Or click the **Customers** menu, **Write Letters**. The Write Letters Wizard opens, as shown in Figure 8.12.

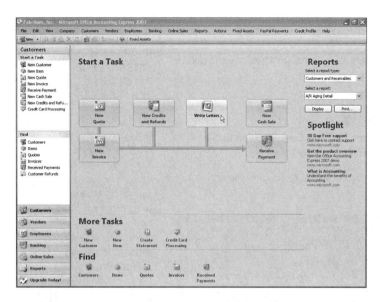

FIGURE 8.11 Use Express's letter-writing capability to write vendors, customers, or employees.

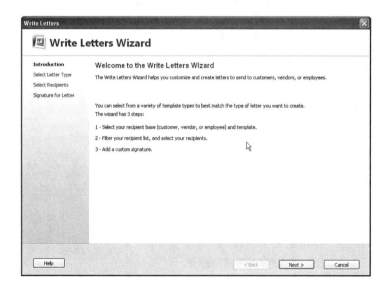

FIGURE 8.12 The Write Letters Wizard walks you through the steps of creating letters within Express.

Pay Sales Tax

View the sales tax liability, edit if it is inaccurate, and then pay the taxing authority.

View Sales Tax Liability

To view the Sales Tax Liability report, click the **Company** menu, **Sales Tax**, **View Sales Tax Liability**, as shown in Figure 8.13.

Click the **Modify Report** button, shown in Figure 8.14, on the report to make changes.

TIP

REVIEW SALES TAX SETTINGS FOR PROBLEMS

If the sales tax is off more than a few cents, figure out why; don't ignore it. Click the **Company** menu, **Sales Tax**, and review each menu item for accuracy. If you still cannot find the problem, write down the logic of how sales tax should be calculated, review each sales tax transaction to decide what type of sales tax is off, and then work through the setup steps in the section "Sales Tax Setup" in Chapter 5, "Company Setup," until you find the problem.

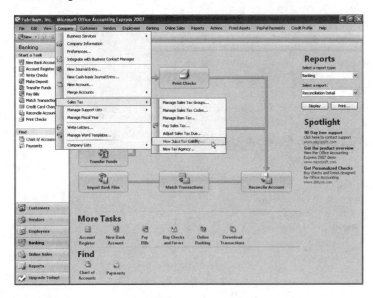

FIGURE 8.13   Open the sales tax report to see how much is owed.

Adjust Sales Tax Due

How much is sales tax off? If the amount is pennies or the taxing authority is giving you a discount for early payment, adjust it using the Adjust Sales Tax form.

To open the Adjust Sales Tax form, shown in Figure 8.15, click the **Company** menu, **Sales Tax**, **Adjust Sales Tax Due**, as shown earlier in Figure 8.13. The Adjust Sales Tax window opens.

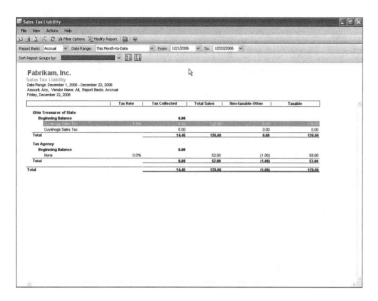

FIGURE 8.14 Modify and filter the sales tax report to show exactly what you need.

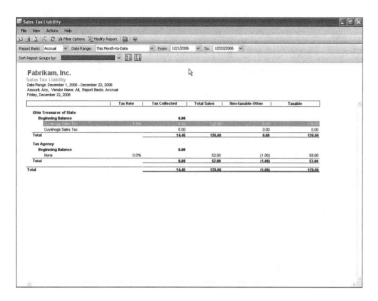

FIGURE 8.15 Adjust sales tax if it is off.

To adjust the sales tax, enter the following information:

- **Date Effective**—Today's date shows. If a different date is needed, type the date or click the drop-down arrow and choose a date from the calendar.

- **Journal Entry No.**—Increments automatically but can be changed. However, changing the number is not recommended.

- **Tax Income or Expense**—Select the income or expense account the adjustment should affect. Either click the drop-down list arrow and choose the correct financial account from the list, or start typing the financial account. Type the name or the account number, and the name will appear. When you're finished, press the **Enter** or **Tab** key. You can add new accounts by clicking on the first line in the drop-down list.

- **Tax Code to Adjust**—Click the drop-down list arrow and choose the correct tax code from the list, or start typing the account and the full name will appear. When you're finished, press the **Enter** or **Tab** key.

- **Adjustment**—Click the **Increase** button to increase the tax owed, or click the **Decrease** button to decrease the tax owed.

- **Amount**—Enter the amount of the increase or decrease.

- **Memo**—Enter comments concerning the adjustment.

When the adjustment is complete, click the **OK** button. The information is saved and the window closes.

Pay Sales Tax

After viewing the sales tax liability and adjusting it if necessary, pay the sales tax via cash, credit card, checking, or online banking.

To open the Pay Sales Tax window, shown in Figure 8.16, click the **Company** menu, **Sales Tax**, **Pay Sales Tax**.

To pay sales tax, enter the following information:

- **Date**—Today's date shows. If a different date is needed, click the drop-down arrow and choose a date for the calendar.

- **Pay From**—(Required) Enter the financial account. Click the drop-down list and choose the correct cash, bank, or credit card account; or start typing the financial account name or number and the full name will appear. When you are finished, press the **Enter** or **Tab** key.

- **Payment Method**—(Required) Click the drop-down list arrow and choose **Cash**, **Check**, or **Credit Card**. Alternatively, start typing the payment method and the full name will appear. When you're finished, press the **Enter** or **Tab** key. If online banking is enabled, the Electronic Payment option is also available.

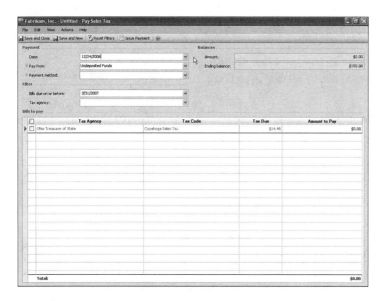

FIGURE 8.16   Pay the sales tax due.

The Bills to Pay section shows all sales tax bills due. Limit the bills that appear by using the **Filter** section. The **Bills Due On or Before** and **Tax Agency** fields may be left blank.

- **Bills Due On or Before**—Type in a date or click the drop-down arrow and choose a date from the calendar. Only bills on or before this date will show in the Bills to Pay section. To delete particular information, highlight it in **Bills Due On or Before** and then press the **Delete** key.

- **Tax Agency**—Click the drop-down list arrow and choose the tax agency, or start typing the tax agency and the full name will appear. Only bills for this tax agency will appear. To delete particular information, highlight it in **Tax Agency** and then press the **Delete** key.

Use the **Reset Filters** button to clear both filters.

The Amount field is not editable. It shows the amount to pay and updates when the bills are checked or unchecked in the Bills to Pay section.

The Ending Balance field is not editable. It shows the ending balance in the Pay From *Financial Account* field you chose earlier. This balance changes when a bill is checked or unchecked in the Bills to Pay section.

The Bills to Pay section shows one bill per row. The Tax Agency, Tax Code, and Tax Due fields are not editable on this form.

Click the **Select All** check box to select all bills for payment. The bills to be paid have a checkmark. Uncheck a specific bill to stop paying it. Checkmark a bill to pay it.

- **Amount to Pay**—The dollar amount of the payment.
- **Total**—This field calculates automatically and is not editable.

When a payment is complete, do one of the following:

- Click the **Save and New** or **Save and Close** button to save the information.
- Click the **Issue Payment** button to record a cash, check, or credit card payment, and to start the check-printing process.

Express automatically asks to save the information before issuing payment. Click the **OK** button.

> **CAUTION**
>
> **DON'T CANCEL**
>
> After you click the **Issue Payment** button and save the information by clicking the **OK** button, the bill might be marked as paid, even if you click the **Cancel** button later.

Accountant Review

Your accountant will want to see your information and reports and assist you with taxes, either monthly or quarterly. There are two important decisions to make.

First, decide how to send the accounting information to your accountant:

- **Manually**—Mail a CD, DVD, or report.
- **Manually Online**—Transfer the file using an email attachment. This is normally not a secure method.
- **Office Live**—Both the accountant and client must sign up for a Windows Live (Passport) account. Office Live uses encryption to transfer the file securely.

Second, you need to know the type of information to send to your accountant:

- A printed report showing only what the accountant requests
- A company backup using the Send Books button
- An accountant's version using the Send Books button

Here are some guidelines to help you decide how to send the information and the type of information to send.

For most companies, the best transfer method is Office Live. Ask your accountant to sign up for Office Live. If the accountant is willing to use Office Live, you must sign up for Windows Live (also called Passport) to enable Accountant Transfer. Accountant Transfer allows secure transfer of your company data.

If this is not possible, password-protect the data and send it via email. Be sure to compress the file into a `.zip` file before sending it—right-click the file, click **Send To**, and then select **Compressed (Zipped) File**. Send the compressed file as an attachment. The accountant must then send back the changes via email, fax, or mail as a written journal entry that you will enter.

When transferring a company backup, use Send Books because the file size is substantially smaller than a backup, and the accountant may make changes to your books without sending you a written journal entry for you to enter into Express.

If Send Books is used, the accountant makes the journal entry, sends the file back to you, and then your records are automatically updated with the changes. Send Books is easier, but can you run your business without affecting transactions that the accountant has? Most small businesses want to immediately deposit checks that affect invoices the accountant is reviewing, or reconcile their bank accounts.

Send Books limits what you can do while the accountant has your data. For this reason, you might want to click the **File** menu, **Accountant Transfer**, **Cancel Transfer** after sending or emailing the file. This cancels the limitations placed on your copy of the data and does not allow you to receive the file from your accountant. However, your accountant can still review your books. In this case, be sure to tell your accountant that you cancelled the transfer and ask that your accountant's written journal entry be faxed, emailed, or mailed. When you receive the changes, you will enter them into Express yourself.

If you do not understand how to make a journal entry and your accountant is unable to show you, do not cancel Send Books. This allows the accountant to create a journal entry in Express for you before sending back the books.

For Accountants Only—Setting Up Office Live

To view client files as an accountant, open Accountant View, as shown in Figure 8.17, after installing Microsoft Office Accounting 2007 Professional or Express.

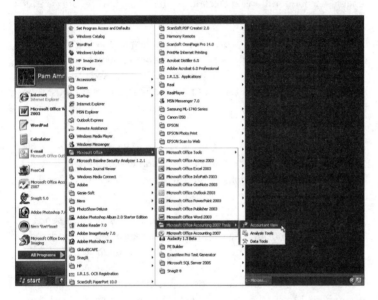

FIGURE 8.17   The accountant opens a separate program that comes with Express called Accountant View.

The accountant may view client files transferred by methods other than Office Live, but Office Live allows secure transfer of the data between client and accountant, regardless of the file size. Emailing the data file is usually not secure. In addition, an email transfer might not work if either the client or the accountant does not have sufficient room in their mailbox.

Click the **Sign Up for Online Transfer** button, shown in Figure 8.18. Internet Explorer opens the Office Live website, shown in Figure 8.19.

The accountant clicks **Sign Up for Online Transfer** while connected to the Internet.

Sign Up for Online Transfer

Add Client ┐ ┌ Sign In

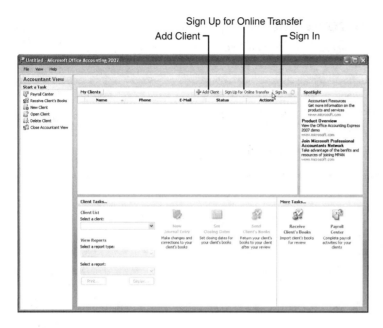

FIGURE 8.18   First, sign up for online transfer.

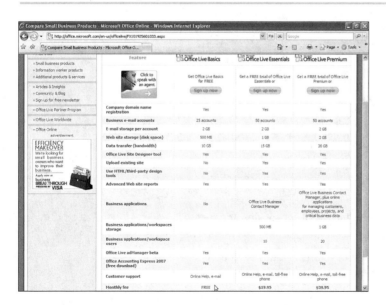

FIGURE 8.19   Office Live Basics is free.

Sending Files to the Accountant

Because Send Books limits the functions you can use while the accountant has your data, coordinate the best time to send the books to your accountant to receive them back quickly. If your accountant cannot return your books within a week, at the very most, use Send Books to send a backup to your accountant instead, and then use **Cancel Transfer** to continue using your data.

There are two options for using Send Books—Manual and Office Live.

To open Send Books, click the **Send Books** button, shown in Figure 8.20.

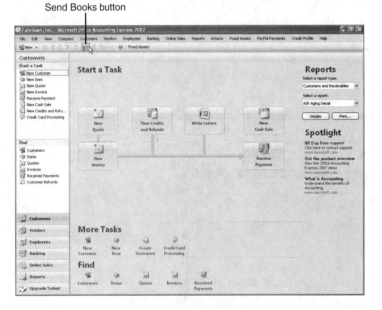

FIGURE 8.20   Open Send Books.

The first time this method is used, the client must send a file to the accountant manually, either by emailing the file or copying and then mailing it to the accountant.

If this is the first Accountant Transfer, or if you need to send the file manually, click the **Send Books Manually** button, as shown in Figure 8.21, and then click the **Next** button.

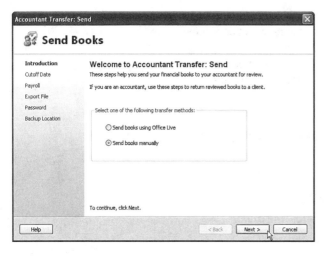

FIGURE 8.21   The first time, the books must be sent to the accountant manually.

To send the books online using Office Live, click the **Send Books Using Office Live** button, and then click the **Next** button. The Windows Live sign-in window opens. Create an account if you don't already have one, and then sign in to Windows Live.

To choose a cutoff date, click the drop-down arrow, and then choose the correct date from the calendar, as shown in Figure 8.22.

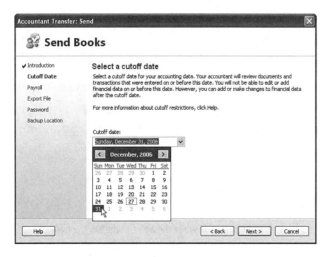

FIGURE 8.22   Select a cutoff date.

While the accountant has the books (using Send Books), any transactions affecting a transaction before the cutoff date cannot be entered. For example, if the cutoff date is December 31 and you receive a customer check on January 5 for an outstanding invoice dated December 3, you will not be able to enter the deposit until you receive the books back from the accountant because the deposit affects a transaction before the cutoff date.

The following lists work you cannot perform while the accountant has your books:

- Editing or adding transactions before the cutoff
- Taxes affecting transactions before the cutoff
- Bank reconciliation of transactions before the cutoff
- Check printing of transactions before the cutoff

In addition, you cannot change the fiscal year or company information, or add online banking.

As shown in Figure 8.23, to have your accountant run payroll, click the **My Accountant Will Run Payroll** button, and then click the **Next** button.

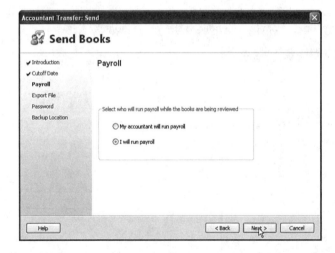

FIGURE 8.23   Decide whether you or the accountant will run payroll while the accountant has the books.

If you want to run payroll, click the **I Will Run Payroll** button, and then click the **Next** button.

Choose the location for the file that will be sent to the accountant, and then click the **Next** button, shown in Figure 8.24.

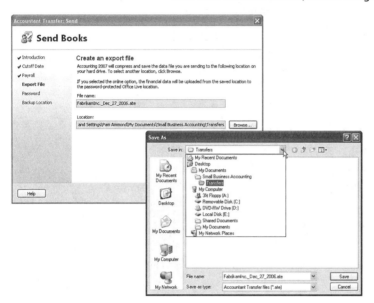

FIGURE 8.24   Decide where Express should put the file.

Optionally, add a strong password to the file, and then click the **Next** button, as shown in Figure 8.25. A strong password is at least seven characters long and contains uppercase and lowercase letters, numbers, and symbols.

In the last step, select a location for the backup file and click the **Export** button, as shown in Figure 8.26. Express backs up the company data and then creates the accountant's file. Wait while the backup completes and the accountant's copy is created.

The easiest way to manually transfer the accountant's file this first time is to use Microsoft Outlook or another email program. The file will have today's date and an .ate extension. Right-click the file, **Send To**, **Compressed (Zipped) Folder**. This compresses the file. Open the email program, create a new message, enter the accountant's email address, the subject, and a message, and then attach the zipped file.

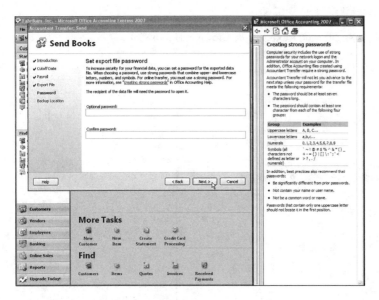

FIGURE 8.25 Optionally, add a password. Then REMEMBER it! The password must also be given to your accountant.

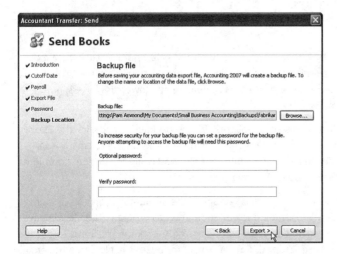

FIGURE 8.26 Express creates a backup of company data and then creates a file to send to the accountant.

Accountant Receives Files

The accountant receives the zipped file, right-clicks the file, and then uncompresses it. The file will have an .ate extension and reside on the accountant's computer.

To receive a client's file:

1. In Accountant Transfer, click **Receive Client's Books**, shown in Figure 8.27. Or click the **File** menu, **Accountant Transfer**, **Receive Client's Books**. The Accountant Transfer: Receive window opens.

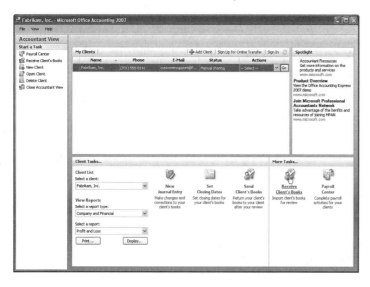

FIGURE 8.27   Receive the client's books.

2. Click the **Next** button.

3. Click the **Browse** button to locate the file, and then highlight the file and click the **Open** button.

4. Click the **Next** button.

5. Enter a password, if necessary, and then click the **Next** button.

6. Type a name for the new company and click the **Save** button, as shown in Figure 8.28.

7. Click the **Import** button. The Create New Company window appears if the company does not already exist. Click the **Yes** button to create the company.

8. Wait while the company data transfers. Then click the **Finish** button.

The accountant cannot change entries after the cutoff date, or add or delete customers or vendors.

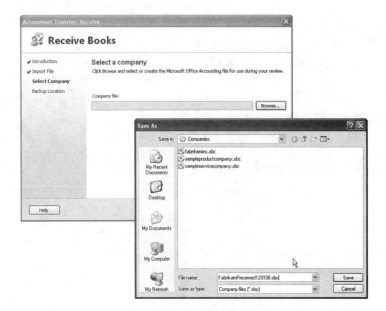

FIGURE 8.28 Enter a name for the client's file.

Accountant Creates Journal Entries and Returns Books

If Send Books with a cutoff date was used to send the client's books to the accountant, the accountant can create journal entries in the client's file and then return the file to the client.

If Send Books was not used, the client's file is not returned to the client. The journal entry is written down and sent using email, fax, or mail, and the client enters the journal entry. Alternatively, the accountant visits the client to enter the journal entry.

▷   See "New Journal Entry," page 239.

If Send Books was used, click **New Journal Entry**, shown in Figure 8.29, and create the necessary journal entries. The date of the journal entry must not be after the cutoff date.

When finished, click **Send Client's Books**, shown in Figure 8.29, to return the books to the client. The Accountant Transfer: Send window opens. Choose manual or Office Live transfer, select the file, optionally enter a password, and then select the backup location. The file backs up and is saved to the hard drive or sent to the client using Office Live.

New Journal Entry   Send Client's Books

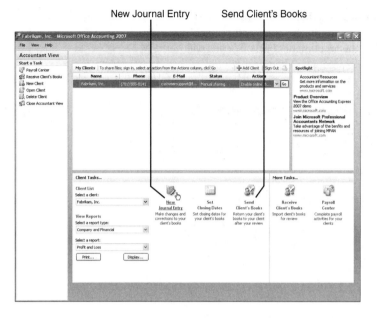

FIGURE 8.29   If Send Books was used, the accountant can enter a journal entry before sending the books back to the client.

Client Receives Files

To receive the books from the accountant:

1. Click the **Receive Books** button, shown in Figure 8.30.

2. Click the **Next** button.

3. Click the **Browse** button to locate the file, highlight it, and click the **Open** button.

4. Click the **Next** button.

5. Enter a password, if necessary, and then click the **Next** button.

6. Locate the correct company.

7. Click the **Import** button.

8. Wait while the company data transfers. Then click the **Finish** button.

If you need to enter transactions and can't because of Accountant Transfer, cancel the transfer. As shown in Figure 8.31, click the **File** menu, **Accountant Transfer**, **Cancel Transfer**. Remember to tell your accountant to send you the changes on paper instead of using Accountant Transfer.

The limitation of using **Cancel Transfer** is that the accountant must email, fax, or mail any changes to you so that a journal entry can be added to Express. Do not restore the accountant's backup or you will lose work that was added while the accountant had the backup.

Receive Books button

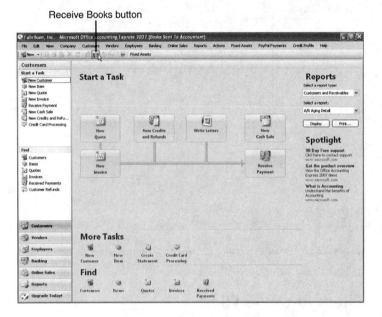

FIGURE 8.30   Receive the files from the accountant. Adjusting journal entries were already made by the accountant!

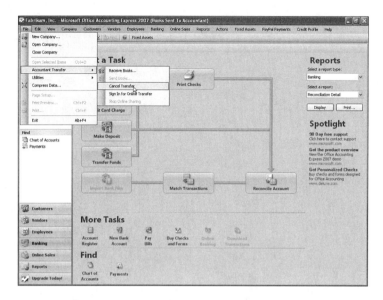

FIGURE 8.31   What happens if the accountant takes too long to send the books back and you must enter transactions before the cutoff? Cancel the transfer!

WHAT YOU'LL LEARN

- PayPal, eBay, Equifax, and ADP Payroll Add-Ins
- Modifying Express to Your Specialized Needs
- Creating Form Letters
- Use Online Banking for Easier Reconciliation and Bill Paying
- Using Express With Access, Excel, and Word

Advanced Features

Advanced features are the nonessential but extremely useful and unique features of Express. The third-party add-ins; integration with Access, Excel, Word, your local bank and credit card processor; and the advanced programming mean that Express is practically limitless. Here's where Express differentiates itself from the competition.

Add-Ins

If you are looking for additional import capabilities from other products, specialized uses of Express (for example, by a manufacturer or distributor), or for additional features (for example, additional integration with shippers), contact these third-party vendors.

To view additional Express add-ons, click the **Company** menu, **Business Services**, **Find Software Add-Ons**, as shown in Figure 9.1. This opens Internet Explorer to an address of

http://directory.partners.extranet.microsoft.com

Then search for Small Business Accounting or Office Accounting products. There are more than 40 add-on products.

PayPal

PayPal can receive or send money for you using the Internet. PayPal integration with Express means you can add a PayPal button to your emailed invoices. Customers can click the **PayPal** button to send payment. Using PayPal, you can receive payment faster and accept credit cards less expensively than through traditional methods. Download PayPal payment information to create an Express transaction—no retyping is necessary.

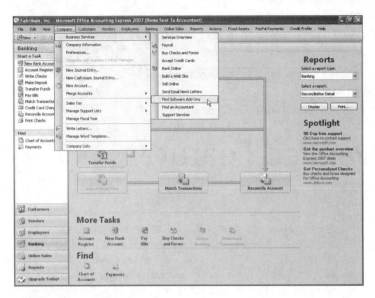

FIGURE 9.1   Other companies have increased Express's capabilities even further. Take a look!

Io set up PayPal:

1. As shown in Figure 9.2, click the **PayPal Payments** menu, and
   select **PayPal Settings**. The PayPal Payment Settings window,
   shown in Figure 9.3, opens.

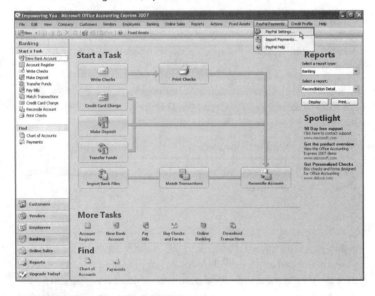

FIGURE 9.2   Set up PayPal in Express.

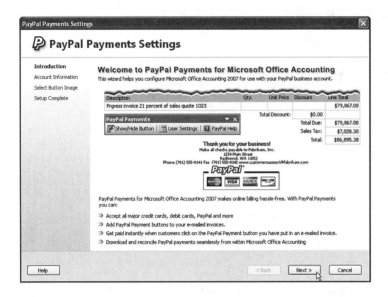

FIGURE 9.3   PayPal settings.

2. Click the **Next** button.

3. Enter your PayPal email address, and then click the **Next** button.

4. Choose the appearance of the PayPal button that appears on invoices, and then click the **Next** button.

5. Click the **Finish** button to close the PayPal Payment Settings window. Three accounts will be added to Express:

   - PayPal vendor account for PayPal charges

   - PayPal customer account for customers who are not already set up in Express

   - PayPal Expense Account for posting PayPal expenses

You can now email invoices with the **PayPal** button on them (see "New Invoice" in Chapter 6, "Basic Accounting Transactions") and import customer payments.

To download PayPal activity:

1. Open Internet Explorer and go to paypal.com.

2. Log in with your ID and password.

3. Click the **History** tab, and then click the **Download My History** link, shown in Figure 9.4.

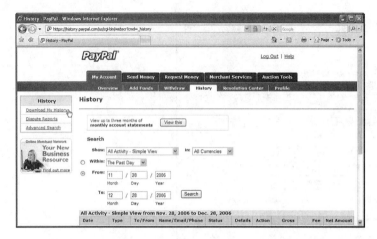

FIGURE 9.4   First, go online to your PayPal account and download the history.

4. Choose the correct dates for the activity to download. Click the
    File Types for Download drop-down list arrow and choose
    Comma-Delimited - All Activity. Click the **Download History**
    button.

5. Save the document where you can find it.

6. Click the **PayPal Payments** menu and select **Import Payments**,
    as shown in Figure 9.5.

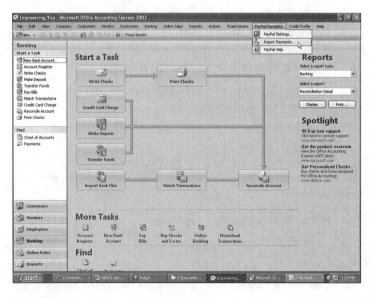

FIGURE 9.5   Import customer payments.

7. Click the **Next** button.

8. Click the **Browse** button to locate the file. The Open window appears. Find and highlight the downloaded PayPal file, and then click the **Open** button. The Open window closes.

9. In the Import PayPal Payments window, click the **Next** button.

10. Enter any write-offs, and then click the **Next** button, shown in Figure 9.6.

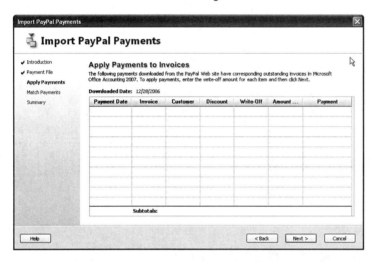

FIGURE 9.6 If Express finds payments that match invoices, they appear on this screen.

11. For items that did not match an invoice, choose a customer to which the payments should apply, as shown in Figure 9.7. Then click the **Next** button.

12. View the Transaction Summary, and then click the **Finish** button.

Equifax

Equifax is a credit reporting service. After you sign up, you can view your company's credit report, and customer and vendor credit data and risk ratings.

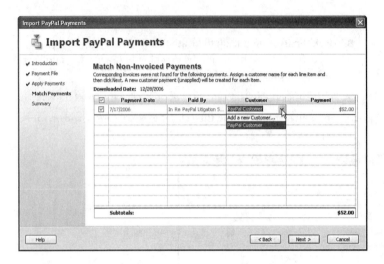

FIGURE 9.7   Match any remaining payments to customers.

To sign up with Equifax to receive credit profiles, do the following:

1. As shown in Figure 9.8, click the **Credit Profile** menu, and select **Sign Up for Credit Profile**. The Equifax Credit Profile Service Wizard opens. Click the **Next** button.

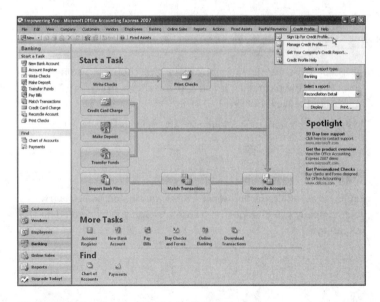

FIGURE 9.8   First, sign up with Equifax.

2. Choose the service, as shown in Figure 9.9, from a free trial sub-scription to $99.95 per month for up to 300 customers and vendor profiles. A single profile is $4.95. Click the **Next** button.

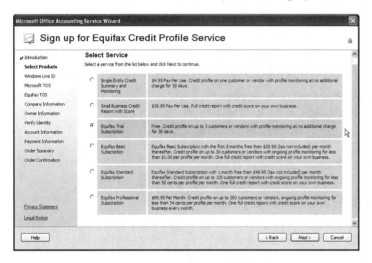

FIGURE 9.9   Choose the credit profiling service.

3. Enter your Windows Live ID. You can sign up if you do not already have one. Click the **Next** button.

4. Read the Microsoft agreement and type the words I Agree if you agree. Click the **Next** button.

5. Read the Equifax agreement and type the words I Agree if you agree. Click the **Next** button.

6. Enter your company information, including your name, address, phone number, tax ID, and email address. Click the **Next** button.

7. Enter the owner information, including name, address, phone number, Social Security number, driver's license number, and date of birth. Click the **Next** button.

   Equifax then checks the information you entered against its records. If their records do not match, you must call them and fax in your current records for verification, which takes three to five days.

8. Enter the account information containing the name, address, phone number, and email address for the person managing the Equifax account. Click the **Next** button.

9. If you ordered a service requiring payment, enter the credit card and billing address information. Click the **Next** button.

10. On the Order Summary page, review your order, and then click the **Confirm** button.

11. On the Order Confirmation screen, click the **Finish** button.

Now that your company has an Equifax account, you can

- Click the **Credit Profile** menu, **Manage Credit Profile** to view and modify the customers and vendors whose credit profile you have requested. In addition, you can change service levels or cancel the service.

- Click the **Credit Profile** menu, **Get Your Company's Credit Report** to view a current credit report and all past credit reports.

- Open a customer or vendor, and then click the **Get Credit Data** button, shown in Figure 9.10, to obtain a credit profile, or click the **View Credit Alerts** button to see credit alerts.

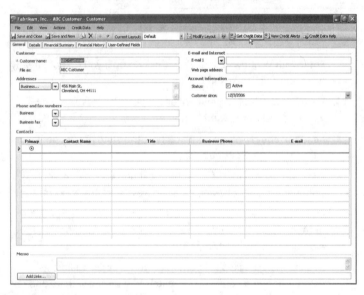

FIGURE 9.10   Each customer and vendor screen has buttons to obtain a credit profile and credit alert.

Sell Online

eBay is an online website where people sell and buy products and services. Express integrates with eBay to assist in listing items and downloading sales transactions.

SET UP TO SELL ONLINE

Get ready to sell on the Internet!

To sign up for online sales:

1. Click the **Online Sales** menu, **Set Up to Sell Online**, as shown in Figure 9.11.

   Or click the **Company** menu, **Business Services**, **Sell Online**.

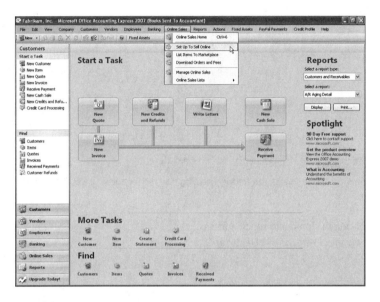

FIGURE 9.11   Set up to sell online.

2. Click the **Next** button, shown in Figure 9.12, in the Marketplace Services window.

3. Using Windows Live ID (previously called Passport), enter your ID and password to sign in.

4. Choose a plan:

   - **Marketplace Services Basic**—Up to 20 listings per month free.

   - **Marketplace Services Standard**—$9.95/month for up to 200 listings per month. More than 200 listings is $.05 per listing. Use your credit card to sign up and cancel at any time.

   Click the **Next** button.

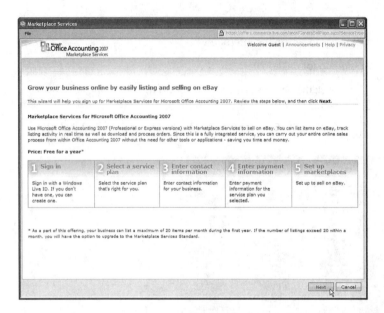

FIGURE 9.12 The Marketplace Services Wizard walks you through signing up. Free for one year, you can sell up to 20 items per month on eBay.

5. Verify your name, address, phone number, and email address. View the agreement, and then click **I Accept** or **I Decline**. Click the **Next** button.

6. Click the **Sign Up** button on the marketplace service to set up. Currently, eBay is the only service shown.

7. Click the **Next** button, shown in Figure 9.13, in the eBay Download Options window.

8. Click the **Next** button, and eBay opens. Sign in to eBay using your eBay ID and password. Review the Microsoft agreement, and then click the **Agree and Confirm** button if you agree.

9. The Accounting Confirmed window opens. Click the **Next** button.

10. In the Manage Order Downloads window, choose one of the following:

   - Only Download Orders Listed Through Microsoft Office Accounting

   - Download All Orders from a Specific Date—Enter the month, day, and year

   Click the **Next** button.

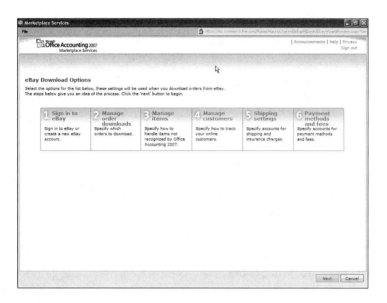

FIGURE 9.13   Set up eBay to work with Express.

11. In the Manage Items window, choose one of the following:

- Track Unrecognized Items Individually—This means that a new item is created in Express when you sell an item on eBay that has not already been entered as an item in Express

- Track All Unrecognized Items As a Single Item Called eBay Sales

Click the **Next** button.

12. In the Manage Customers window, choose one of the following:

- Track Unrecognized Customers Individually—This means a new customer is created in Express when you sell an item on eBay to a customer that has not already been entered in Express

- Track All Unrecognized Customers As a Single Customer Called eBay Customer

Click the **Next** button.

13. In the Manage Shipping and Insurance window, specify the Express Accounts. Select an existing account or add a new account for

   - **Shipping**—eBay shipping charge
   - **Insurance**—eBay shipping insurance charge
   - **Additional charges**—eBay additional charges

   Click the **Next** button.

14. Figure 9.14 shows that in the Manage Payment Methods window, you can specify the Express payment methods and accounts. For each payment method—PayPal, check, cashier or money order, and credit card—choose an Express payment method and account.

   Click the **Next** button.

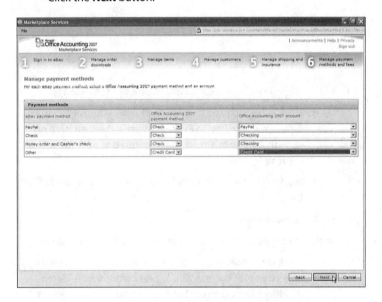

FIGURE 9.14   Match eBay accounts and payment methods to Express.

15. In the Fees window, shown in Figure 9.15, choose whether to download eBay fees from a specific date (no older than three months ago) and PayPal fees. If fees are downloaded, choose vendors and accounts to use.

   Click the **Finish** button.

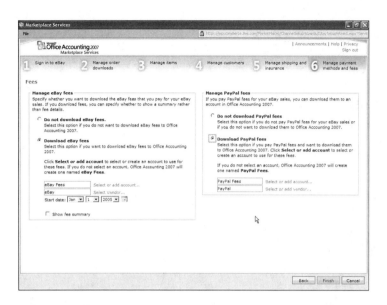

FIGURE 9.15   eBay and PayPal fees can be downloaded into Express.

16. In the Setup Complete window, click the **Close** button. You are finished with setup and ready to sell items and download sales.

LIST ITEMS TO MARKETPLACE

Enter all the information needed to sell an item on the Internet.

To sell items on eBay, do the following:

1. Click the **Online Sales** menu, **List Items to Marketplace**, as shown in Figure 9.17.

2. As shown in Figure 9.18, checkmark the check box of the item(s) to sell. Click the **Next** button.

3. Log in using your Windows Live ID and password.

4. In the Select a Marketplace window, choose the location (eBay, in this case), and then click the **Next** button.

5. In the Review and List window, all the items that you previously chose to sell appear.

- Click the **Remove** link, shown in Figure 9.19, to delete an item from the list of items to sell.

CAUTION

DOUBLE-CHECK BEFORE USING

Before using Marketplace the first time, be sure to check your settings. Click **Online Sales**, **Manage Online Sales**. Log in using your Windows Live ID. Click the **eBay Account Settings** tab, shown in Figure 9.16.

- Click the **Preview** button to view how the item will look when it is listed.

- Click the **Edit** button to add additional information about the item before listing it.

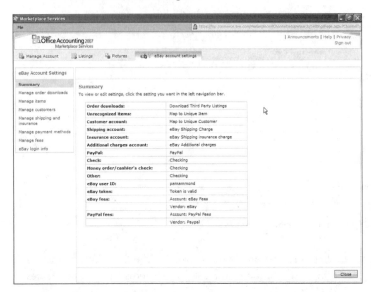

FIGURE 9.16   Check your Marketplace settings before selling or downloading transactions.

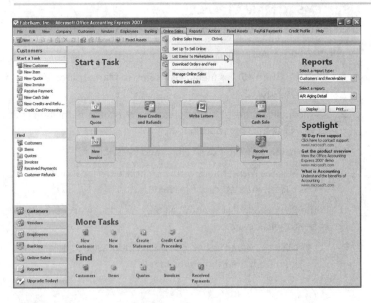

FIGURE 9.17   List your items on eBay.

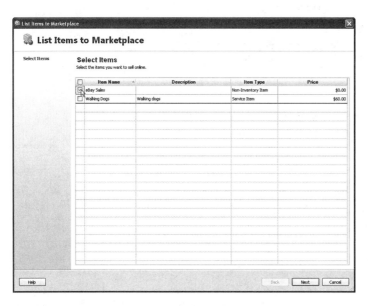

FIGURE 9.18   Select an Express item to sell.

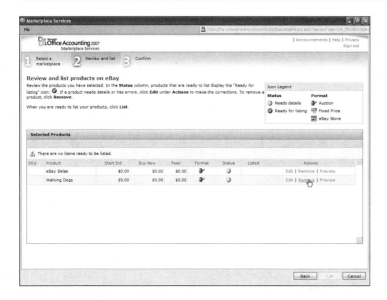

FIGURE 9.19   Delete items that should not be listed and edit items to be listed.

The edit window has all the options needed to list an item on eBay. Be sure to complete the settings in the **Shipping and Taxes**, **Locations**, **Payment**, and **Upgrades** tabs, shown in Figure 9.20.

Settings tabs

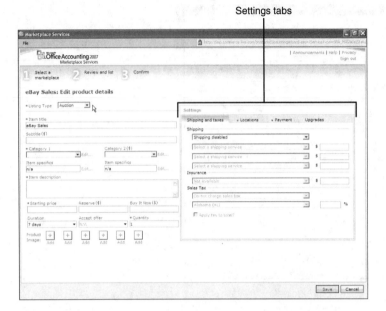

FIGURE 9.20 Click a settings tab and fill in all the item information needed to properly list the item on eBay.

Information eBay lists for free includes

- Listing type—Auction, Fixed Price, eBay Store
- Item title
- Category
- Item specifics (two)
- Item description
- Starting price
- Duration
- Accept offer
- Quantity
- Product pictures (six)
- Shipping
- Insurance
- Sales tax
- Item location
- Country

- Ship to locations or pick-up only
- Payment methods
- Additional payment instructions

eBay charges extra for

- Item subtitle
- Category 2
- Reserve
- Buy It Now
- Upgrades: Gallery, Bold, Border, Highlight, Featured Plus, Gallery Featured, Home Page Featured, Show As Gift

To add pictures, click the picture's **Add** link, shown in Figure 9.21, and then browse to find the correct photo—either online or on your computer.

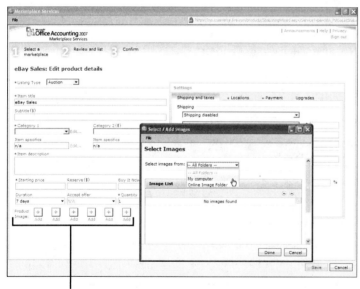

Product Image Add link

FIGURE 9.21   Adding a picture is easy.

After entering the eBay information and clicking the **Next** button, fix any errors, shown in Figure 9.22, before continuing.

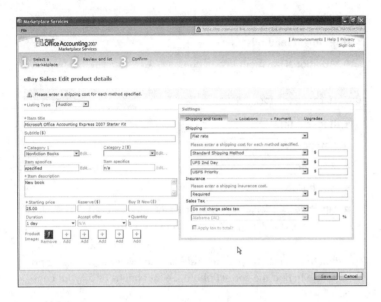

FIGURE 9.22   Fix errors before you continue.

Preview an item, and then edit it as necessary before listing. Click the **List** button, shown in Figure 9.23. A confirmation window appears. Then click the **Close** button.

The item immediately lists on eBay.

DOWNLOAD ORDERS AND FEES

Marketplace orders and fees are downloaded to Express. It is not necessary to enter these transactions manually in Express.

On the Online Sales screen, shown in Figure 9.24, click the **Download Orders and Fees** button.

Or, click the **Online Sales** menu, **Download Orders and Fees**.

Express synchronizes with the online marketplace and downloads any orders. If errors are listed, click the **View Error Details** button.

Orders can be viewed in Express's Online Orders List. Click the **Online Sales** menu, **Online Sales Lists**, then **Online Orders**. The Online Orders List opens.

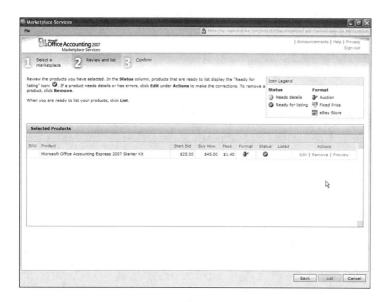

FIGURE 9.23 Remove, edit, or preview before listing the items.

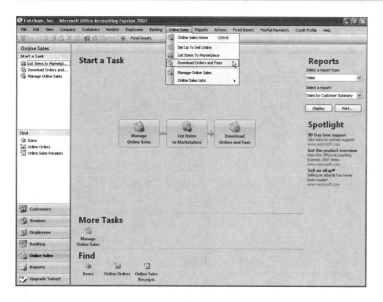

FIGURE 9.24 Download eBay orders and fees.

Forms Modification

Use forms to enter information into Express. After entering the form information, print the form using a Microsoft Office Word template.

Modifying Entry Forms

Modify entry forms to match your printed forms for ease of data entry. Change the name and location of group headers; change the name of fields; or change, add, or delete fields on the form.

For example, your invoice might have the **Date** in the upper-left corner instead of the upper-right corner, **Color** is added to each line item, the field name **Reference** changes to **Purchase Order**, and **Salesperson** is never used and must be removed. All these changes are possible in Express.

Some payment forms cannot be modified.

As shown in Figure 9.25, to modify the layout of a data entry form, open the form and then click the **View** menu, **Modify Layout**.

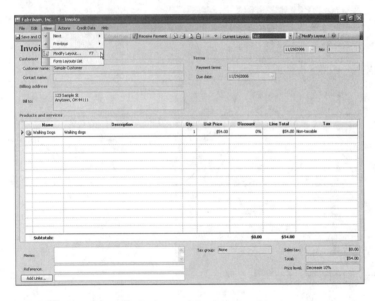

FIGURE 9.25   Modify the layout of the data entry form.

ADDING FIELDS

To add a custom field, before clicking the **View** menu, **Modify Layout** on the form, the field must be added to a vendor or customer record. Add a new field

- To Customers for Quotes, Invoices, Cash Sales, and Customer Credit Memos

- To Vendors for Bills, Vendor Payments, Cash Purchases, and Vendor Credit Memos

Add custom fields to Tax Agency, Items, and Employees; they are not used on other forms.

Open the customer, vendor, item, or employee record, click the **User-Defined Fields** tab, and click the **New Fields** button, shown in Figure 9.26. Checkmark **Text**, **Multi-line Text**, **Date**, **Number**, or **Check Box**. Type the name of the field. Then click the **Close** button. The field is added.

User-Defined Fields tab

New Fields button

FIGURE 9.26   Add a custom field.

Employee user-defined fields are available for Time Report. Open the report, click the **Modify Report** button, click **Columns**, and then check-mark the user-defined field.

You can modify lists to show user-defined fields. Open the list. As shown in Figure 9.27, click the **View** menu, **Add/Remove Content**. The Modify Layout window opens. Click an **Available Fields** field to add to the form. The field highlights. Click the **Add** button to move the field from **Available Fields** on the left to **Show These Fields in This Order** on the right. To remove a field, click the field on the right side and click the **Remove** button.

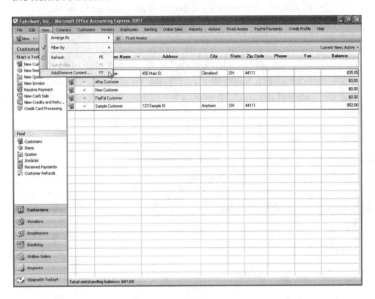

FIGURE 9.27   Change fields on a list.

Open the form requiring a new field. Click the **Modify Layout** button.

Click the drop-down list arrow to select the correct Form Section, and then click an **Available Fields** field, shown in Figure 9.28, to add to the form. The field highlights. Click the **Add** button to move the field from **Available Fields** on the left to **Show These Fields in This Order** on the right. To remove a field, click the field on the right side and click the **Remove** button.

Click the **Preview** button to view the placement of the field on the form. If necessary, click the **Move Up** or **Move Down** button to reposition the field. Then click the **OK** button. The Save Layout window appears. Save the form as a new form or update the current form.

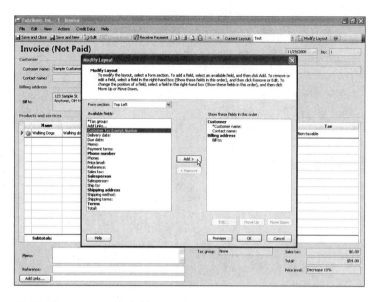

FIGURE 9.28 Add a field to the data entry form.

CHANGING FIELD NAME AND POSITION

Change the position or name of a field to better suit your company's needs.

Open the form requiring a new field. Click the **Modify Layout** button.

Click the drop-down list arrow to select the correct Form Section, and then click a field or header to be changed. The field or header highlights. Click the **Edit** button, shown in Figure 9.29. An Edit Field Name window opens. Type in the new field name, and then click the **OK** button. The name of a field with multiple options (for example, the **Phone** field) cannot change.

Click the **Preview** button to view the placement of the field or header on the form. If necessary, click the **Move Up** or **Move Down** button to reposition the field or header. Then click the **OK** button. The Save Layout window appears. Save the form as a new form or update the current form.

REMOVING FIELDS

Remove a field from a form when it is no longer necessary.

Fields with an asterisk (*) before the name are required and may not be removed.

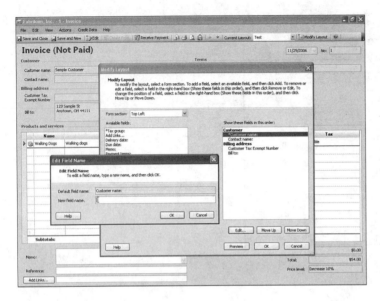

FIGURE 9.29 Change the name of a field.

Open the form requiring a deleted field. Click the **Modify Layout** button.

Click the drop-down list arrow to select the correct Form Section, and then click a field or header to change in **Show These Fields in This Order** on the right. The field highlights. Click the **Remove** button, shown in Figure 9.30. The field or header moves to the **Available Fields** area on the left. Then click the **OK** button. The Save Layout window appears. Save the form as a new form or update the current form.

REMOVE/EXPORT/IMPORT FORM

Manage your forms by removing unused forms, exporting forms for use in other programs, or importing forms from other programs.

Unused forms may be deleted or exported. Click the **Company** menu, **Manage Support Lists**, **Form Layouts List**. As shown in Figure 9.31, the Remove Form Layout window opens. Highlight a form. Then click the **Remove** button to delete it, the **Export** button to save it as an .xml file, or the **Import** button to open a previously exported .xml file to use as a form.

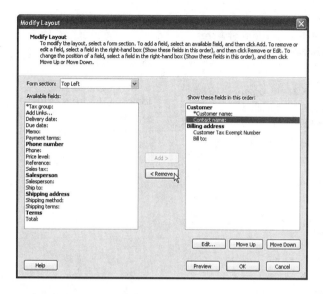

FIGURE 9.30 Remove a field.

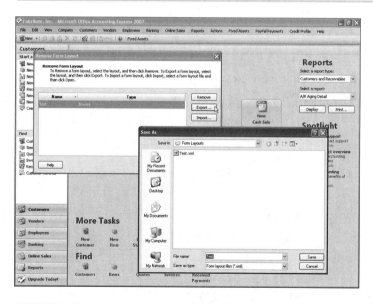

FIGURE 9.31 Remove, import, or export a form.

Modifying Printed Forms

Printed forms can be modified using Microsoft Office Word. Use a theme, add a logo, or add, delete, and move fields.

Word versions before 2002 will not modify templates. Word 2002 (Office XP) offers less form modification than later versions of Word, allowing only the deletion of fields and the addition of a company logo and slogan.

Printable forms using Word 2003 or later are XML documents, also called *smart documents*. Add, edit, and delete fields (called *tags*), add line-item fields, and add a company logo and slogan. Additional modification and creation of new forms not based on existing templates is possible if you are an XML programmer.

The following printed forms may be modified:

- Credit Memo
- Customer Statement
- Invoice
- Online Order
- Online Sales Receipt
- Packaging List
- Sales Receipt
- Quote

After you modify a template, you must save it under a new name.

To modify a printed form, click the **Company** menu, **Manage Word Templates**, as shown in Figure 9.32. The easiest way to proceed is to modify an existing Word template.

Click a template to highlight it, and then click the **Modify** button, shown in Figure 9.33. Or, to create a new printable form, click the **Create** button.

Microsoft Office Word opens with the template showing.

Click the **Show/Hide Button** button, shown in Figure 9.34, to add or remove the PayPal button.

To add your logo to a form, as shown in Figure 9.35, right-click **Your Logo Here**, and then click **Show Picture Toolbar**. The Picture toolbar appears. Click the **Insert Picture** button. Browse to locate your logo, and then resize it for your needs.

> TIP
>
> **SAVE AS BEFORE CONTINUING**
>
> Before modifying your template, use **Save As** to give it a new name. Make sure you do not modify the original template.

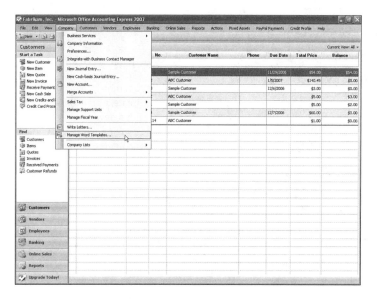

FIGURE 9.32   Modify printed forms through Word templates.

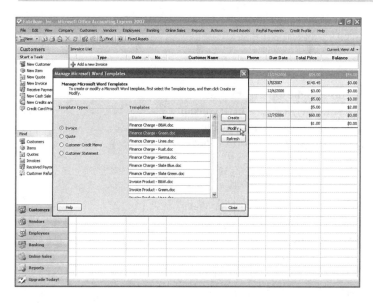

FIGURE 9.33   Unless you are an expert, modify an existing Word template.

Logo   PayPal Payments Show/Hide Button toolbar

Document Actions
Task pane

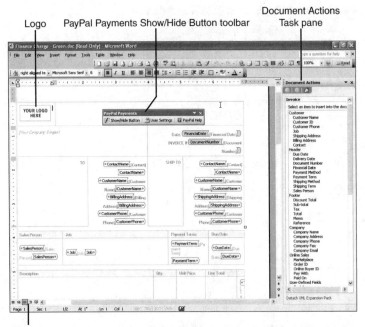

New Fields button

FIGURE 9.34   Add your logo; add or remove the PayPal payment button; add, edit, or delete fields; or change the position of fields.

To add text (not a field), move your cursor to the top left of the text area and drag to the bottom right. Alternatively, click the **Insert** menu, **Text Box**. A rectangular text box area appears and the Text toolbar appears. As shown in Figure 9.36, type in the word(s) to add. Change the font type, size, attributes, and alignment if desired.

To add a field from Express:

1. If the Document Actions Task pane isn't showing, click the **View** menu and make sure that **Task Pane** is checked. Click the drop-down list at the top of the Task pane, and then click **Document Actions**.

2. Click the form where you want the new field located, and then click the field in the **Document Actions** list. The field appears on the form. Move the field or add text attributes if desired. Save the form before exiting Word.

Picture toolbar

Insert Picture button

Logo

New Fields button

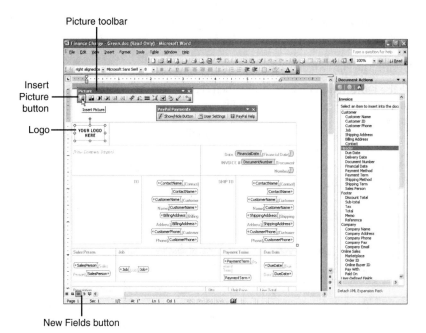

FIGURE 9.35 Easily add your logo!

Font Size — Bold button

Font Type — Align Center button

Text toolbar

Text box

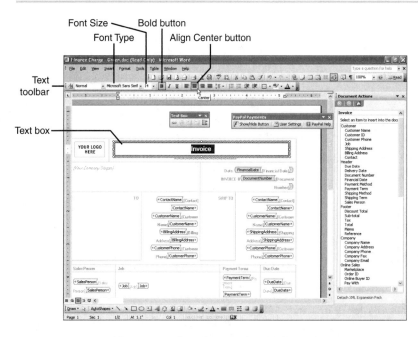

FIGURE 9.36 Add text to your form; for example, add the word *Invoice* at the top.

Follow these steps to use your new template:

1. Open a form.

2. Click the **File** menu, **Print**. The Print window opens.

3. In Print Options, click the **Word Template** button, and then click the **Templates** button, shown in Figure 9.37. The Select Word Templates window opens.

FIGURE 9.37   Print the form using a customized template.

4. Scroll down to your template and select it. Click **Select** to close the window.

5. Click **OK** to print.

Letter Templates

Create custom form letters or modify an existing form letter.

Follow these steps to create a custom form letter:

1. Click the **Company** menu, **Write Letters**, as shown in Figure 9.38. The Write Letters Wizard opens.

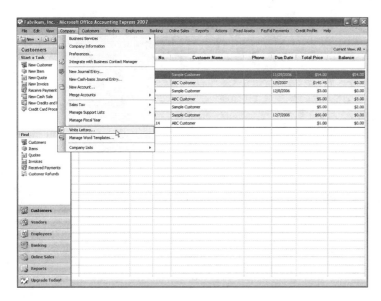

FIGURE 9.38 Create a custom form letter to send to all or select customers, vendors, or employees.

2. Click the **Next** button.

3. Select the recipient by clicking the **Customer**, **Vendor**, or **Employee** button.

4. Choose the letter template by clicking it to highlight it. Click the **Modify** button to modify the letter if necessary. Alternatively, click the **Create** button to create a new template.

5. Click the **Next** button.

6. Select specific customers, vendors, or employees. Then click the **Next** button, shown in Figure 9.39.

7. Use the standard signature or modify it. Then click the **Create Letters** button. The customized form letters display in Word.

8. Click the **Print** button to print the letters.

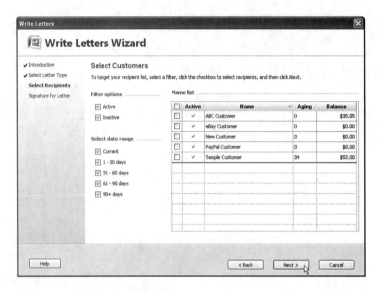

FIGURE 9.39 Choose the customers to receive letters.

ADP Payroll

For $169 per year, ADP Payroll

- Calculates payroll

- Calculates payroll taxes—federal, state, and local

- Allows you to print payroll tax forms, payroll checks, and stubs

- Uses automatic deposit if your bank handles it

- Provides automatic tax reminders

- Integrates with Office Accounting

- Uses the timesheets in Office Accounting

For an additional $60 per year, ADP prepares electronic tax returns and files them.

Click the **Employees** menu, **Online Payroll, Sign Up for Payroll Service**, as shown in Figure 9.40. Internet Explorer opens to the website shown in Figure 9.41.

When signing up for ADP Payroll, the sign-up forms are populated with the information in Express. Initial setup involves company and employee information, pay frequency, optional direct deposit, taxes, and up to 20 earnings and 20 deductions.

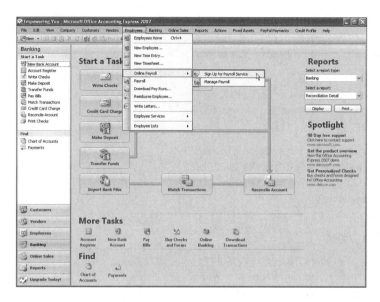

FIGURE 9.40 Sign up today for worry-free ADP payroll.

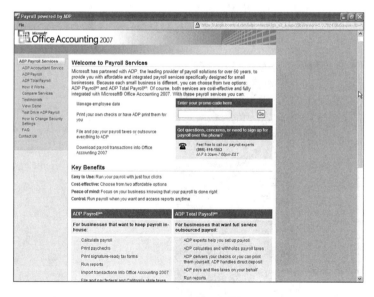

FIGURE 9.41 The ADP Payroll website.

To run a payroll, either type in the hours or import Express's timesheet (see "Employees" in Chapter 6). Preview the data and edit it before running payroll.

ADP calculates the taxes and sends them back to Express. You can edit the information and print checks or use direct deposit (ADP does not charge for direct deposit, but your bank might charge you). A journal entry automatically records each payroll.

Full reports are available, including payroll summary and detail, earnings, deductions, paid time off, workers compensation, and more. View, print, or export the reports to Excel.

Tax forms are completed with your information and can be edited. When a figure is edited, the forms are automatically recalculated. You can print completed tax forms, including 940, 941, and W-2 forms. All federal, state, and local forms are available.

Accountant's ADP Payroll

ADP Payroll for accountants does not handle direct deposit, and currently does not provide online filing of returns. Otherwise, it provides everything the client's ADP Payroll handles. Checks and tax forms print at the accountant's office, not at the client's office.

In Windows, click the **Start** menu, **All Programs**, **Microsoft Office**, **Microsoft Office Accounting 2007 Tools**, **Accountant View**, as shown in Figure 9.42. Accountant View opens.

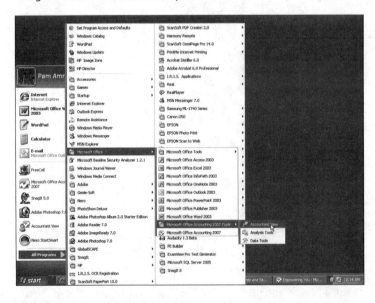

FIGURE 9.42   Open Accountant View.

Click the **Payroll Center** button or the **Payroll Center** link to sign up, as shown in Figure 9.43.

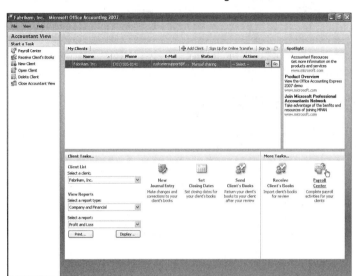

FIGURE 9.43   Your accountant uses Accountant View for journal entries and payroll.

The accountant's version of ADP Payroll, shown in Figure 9.44, costs $99 per year, plus $9.99 per client per month.

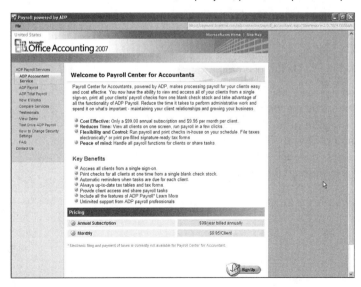

FIGURE 9.44   Open Payroll Center.

Preprinted Checks and Forms

You can buy checks and forms online that are preprinted with your company information.

As shown in Figure 9.45, click the **Company** menu, **Business Services**, **Buy Checks and Forms** to buy checks and forms online.

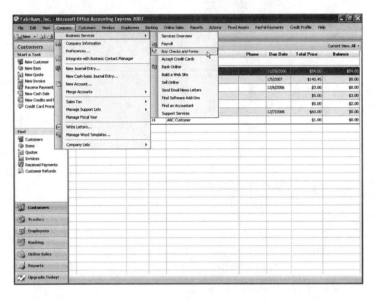

FIGURE 9.45 Buy checks and forms online.

You can buy checks, forms, labels, stationery, tax forms, envelopes, and more on the website shown in Figure 9.46.

To print a form using a preprinted form, load the form into the printer. Then click the **File** menu, **Print**. Click the **Pre-printed Form** button to select it. If necessary, click the **Alignment** button, shown in Figure 9.47, to align the paper properly. This enables you to move the print in 1/100th increments to perfectly align the text on the form.

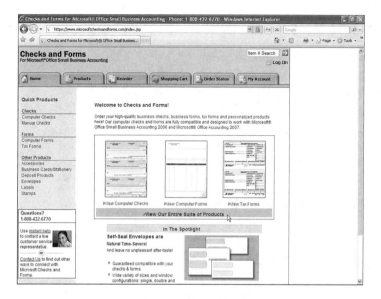

FIGURE 9.46   The website for buying checks and forms.

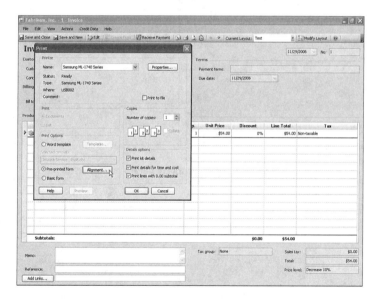

FIGURE 9.47   Choose Pre-printed Form in the Print window.

Credit Card Processing

Payment Services for Express allows you to accept customer credit cards using your existing merchant account or through PayPal or Chase. Handle all credit card processing from within Express without using an expensive terminal or manually reentering transactions.

To accept credit cards, click the **Company** menu, **Business Services**, **Accept Credit Cards**. Or click the **Customers** menu, **Credit Card Processing**, **Sign Up for Credit Card Processing**, as shown in Figure 9.48. Internet Explorer opens the website shown in Figure 9.49.

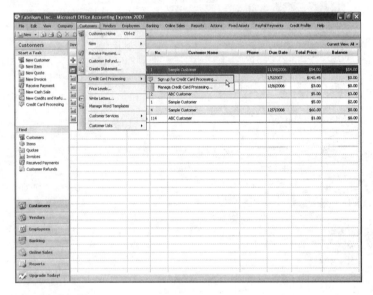

FIGURE 9.48   Use your existing credit card merchant account, or sign up for credit card processing through PayPal or Chase.

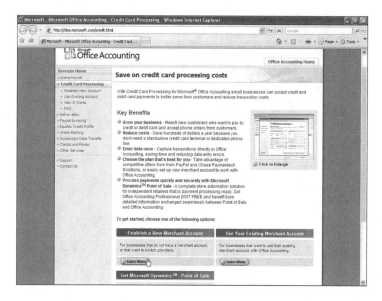

FIGURE 9.49 Choose the best credit card processing option for your company.

> **CAUTION**
>
> **SET UP THE BANK ACCOUNT FIRST**
>
> Click **Banking**, **New Bank Account** and set up the bank in your accounts first, before setting it up online.

Bank Online

Online banking enables you to transfer funds between accounts, pay bills online, and download and match transactions.

Set Up Online Banking

You enable online banking using the Online Banking Wizard.

To view a list of banks, click the **Banking** menu, **Bank Online**, **Set Up Online Banking**, as shown in Figure 9.50. Internet Explorer opens the Online Banking website.

Click **Compatible Banks** on the left side, shown in Figure 9.51, to see a list of banks that are compatible with Express.

For best results, choose a direct connect bank from the list on the right side. Express can import transactions from banks using the .ofx Microsoft Money format, but the direct connect method is preferable. Only the direct connect method permits you to transfer funds between accounts and pay bills online from Express. Click the **Refresh** button to update the bank lists.

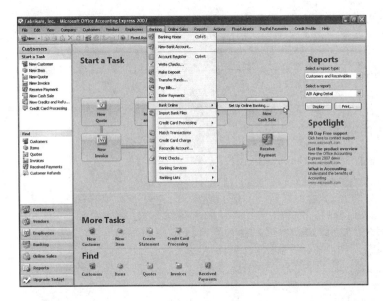

FIGURE 9.50 Set up online banking.

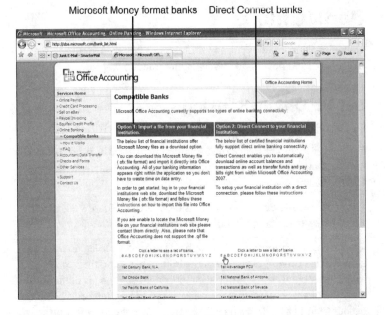

FIGURE 9.51 Choose a bank, preferably from the right side.

To set up online banking, click the **Banking** menu, **Bank Online**, **Set Up Online Banking**. The Bank Online Wizard opens.

Set up online banking for one bank account at a time. For each additional bank account, return to the wizard.

Complete the following information using the wizard:

1. At the welcome screen, click the **Next** button, shown in Figure 9.52.

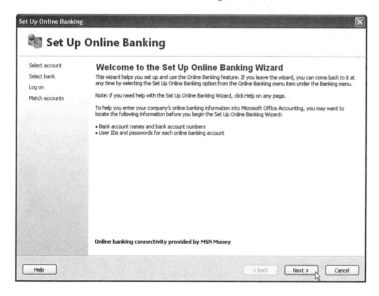

FIGURE 9.52   Complete the Online Banking Wizard.

2. Choose the correct bank account and click the **Next** button.

3. Choose the correct bank from the list. Click the **Next** button.

4. The bank account is found. Click the **Next** button.

5. Choose how far back to download transactions, and then click the **Next** button.

6. The Setup Overview screen opens. The account is now set up for Transaction Download, Pay Bills, and IntraBank Transfers. Click the **Close** button.

Download Transactions

Download transactions from your bank to match them in Express:

1. From the **Banking** screen, click the **Download Banking Transactions** button. Or click the **Banking** menu, **Bank Online**, **Download Transactions**, as shown in Figure 9.53.

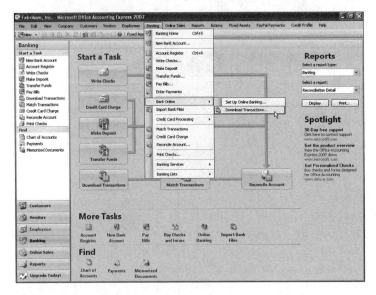

FIGURE 9.53   Download banking transactions.

2. Click the **Match Transactions** button on the Banking screen to open the window shown in Figure 9.54.

3. Click the **Save** button when done.

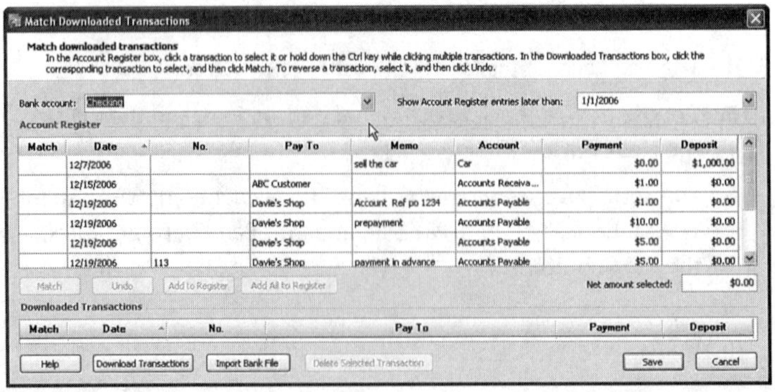

FIGURE 9.54   Match the transactions in Express with the online bank transactions.

Office Live

Microsoft Office Accounting Express 2007 is part of the Office family of products. Another product within that family is Office Live. Use Office Live to transfer your accounting data to your accountant, set up a website as an online storefront, email newsletters, and for email. Sign up for Office Live from multiple places within Express, one of which is shown in Figure 9.55.

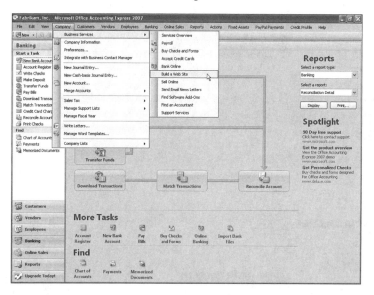

FIGURE 9.55   Sign up for Office Live to set up a website or email, or to email newsletters.

Office Integration

Express works with many Office products:

- **Word**—Microsoft Word is used to create letters and other documents. From within Express, write Word letters that use data from Express customers, vendors, and employees (See "Letter Templates" in this chapter.) Use Word to modify or create new printed Express forms. (See "Modifying Printed Forms" in this chapter.)

- **Excel**—Excel is a spreadsheet used to analyze data. Send Express reports to Excel for analysis. (See "Export to Excel" in Chapter 7, "Accounting Reports.") Import data from Excel into Express. (See "Excel Import" in Chapter 4, "Importing Data.") Use Analysis Tools to create Excel pivot tables for sales and purchase analysis.

- **Access**—Access is a database, like a huge filing cabinet of data that can be added to using forms you create, and analyzed and sorted using reports you create. Use Analysis Tools to create Access databases and reports for vendors, payments, items, invoices, employees, customers, and profit and loss.

  To open Analysis Tools, click the **Start** menu, **All Programs**, **Microsoft Office**, **Microsoft Office Accounting 2007 Tools**, **Analysis Tools**, as shown in Figure 9.56.

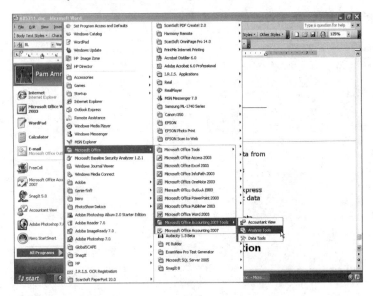

FIGURE 9.56   Open Analysis Tools from the Start menu.

  Use Analysis Tools, shown in Figure 9.57, to create Excel pivot tables and Access databases and reports to analyze data further.

- **Outlook 2007 with Business Contact Manager (BCM)**—Outlook is an organizer, scheduler, contact manager, and email program. After it is linked, add customers, vendors, and items in either Express or Outlook and they appear in the other.

  Quotes and invoices in Express show as Account and Opportunity records in Outlook, and Outlook account and opportunity records can be used to create quotes and invoices in Express. Outlook appointments, phone logs, and tasks can be used as Express time entries and billed. Customer and vendor financial history appears in Outlook.

FIGURE 9.57 Analysis Tools comes with Express but is a separate program.

The user must be the database owner and have administrator permissions to integrate with Express. Versions earlier than Outlook 2007 are not compatible with Express 2007.

To integrate with Outlook BCM, click the **Company** menu, **Integrate with Business Contact Manager**, as shown in Figure 9.58.

To start the wizard, click the **Next** button, shown in Figure 9.59.

Advanced Programming

Microsoft Office Accounting 2007 has almost unlimited capabilities due to the Software Development Kit (SDK) available as a free download from Microsoft:

http://www.microsoft.com/downloads/details.aspx?familyid=1B7C5F43 -2BAE-4103-9457-66B49EF6799A&displaylang=en

If you are a programmer, the SDK will help you write additional reports and forms and provide additional capabilities for Express.

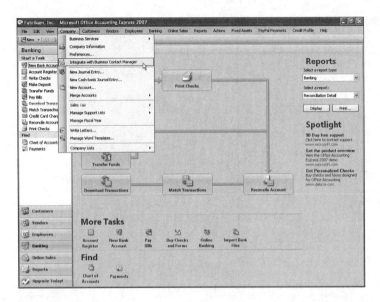

FIGURE 9.58   View Express information within Outlook—customers, vendors, and items.

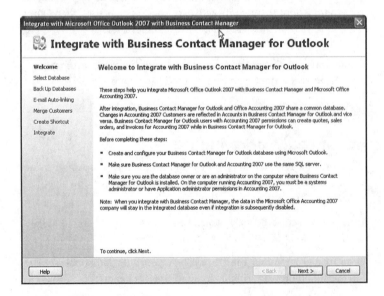

FIGURE 9.59   The Outlook Business Contact Manager Wizard guides you through setup.

WHAT YOU'LL LEARN

- Do's and Don'ts to Prevent Problems
- Common Problems and Solutions
- How to Use Express Data Tools to Back Up and Restore
- Recovering from Problems

Troubleshooting

Now that you know how to use Express, you can learn what to do if something goes wrong. In this appendix, you will view common errors and their solutions. In addition, you'll learn how to back up data and what to do if catastrophe strikes.

Preventing Problems

The following are general computer tips and things to avoid when using Express.

DO:

- Hold a CD by its edge and avoid fingerprints and scratches on the shiny side.
- Close all programs, such as Express, before shutting down the computer.
- Make sure all power switches (Uninterruptable Power Supply [UPS], power strip, monitor, rear computer power switch, and front computer power switch) are turned on and all cables are connected properly.
- Place a CD in the CD tray with the label side facing up (in almost all cases).
- Close other programs for best performance.
- Write down the product key or keep it in a safe place.
- Treat the CD tray gently. Use the open/close button instead of pushing the tray.

DON'T:

- Smoke near the computer. Smoke can damage the computer and shorten its life.
- Use the computer in extreme heat or cold. High and low temperatures can damage the computer.

When performing an operation in Express, it can take awhile. Be patient. Don't click the button multiple times; this can cause problems.

Errors and Resolutions

Microsoft offers several discussion groups on small business accounting, for general questions and programming development, at

http://www.microsoft.com/office/community/en-us/default.mspx

This book includes some of the most frequent Microsoft Office Accounting questions and their answers. You can search online for answers to your specific questions, or post questions. Community members and Microsoft employees frequently answer questions within a day or two.

Problem: When viewing a list of transactions, the transaction I am looking for is not in the list; but it should be.

Cause: The list has been filtered.

Solution: Click the **Current View** drop-down list arrow in the top-right corner of the list. Select **All**. All transactions now appear.

Problem: When trying to install Microsoft Accounting Express 2007, an error message appears stating that MOA7024Express.exe is not a valid Win32 Application.

Cause: The program file might not have downloaded correctly. The file on the CD might be corrupt, if you're using the CD.

Solution: Download the file again or get a different CD. When downloading and installing, make sure that unnecessary programs are not running.

Do the following before downloading and installing:

- Close unnecessary programs.
- Open Internet Explorer. Choose **Internet Options** and click the button to remove temporary files.

Problem: Importing from versions of QuickBooks other than 2004–2006 Pro, Premier, and Accountant doesn't work.

Cause: Those are the only versions of QuickBooks fully supported with all data, including transactions. 2002–2006 Basic, Pro, Premier, and Accountant import the master records.

Solution: Either convert the files to a supported version of QuickBooks or look for an add-in program that allows Express to import these files.

Problem: The bank list does not contain the bank you use.

Cause: Not all banks are on the list.

Solution: Download the account data in the Microsoft Money or `.ofx` format and import the file into Express. Then contact your bank to request that it add support for Microsoft Office Accounting 2007.

Problem: When trying to sign up to sell online with a Passport account, an error message appears stating that the Passport Network is experiencing technical difficulties, but the account works on other websites.

Cause: The company name might contain a special character, such as an apostrophe, that causes problems with the Online Sales feature.

Solution: Change the company name to use only letters and numbers, and try again.

Problem: The payment option I use, such as online bill payment, isn't listed.

Cause: Express doesn't automatically integrate with all types of payments.

Solution: Use the check payment method and enter a description such as `Online Bill Payment 01`. Do not print the check. Instead, click **Save and Close** to file the check without printing it.

Problem: Sending your files to your accountant causes you to lose access to them.

Cause: The Accountant Transfer function causes the company to enter a limited access mode so that you don't interfere with work your accountant is performing.

Solution: Wait until you receive the files from your accountant. Or, if the Accountant Transfer function was started accidentally, click the **File** menu, **Accountant Transfer**, **Cancel Transfer**.

Problem: SQL errors: `Cannot connect to database, SQL is unavailable.`

Cause: SQL Server might not be running.

Solution: Check to see whether SQL Server is running by doing the following:

1. Click the **Start** button.

2. Click the **Control Panel** menu item.

3. Click the **Administrative Tools** menu item.

4. Click the **Services** menu item.

5. Check SQL Server (MSSMLBIZ).

If SQL Server (MSSMLBIZ) is not running, start it, or reboot the computer and MSSMLBIZ might start.

Data Utilities

To prevent and recover from data errors, use the Data Utilities options.

To open the Data Utilities window, click the **File** menu, **Utilities**, **Data Utilities**, as shown in Figure A.1. The Data Utilities window opens.

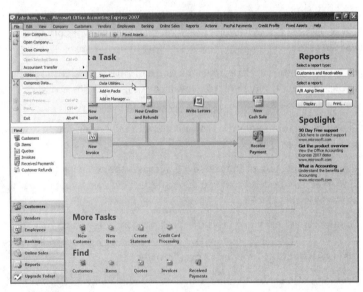

FIGURE A.1   Open the Data Utilities window.

Backup

Creating backups of your data enables you to use the rest of the tips in this chapter. You cannot restore data and recover from errors as easily without frequent backups.

Express reminds you to back up. Or, back up any time you feel more data has been entered than you want to reenter if a problem occurs.

CREATING A BACKUP

Create a backup to prevent loss of data.

To open the Backup window, click the **Backup** button, shown in Figure A.2. Or, if you are not ready to back up your company, click the **Close** button.

Basic Tools tab ———

FIGURE A.2 The Data Utilities window contains all the options related to your company's information.

To create a backup of your company's data, do the following:

1. Use the **Browse** button, shown in Figure A.3, to select the location you want to use for the backup file.

   Type in the name of the file to use, click on a file, or use the default filename that shows up automatically in the **Backup File Name** section.

2. For extra security, enter a password in the **Password** section. Write down the password in a safe place.

3. If you entered a password, reenter it in the **Verify Password** section.

4. Click the **OK** button to create a backup file of the company that is currently open.

FIGURE A.3   The Backup window enables you to back up your company data and protect it with a password.

Rebuild, Repair, and Restore Data

If you encounter a problem with company data, have Express fix the problem. Repair the data if there is an error, rebuild the data if a company file was accidentally deleted, or restore the data from a backup, if one exists.

REBUILDING A COMPANY FILE FROM THE DATABASE

If a company file was accidentally deleted, rebuild it from the Express database.

Click the **Rebuild** button, shown in Figure A.4, to open the Rebuild Company File window.

To rebuild a deleted company file, select the company name containing the company's most recent database version from the list and click the **Rebuild** button, shown in Figure A.5, to start the rebuilding process.

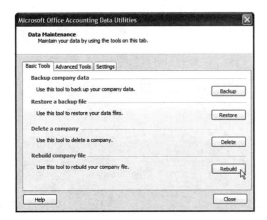

FIGURE A.4   Open the Rebuild Company File window.

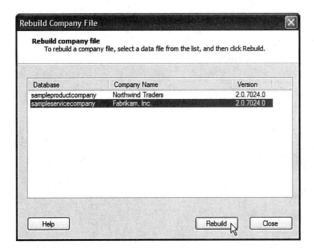

FIGURE A.5   Rebuild a deleted company file from the Rebuild Company File window.

REPAIRING THE DATABASE

If a database has errors, Express can try to repair it.

To open the Repair Database window, click the **Advanced Tools** tab, and then click the **Repair** button, shown in Figure A.6.

FIGURE A.6   Open the Repair Database window.

To repair a database, do the following:

1. You cannot repair a database for a company that is currently open. Switch to another company or open a sample company first.

2. Select the company name containing the company's most recent database version.

3. Click the **Repair** button, shown in Figure A.7.

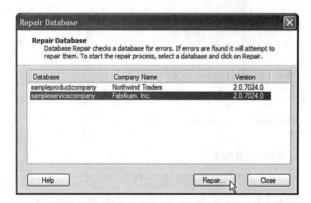

FIGURE A.7   Use the Repair Database window to repair a database that has errors.

4. Express asks whether you want to continue. Make sure that the database is not in use, and then click the **Yes** button, shown in Figure A.8, to start repairing the database.

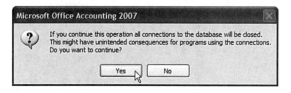

FIGURE A.8   Click the Yes button.

RESTORING DATA

If the other options for fixing data fail, restore from a backup. This should be the last resort because changes made since the last backup will be lost. At least one backup must exist for the Restore option to work.

Click the **Restore** button, shown in Figure A.9, to open the Database Restore window.

To restore a backup and recover data, do the following:

1. Click the **Browse** button next to **Backup File Name**, shown in Figure A.10, to select the backup to restore. Choose the backup containing the most recent data.

2. Click the **Browse** button next to **Restore Backup File To**, and select the company file to be restored. Enter a new filename to avoid accidentally overwriting a file you want to keep.

3. If the backup is protected by a password, enter the password in the **Password** section.

4. After you have filled out the information, click the **OK** button to start the restoration process.

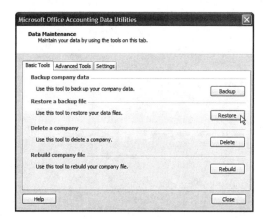

FIGURE A.9   Open the Database Restore window.

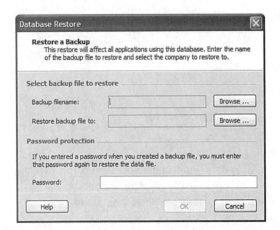

FIGURE A.10 The Database Restore window enables you to restore a backup created previously.

Data Compression

To improve performance, Express can compress company data that is no longer used. Use data compression if the company contains many old entries or is working slowly. Do not use data compression to save space on the computer. Doing so will actually use more space because data compression creates a backup and other files. It might increase Express's speed, but it does not save space.

To start the Compress Data Wizard, click the **File** menu, **Compress Data**, shown in Figure A.11. The Compress Data Wizard opens.

Click the **Next** button, shown in Figure A.12, to start the Compress Data Wizard.

Express will not compress

- Data in a fiscal year that is not closed
- Payroll transactions
- Open or partially paid vendor bills
- Open or partially paid invoices
- Other open or unapplied entries
- Undeposited funds

> CAUTION
>
> **USE CAUTION WHEN COMPRESSING DATA!**
>
> Do not compress data unless the data will not be used in future reports and transactions! If the data is later restored, any changes made since the compression will be lost.

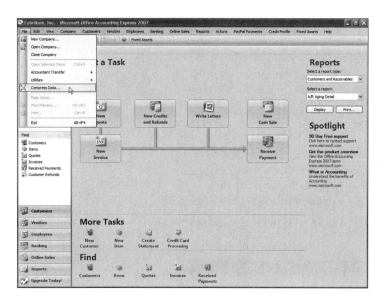

FIGURE A.11   Open the Compress Data Wizard.

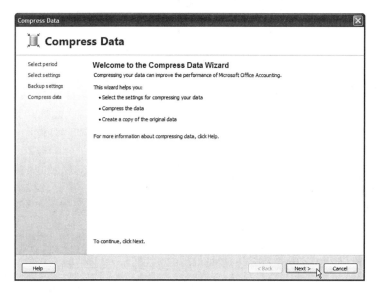

FIGURE A.12   The Compress Data Wizard introduction screen shows how the wizard guides you through choosing settings, backing up the company, and compressing the data.

The financial period to be compressed must be in a properly closed fiscal year. Decide whether you want to compress unreconciled imported bank and credit card statements. If your company does not reconcile these statements using Reconcile Account in Express, you might want to compress them if there is a large number of them. Or you can reconcile all accounts before compressing.

To use the Compress Data Wizard, do the following:

1. All data from the first day of the first fiscal year to the end date will be compressed. The start date is always the first day of the first fiscal year and cannot be changed. Select an end date in a closed fiscal year (including the last day of a closed fiscal year).

2. Click the **Next** button, shown in Figure A.13. The Select Settings portion of the wizard opens.

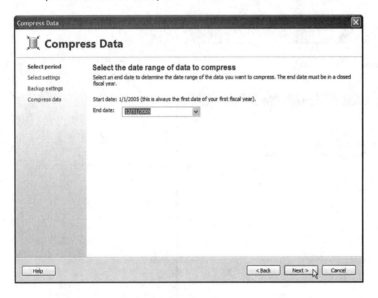

FIGURE A.13   Compress data between the starting and ending dates.

To select data compression settings, do the following, as shown in Figure A.14:

1. If you decide to compress unreconciled bank and credit card statements, click the Compress Unreconciled Bank and Credit Card Statements **Yes** button; otherwise, click the Compress Unreconciled Bank and Credit Card Statements **No** button.

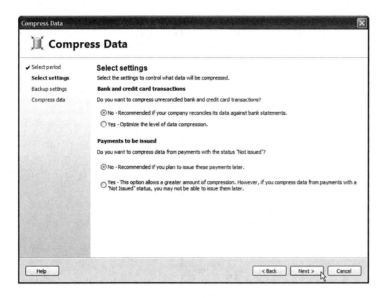

FIGURE A.14 Select the data compression settings carefully. If you're unsure, select No for both options.

2. Because compressing payments that have not been issued might make them impossible to issue, click the Compress Payments Not Issued **No** button. Express will still compress payments that have already been issued.

3. Click the **Next** button. The Select Backup Settings portion of the wizard opens.

To create the backup and start compressing data, do the following:

1. Click the **Browse** button, shown in Figure A.15, to select the location to use for the backup file.

   Type the name of the file you want to use, click on a file, or use the default filename that displays in the **Backup File Name** section.

2. For extra security, enter a password in the **Password** section. Write down the password in a safe place.

3. Only if you entered a password, reenter it in the **Verify Password** section.

4. Click the **OK** button to create a backup file of the company that will be compressed.

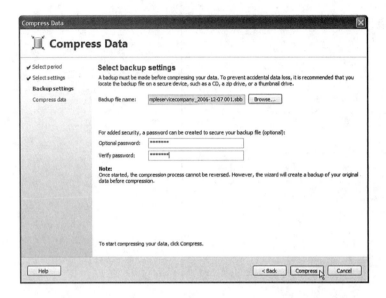

FIGURE A.15   Select backup settings to archive your data before compressing it.

5. To change settings previously entered, click the **Back** button.

   Or, to cancel the data compression process altogether, click the **Cancel** button.

6. When the choices are correct for your needs, click the **Compress** button to compress the data.

Before the Compress Data Wizard finishes compressing the data, it creates an archived backup of the company database, an archived backup of the company file, and a compression journal. This compression journal can be viewed as a line item under the accounts in which entries were compressed, and on reports that contain compressed entries. Compressed entries can be changed only by restoring a copy of the database archive. This is the same as restoring a backup—changes made since data compression will be lost.

When Express finishes compressing the company data, it displays a message about how much it was able to compress. Express might perform hidden routines that significantly slow down the computer after compression. If this happens, close Express and reboot the computer after data compression.

About Data Files

Data files can have different extensions (an extension is the three characters after the period in a filename) and can be located in different areas of your computer's hard drive, based on how the files are used. Table A.1 shows extensions, how the files are used, and their typical locations.

Table A.1   Data File Extensions Explained

Data File Extension	Description
.sbd	The main data file. It is located in the Program Files\Microsoft SQLServer\MSSQL$MICROSOFTSMLBIZ\Data folder.
.sbc	A shortcut pointing to the data file. It is located in the administrator's My Documents\Small Business Accounting 2007\Companies folder.
.sbl	A log file, created when creating a new company or restoring from a backup. It is located in Program Files\Microsoft SQLServer\MSSQL$MICROSOFTSMLBIZ\Data folder.
.log	A log file, created when repairing, upgrading, or importing data, bank transactions, or payroll transactions. It is located in the administrator's My Documents\Small Business Accounting 2007\Logs folder.
.sbb	The uncompressed backup file. It is located in the administrator's My Documents\Small Business Accounting 2007\Backups folder.
.zip	The compressed backup file. It is located in the administrator's My Documents\Small Business Accounting 2007\Backups folder.
.ate	The compressed backup file sent to the accountant. It is located in the administrator's My Documents\Small Business Accounting 2007\Transfers folder.
.ati	The compressed backup file sent from the accountant to the client. It is located in the administrator's My Documents\Small Business Accounting 2007\Transfers folder.

Moving or Copying the Company Data

To move or copy the company data, it must be detached before moving and reattached before using (see Figure A.16).

Advanced Tools tab

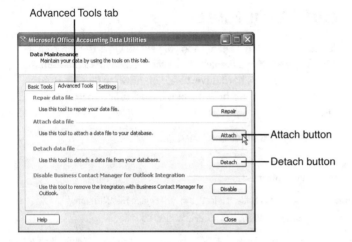

———Attach button

———Detach button

FIGURE A.16   The company data is stored in the SQL database.

Help Resources

Help is available from the Express Help menu and online from Microsoft, search engines, and other websites.

The Help Menu

The first place to look for help is from the Help menu within Express. Click on the **Help** menu in the upper-right corner of the Express screen. The Help menu includes

- **Microsoft Office Accounting Help**—The main Help function for Express. It has five buttons in the upper-left corner:

    - **Previous**—Takes you to the last help screen viewed.

    - **Next**—Takes you to the next help screen.

    - **Refresh**—Redisplays the screen.

    - **Home**—Takes you back to the main Help screen.

    - **Print**—Prints the current page.

    There are three menus:

    - **Contents**—Shows topics organized by category.

    - **Index**—An alphabetical listing of help topics. You can search it by typing a term in the search box or by scrolling through the list of topics.

- **Search**—Searches all the information contained in Help. There are three option check boxes at the bottom of the Search menu, on the left side:

  Search Previous Results—Allows searching again using the most recent results if the initial search produced too many results.

  Match Similar Words—Searches for words that are close to the word entered, in addition to the word itself. For example, searching for the word *work* would find answers with the word *work* as well as the words *works*, *worked*, and *working*.

  Search Titles Only—Only searches for the word in the titles of the help sections.

- **Help with This Window**—Shows help information about the open Express window.

- **Office Online**—Opens the main Microsoft Office website in a web browser. It requires an active Internet connection. Browse the website until you find the link that says Products, and then the link that says Accounting.

- **Check for Updates**—Opens the Microsoft website and requires an Internet connection. It checks that Express is up to date and prompts you to download updates if it is not.

- **Activate and Register Product**—Enables you to activate and register Express, if you have not already (see "Registration" in Chapter 3, "Registration and Setup Wizard," for details).

- **Upgrade to Professional**—Lets you upgrade your copy of Express.

- **Contact Us**—Contact information for Microsoft services and Microsoft product support. It opens in a web browser and requires an Internet connection.

- **Support Services**—Contact information for Microsoft support. It opens in a web browser and requires an Internet connection.

- **Find an Accountant**—Searches for members of the Microsoft Professional Accountants' Network (MPAN) by ZIP code. It opens in a web browser and requires an Internet connection. Certified members appear first on the list.

- **Community**—Opens the Office Accounting Newsgroup menu item, a collection of questions and answers from Office Accounting users, experts, and Microsoft. It opens in a web browser and requires an Internet connection.

- **Customer Feedback Options**—Opens the Customer Feedback Options window, which describes the feedback options and allows the settings to be changed. This item relates to whether to allow Microsoft to collect anonymous data on program use and computer specifications.

- **Submit Feedback**—Used to submit a suggestion or other feedback to the Microsoft Community, which is then publicly posted for people to vote on. It opens in a web browser and requires an Internet connection.

- **About Microsoft Office Accounting**—Contains information about Express, the product code and registration information, the software license, and a link to Microsoft Support, which opens in a web browser and requires Internet access.

Microsoft Help Resources

Another place to look or help is the Microsoft family of websites:

http://www.ideawins.com

A Microsoft website specifically for Microsoft Office Accounting Express. It provides information about Express and links to support.

http://support.microsoft.com

The Microsoft Knowledge Base. Receive help with Express by searching the Knowledge Base for Accounting 2007, and receive help for Windows problems by searching for your specific operating system; for example, Windows XP or Windows Vista.

http://www.microsoft.com

The main Microsoft website. Search for Accounting 2007 and find all the Microsoft pages relating to Express.

Other Online Resources

Use a search engine, such as Windows Live or Google, to look for help.

Go to:

http://www.live.com

or:

http://www.google.com

Type your search term and view the results.

Book-Specific Resources

If you have questions or comments about the book, please visit the author's website:

http://www.empoweringyou.com

or email:

pam@empoweringyou.com

Corrections to the book are posted, along with additional resources.

Glossary

Access   A Microsoft database program that acts like a filing cabinet and can be manipulated. Forms and reports can be programmed to use with the data.

accountant transfer   Used to send a file with the company information to the accountant for review. The accountant can make changes, and then send the file back.

Accountant View   A separate program for accountants and included with Express. Accountant View allows accountants to manage clients and their books.

activate; activation; registration   Activation verifies your software is legitimate. Registration sends your contact and company information to Microsoft. Express activates and registers the product online in one step. Express can be used up to 25 times before activation and registration.

add-ins   Additional features that Microsoft or another company provides for Express. Express comes with the Fixed Asset Manager, PayPal Payments, Equifax Credit Profile, and ADP Payroll add-ins. Fixed Asset Manager is disabled in Express.

anti-spyware   A software program that prevents recording and sending personal information without your consent.

antivirus   A software program that prevents your computer software from being altered without your consent.

audit   Verify the company's account balances and transactions.

audit trail   A record of transactions and corrections.

backup   A copy of the information on a computer.

balance sheet   Shows what the company owns or is owed (assets), what it owes to others (liabilities), and what is left over for the owner (equity).

cancel transfer   Stops accountant transfer after a file has been sent and before it is received back from the accountant. This allows company transactions to be made again.

cash flow statement; statement of cash flow   Shows money moving into and out of a business. Because insufficient cash is one of the biggest reasons small businesses fail, keep a close watch on this report.

cost of goods sold   The direct costs of what was sold.

credit   One line in a transaction with a dollar amount.

credit rating   Creditworthiness of customers.

customer statement; statement   Shows a customer the amount it owes the company and the transactions for that period.

data type   The format and characteristics of an item of data. For example, the integer data type cannot contain a letter.

debit   One line in a transaction with a dollar amount.

default   The provided answer, typically recommended, which is used if you don't replace it.

desktop   In Windows, the full screen area showing before programs open.

dialog box   An area of the screen that opens in a square window to warn, inform, or ask a question.

display resolution; LCD resolution; monitor resolution   The viewable dots in a 1" by 1" area of the display.

download   To move a copy of a program from the Internet to your computer.

drag   While the mouse pointer is over an object, click and hold the left mouse button, and then move the mouse in the direction you want to shift the object.

email   Letter-writing over the Internet.

equity; owner's equity; shareholders equity   What the company owns or is owed (assets) less what it owes to others (liabilities).

Excel   A Microsoft spreadsheet containing rows and columns of information.

expense   The indirect costs of staying in business.

financial statement A document comprised of the balance sheet, income statement, and cash flow statement.

firewall; blocking; Internet access; security warning Stops malicious users and programs from entering or leaving a computer. Warns you when an attempt is made to access your computer or the Internet.

folder A small area on your computer that holds information and that you label with a name.

font A specific style of type.

GB; gigabyte A unit of storage, in billions of bytes.

GHz; gigahertz The speed rating of your computer in billions of cycles per second.

hard disk Where the computer programs and data are physically stored in your computer.

ideawins.com The Internet location for Microsoft Office Accounting Express 2007. Contains frequently asked questions, the capability to order the Express CD, and to download the program (http://www.ideawins.com).

import; migrate To bring in data from another program.

in balance Debit amounts in a transaction equal credit amounts.

income; net income; net loss; revenue What you sold (income, revenue, your services and products), less the direct costs of what you sold (cost of goods sold), less all the other indirect costs of staying in business (expenses). The end result is net income or net loss.

income statement Shows whether a company is making money. It indicates what you sold (income, revenue, your services and products), less the direct costs of what you sold (cost of goods sold), less all the other indirect costs of staying in business (expenses). The end result is net income, or net loss.

Internet Computers communicating together throughout the world.

journal entry A method of recording a transaction by debiting and crediting accounts, instead of using another Express form. Typically used by accountants to record beginning, adjusting, and closing entries.

liability What the company owes to others.

license agreement   A contract detailing your right to use a particular piece of software.

log   A record of the actions taken by a program. Also lists any errors encountered.

map   To create a connection between an item in one list and a specific item in another list.

master record   An account, customer, vendor, employee, or item record. Does not include transactions.

MB; megabyte   A unit of storage, in millions.

memory   The temporary storage location used by programs running on your computer.

Microsoft Baseline Security Analyzer (MBSA)   An easy-to-use tool used to determine and solve security problems on your computer (http://www.microsoft.com/mbsa).

minimize   To temporarily hide the current program. Click on the program's name at the bottom of the screen to show it again.

My Documents   A folder where you store information on your computer; predefined by Windows XP. Called *Documents* in Vista.

.NET   The .NET Framework is a required component, and is installed with Express, if not already on the computer.

New Company Wizard; Company Wizard; wizard   Helps to automate setup by guiding you through a procedure.

Office   A group of Microsoft software that might contain Access, Accounting Express, Excel, Groove, InfoPath, OneNote, Outlook, PowerPoint, Publisher, Visio, and Word.

Office Live   Microsoft online services. Includes many features, such as a website, domain name, email addresses, and accountant transfer.

OneCare; Microsoft OneCare   Security software from Microsoft that includes a firewall, antivirus, anti-spyware, backup reminders, and periodic tune-ups, all bundled in one product.

opening financial statements   Dated the day immediately before the date Express is used for normal transactions. Shows all financial accounts and their balances.

operating system   Microsoft Windows XP, Windows Server 2003, or Windows Vista is required to run software, such as Express. Other operating systems not supported by Express include MS-DOS, Windows 95, Windows 98, Windows 98 SE, Windows Me, Windows NT, Windows 2000, UNIX, Xenix, Linux, and all Macintosh operating systems.

Outlook   Microsoft email software.

processor   The "brains" of the computer, used to calculate and run software.

product key   A string of letters and numbers identifying a specific copy of the software. Used by Microsoft during activation to verify that a copy is legitimate.

Professional; Microsoft Office Accounting Professional 2007   An upgrade that contains additional features for Microsoft Small Business Accounting 2006 or Microsoft Office Accounting Express 2007.

program   Computer software.

reconcile; reconcile account; reconcile statement   Matching an account in Express with a financial account statement received from a financial institution.

reversing entry   Used to correct an inaccurate transaction, in effect deleting the transaction. Uses a debit for each account credited, and a credit for each account debited in the original transaction.

run   Start.

sales tax liability   The amount of sales tax a company owes.

save   Permanently stores a document in a specific location on a computer.

scrollbar   An area on the side of a window showing your location in a document (top, middle, bottom, left, or right).

Service Pack   A software update between major revisions.

slider bar   A small box, inside the scrollbar, which is moved to change your position within the document.

Small Business Accounting 2006 (SBA 2006)   The previous version before Microsoft Office Accounting 2007. Only upgrades to Microsoft Office Accounting Professional 2007, not Express.

SQL; MSDE; SQL Express; SQL Server 2003; SQL Server 2005
Abbreviation for *Standard Query Language*, and also the place where
Express company data is stored. Express comes with SQL Express, a
smaller version of SQL Server 2005. Express will not run on SQL Server
2003 or MSDE, the versions that work with Small Business Accounting
2006.

subfolder   A small area on your computer, inside another folder,
which holds information and is labeled with a name.

transactions   A recorded event involving an exchange of money or
change in value. A transaction consists of at least one credit and one
debit. Debits must equal credits.

window   A portion of the screen shown as a box.

Windows Live; Passport   Microsoft account service that provides
secure identification.

Word   Microsoft word processing software.

index

Safari
BOOKS ONLINE
ENABLED

THIS BOOK IS SAFARI ENABLED

INCLUDES FREE 45-DAY ACCESS TO THE ONLINE EDITION

The Safari® Enabled icon on the cover of your favorite technology book means the book is available through Safari Bookshelf. When you buy this book, you get free access to the online edition for 45 days.

Safari Bookshelf is an electronic reference library that lets you easily search thousands of technical books, find code samples, download chapters, and access technical information whenever and wherever you need it.

TO GAIN 45-DAY SAFARI ENABLED ACCESS TO THIS BOOK:

● Go to **http://www.quepublishing.com/safarienabled**

● Complete the brief registration form

● Enter the coupon code found in the front of this book on the "Copyright" page

If you have difficulty registering on Safari Bookshelf or accessing the online edition, please e-mail customer-service@safaribooksonline.com.